PUBLISHING

OMF International works in most East Asian countries, and among East Asian peoples around the world. It was founded by James Hudson Taylor in 1865 as the China Inland Mission. Our overall purpose is to glorify God through the urgent evangelization of East Asia's billions, and this is reflected in our publishing.

Through our books, booklets, website and quarterly magazine, *East Asia's Billions*, OMF aims to motivate Christians for world mission, and to equip them for playing a part in it. Publications include:

- contemporary mission issues
- the biblical basis of mission
- the life of faith
- stories and biographies related to God's work in East Asia
- accounts of the growth and development of the church in Asia
- studies of Asian culture and religion relating to the spiritual needs of her peoples

Martin Goldsmith served as a missionary with OMF International in Singapore, Malaysia, Indonesia and Thailand.

Visit our website at *www.omf.org.uk*

Or contact us at OMF International (UK),
Station Approach, Borough Green, Kent, TN15 8BG
Tel: 01732 887299 email: omf@omf.org.uk

301

D0268683

Martin Goldsmith

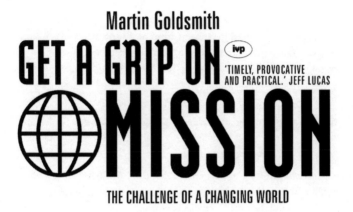

GET A GRIP ON

ivp

'TIMELY, PROVOCATIVE
AND PRACTICAL.' JEFF LUCAS

MISSION

THE CHALLENGE OF A CHANGING WORLD

INTER-VARSITY PRESS
Norton Street, Nottingham NG7 3HR, England
Email: ivp@ivpbooks.com
Website: www.ivpbooks.com

Co-published with OMF International (UK)
First published 2006
Reprinted 2006, 2011

British Library Cataloguing-in-Publication Data
A catalogue record for this book is available from the British Library.

ISBN: 978–1–84474–126–7

Set in Dante 10.5/13pt
Typeset in Great Britain by CRB Associates, Potterhanworth, Lincolnshire
Printed and bound in Great Britain by MPG Books Ltd, Bodmin, Cornwall

Contents

	Introduction	7
1.	Why Christ, not Krishna?	17
2.	What a small world	34
3.	A new centre of gravity	51
4.	Not all missionaries have big noses	67
5.	No bypassing the locals	83
6.	No pith helmets in a concrete jungle	97
7.	Let the airwaves bring good news	114
8.	God never stands still	130
9.	United for mission	145
10.	No ruts in mission	162
11.	Everybody and everything	180
12.	Tailor-made mission – make it fit	198
13.	No more biblical blinkers	217
	Conclusion	233
	Further reading	239

Introduction

'Would you be willing to give a lecture on "Trends in mission for the twenty-first century"'?

This invitation from All Nations Christian College came to me back in 1999 on the eve of the much-trumpeted and brilliantly firework-lit new millennium. My first reaction was somewhat negative. I feared it could be presumptuous to pontificate on the direction Christian mission might take in Britain and around the world in the coming hundred years.

No prophets here

The words of Amos struck a reassuring chord in my heart when he affirmed that he was 'neither a prophet nor a prophet's son' (7:14). Although prophesying was not his official ministry, yet God called him to go and prophesy to his people (7:15). What an encouragement as I faced this invitation! I do not claim in any way to have a special spiritual gift of prophecy, but God could use me to teach in a forward-looking prophetic manner.

It was most encouraging to observe the warm, open-hearted response to the lecture. Since then, others have invited me to share on this vital theme of the practice of Christian mission as we move forward in this twenty-first century. For several years I have given an annual lecture on this topic at All Nations Christian College as well as several lectures at the London Institute of Contemporary Christianity. Both All Nations and LICC attract thinking students of considerable maturity and experience from all over the world, so their questions and comments have stimulated and encouraged me in this Amos-like, non-prophetic lecturing and teaching ministry. It has also been my privilege to share on this topic with international audiences in the course of my ministry in every continent. This has allowed me to see things through the eyes of Christians from other parts of the world.

One still faces the possible rebuke that it is singularly unwise and even arrogant to teach about future developments in the mission of God's church without a specific gift of prophecy. Actually, there are three good reasons why such teaching is possible.

We have the mind of Christ

By his Holy Spirit God may give all of us his insight and understanding. He is the Lord of all history, so he knows what will be the overall directions and movements in the world and in the church. Demonstrating the unique and incomparable wisdom and glory of God, Isaiah asks: 'Who has understood the mind of the LORD?' (Isaiah 40:13). He acknowledges that no mere human being can match our God in his absolute, sovereign power and wisdom. Paul adds an amazing sentence to his quotation of this passage from Isaiah. He, too, confesses that God's judgments and thoughts stand above ours, but he nevertheless declares that the spiritual person 'makes judgments about all things', and then makes the staggering claim that 'we have the mind of Christ' (1 Corinthians 2:15–16).

I confess that I hesitate to make what would be, in my case, such a boastful declaration. I frequently turn Paul's assured statement into a prayer that in his grace God would help me to know something of his mind. Like Paul, I want to think the thoughts of the Lord. In my lectures on mission in the twenty-first century I desire to have the mind of Christ, to know something of what he is planning for the coming years.

Evolution or revolution?

It is rare for history suddenly to move in a totally new direction. Evolution is more common than radical revolution. What appear to be decisive moments of change almost always have their roots in the immediate past. For example, the Roman Catholic Second Vatican Council [1] launched the Catholic Church into new waters, with the Pope leading the way. But actually every new development in that council could be shown to have its roots in previous theological thought or mission practice somewhere in the Catholic Church. For example, although Gustavo Gutiérrez's seminal *A Theology of Liberation* [2] was not published until after Vatican II, political theology was gaining influence much earlier in South America. This was equally true of the radically liberal and politically revolutionary ecumenical conference in Uppsala in 1968. [3] Again, its roots lay in the past, as was evident in all the student riots and demonstrations of that period.

Among evangelical Christians the same is true. The first Lausanne Conference, [4] back in the 1970s, moved us into new thinking and practice in mission worldwide. It thrust African Christian leaders into the forefront of the church's spiritual life, and Latin American theologians were the prime movers in a new biblical understanding. Likewise, the socio-political became accepted for the first time as central to the whole task of Christian mission, together with the spiritual dimensions of evangelism, church-planting and the teaching and edifying of the church. In evangelical circles John Stott became a key advocate of a more holistic approach to mission.

Actually, all three conferences in their particular constituencies were watersheds which caught up streams of thinking among some of their people and brought them into the mainstream of the whole movement.

Similarly, in the New Testament we find that Jesus homes in on some strands of rabbinic or biblical thought which had not previously been centre stage in Jewish life. Thus, for example, the idea that the Messiah would suffer for his people could be traced in some rabbinic thought, but such ideas did not lie at the heart of Jewish thinking at the time of Jesus. The New Testament emphasis on Isaiah 53 would have surprised most Jewish leaders. Neither would they have expected the strong New Testament emphasis on the fact that Jesus has come not only for his own Jewish people, but also for Samaritans and Gentiles. Thus the Gospels show Jesus' purposeful inclusion of the Samaritans in his ministry: he reveals himself to a Samaritan woman in John 4, goes through Samaritan villages *en route* to Jerusalem (Luke 9:51ff.), tells the story of the Good Samaritan (Luke 10:30ff.), and heals a Samaritan leper, who alone of the ten healed men gave Jesus thanks (Luke 17:17–19). For Luke, the Samaritans form a bridge to the wider Gentile world. So in Acts the gospel is to be preached to 'the ends of the earth' (Acts 1:8), but this is preceded by Jerusalem, Judea and Samaria. Yet this international approach can be found also in some Jewish biblical interpretation and rabbinic thought. Thus the Mishnah declares that 'whoever saves a single life, it is accounted to him as if he had saved a whole world' (Mishnah, *Sanhedrin* 4.5).

Thus a Spirit-led and insightful understanding of contemporary mission thinking and practice may open the door to a right view of the future. Future trends can already be seen in contemporary mission.

See what God is doing

The third good reason why it is allowable without presumption or arrogance to teach concerning mission in the twenty-first century picks up on the word 'seen' in our previous sentence. In the Old Testament a prophet was known as a 'seer', one who had his eyes open to see what God was doing. The prophet saw not only what God was doing among his own people Israel, but also the movements of history among the Babylonians and other nations. What the prophet saw formed the basis for his preaching and for his vision of the future. This is true, for example, of the exciting missionary promise that 'the earth will be filled with the knowledge of the glory of the LORD, as the waters cover the sea' (Habakkuk 2:14). This assured, end-time dream of the final goal of our mission is set clearly in Habakkuk's realization of God's impending judgment on the Babylonians.

If we are to understand the directions in which Christian mission is going in this century, we need to keep our eyes open and observe carefully the trends today in God's church and in his world.

Is Christian mission outdated?

For some years the very terms 'mission' and (particularly) 'missionary' have been questioned by more thinking Christian leaders. They are thought to have negative implications in our modern age. There has been much critical propaganda against Christian mission as something linked to imperialism and destructive of national cultures. So it has been suggested that we talk more of 'Christian workers', 'Christian outreach', or other such non-emotive terms.

In recent years the secular world has begun to use the words 'mission' and even 'missionary'. Every organization today has to have its 'mission statement', and people with conviction in spreading their particular views are sometimes described as 'missionary'. No longer are these terms considered pejorative.

Still we have to ask: what is our Christian understanding of mission? The words stem from the Latin *mittere*, 'to send'. Jesus frequently underlines the fact that he was sent by the Father, and he is now sending us to continue and complete the same work that he came to do in the world. 'As the Father has sent me, I am sending you' (John 20:21).

John particularly stresses this concept of being sent. The church worldwide, both in Europe and elsewhere, consists of followers of Jesus who are sent into the world. The title of the popular book *Mission-shaped Church* (Church House Publishing, 2004) sums it up: the church is not called to be a ghettoized, self-centred fellowship, but an outgoing and relevant missionary movement which is constantly recontextualizing for changing cultures. It has been said that the church is the only society which exists for its non-members. All churches need to emulate this dynamic vision. This book largely concentrates on church-planting, but existing congregations also need to adapt for the sake of mission.

Sent for a purpose

So what does mission mean for us today? This wide-ranging question depends on two further interrelated matters. What purpose did God have in sending Jesus into this world? And what are God's ultimate goals for the world?

Jesus: God's missionary

God's purposes in sending Jesus range widely across the whole spectrum of the expression of God's loving grace towards the world and all people. His love desires our salvation in its widest sense, both individually, and corporately as societies within his creation. He came to save by his death on the cross and to bring the fullness of new life (e.g. John 10:10) through his resurrection. It is noteworthy that the apostles thought of themselves as primarily witnesses of the resurrection (Acts 1:22), and they emphasized the resurrection so much that the Athenians mistakenly thought that Jesus and the Resurrection were two foreign gods (Acts 17:18). Paul had been 'preaching the good news' of Jesus and the Resurrection. Christians may rejoice in the glory of the resurrection. Just as God the Father raised the hopelessly cold and dead body of Jesus to new life in the resurrection, so also God will raise us to new life from the hopelessness of sin and spiritual death. The work of Jesus on earth further required the sending of his Holy Spirit to bring his people into the image and likeness of God in holiness and righteousness. As we 'put on the new self, which is being renewed in knowledge in the image of its Creator' (Colossians 3:10), we need the power of the indwelling Holy Spirit.

The task of mission worldwide is some times said to be summed up in the so-called Great Commission of Jesus at the end of Matthew 28. This includes not only the primary task of going into the world in order to 'make disciples of all nations', but also the external forms of the Christian faith in 'baptising them in the name of the Father and of the Son and of the Holy Spirit'. Mission must therefore be more than just evangelism; witness must lead to the planting of visible churches. Disciples and churches then need to be brought into maturity through the biblical teaching of 'everything I have commanded you'.[5]

Already in Matthew 1 Jesus is revealed as Immanuel, God with us. And after the Great Commission the Gospel ends with the repeated assurance that Jesus will be with us always, to the very end of the age (28:20). The comforting reality of Jesus' presence with us in 'all authority' (28:18) is specially needed, since God commits this calling to universal mission to weak disciples, some of whom 'doubted' (28:17). Still today God's Holy Spirit calls ordinary Christians to fulfil his great, worldwide, missionary purposes. Like the women at the resurrection they may be 'afraid yet filled with joy' (Matthew 28:8), doubting yet at the same time believing.

A glorious destination

God's great aim for his world is that there may finally be a new redeemed people and also a new heaven and earth (2 Peter 3:13; Revelation 21:1), in which God will make everything new (Revelation

21:5). As the creator of the world, God never loses his concern for the welfare of all he has created. Paul therefore affirms that God's purposes embrace all people, both Jews and Gentiles. He underlines the fact that he is the God of both Jews and Gentiles, justifying both the circumcised and uncircumcised (Romans 3:29–30). Not only that; Paul also notes that 'the creation itself will be liberated from its bondage to decay and brought into the glorious freedom of the children of God' (Romans 8:21).

Throughout the Bible there is a close connection between the creation and humanity. If Israel sins, the land suffers. If Israel follows the Lord in righteousness, the land flourishes. In redemption, too, Paul is showing that human salvation is closely linked to creation being freed from its corruption. In the great Christological passage in Colossians 1:15–20, Paul again emphasizes the 'supremacy' of Jesus in the context of 'all creation'. Indeed, the passage repeats for emphasis the words 'all things'. God is truly concerned both for the redemption of humanity as the pinnacle of his creation and for the redemption of the natural world.

When God sends us out in mission, therefore, his purposes are spiritual in relation to evangelism with the building and edifying of his church. God's mission also involves us in social, developmental and justice issues, so that humanity in our corporate life may be redeemed. Thus, in the so-called 'Mission Manifesto' of Jesus in Luke 4:18–19, the Spirit of the Lord sends Jesus out in mission for the sake of 'the poor', 'prisoners', 'the blind' and 'the oppressed'. And the climax comes with 'the year of the Lord's favour', the Jubilee Year, which restored the rights of all people every fifty years. The manifesto further underlines Jesus' call to 'preach' and 'proclaim' this 'good news'. So the mission of Jesus and then of his followers is one of preaching and proclamation, but it relates to the needs of the poor and oppressed. Mission must therefore include an active concern for all people, for the social needs of the poor and for the environment, which is created for Christ (Colossians 1:16) and should be kept beautiful for his pleasure.

To boldly go ... everywhere
The words 'mission' and 'missionary' are often sadly misunderstood. Many Christians think of evangelism and witness as appropriate activities in their own country, but 'mission' is only abroad and

'missionaries' are only those people who are sent to another country. Such ideas are not only unbiblical; they are patently inappropriate to the spiritual and social needs of our various home countries. All of us need mission and missionaries.

Of course, we have to take seriously Jesus' coming from heaven to earth, and the apostles' example of going to other countries and to Gentiles as well as to their own Jewish people. International and cross-cultural mission is an integral part of our biblical understanding of Christian mission. But mission in the New Testament involved the apostles going to their own Jewish people in Jerusalem and Judea, as well as going to the Gentiles in the uttermost parts of the earth.

On the other hand, as an Englishman myself, I am very aware of the temptation to insularity in our British churches. We can become so concerned with the needs of our own country, where only a small percentage of people are actively involved in the church, that we lose sight of the wider world. While we need to keep very much in mind the need for mission in our own country and among our own people, we have to remember that Britain is just a small part of God's wider world.

To all people

A major theme of the New Testament is that God's purposes in and through Jesus Christ are for all peoples, both Jews and Gentiles. Although the Old Testament does have a wider vision than just Israel, yet salvation and relationship to God remained fundamentally for the people of Israel and those few Gentiles who joined themselves to Israel as God-fearers or proselytes. Already in the early years of the Christian church the Holy Spirit began to reach out to Gentiles. The Jewish church had therefore to ask serious questions concerning mission. Is the God of Israel really concerned for the salvation and welfare of Gentiles? If so, was it right to evangelize Gentiles? When Gentiles believe in Jesus, must they join themselves to the people of Israel as in the Old Testament? If so, must they follow the law of Israel and even be circumcised? [6]

So already, in the early church, mission was not only to one's own people, but also cross-religious and cross-cultural to all peoples. Today, too, if we are to be biblical in mission, we shall reach out beyond the confines of our own people. Today's mission includes the infinite variety of ethnic-minority communities within our own borders and the wide variety of different cultures even within our own people; the culture of grandparents may differ just a little from that of their grandchildren! People in one part of the country may have a different culture from those in other parts. The educated people may not be the same as those with less formal education, or city people like those who live in villages. Mission reaches out to all people.

Everyone a missionary

As followers of Christ, all of us are sent out in mission. The whole church is called as a body to be active and involved in mission. This is God's supreme purpose for his church. The Westminster Confession rightly underlines the fact that the church's calling is to glorify God. It is therefore our aim that his name should be glorified, not dragged in the mud by casual unconcern and unbelief or by blasphemous misuse of his name as just a swear-word.

Although the whole church is sent by God into the world in witness and mission, it remains true that some Christians will be called for specialized and specific ministries within the wider calling to mission. Thus some will be sent cross-culturally to other cultures or to ethnic minorities within our own land, and some will also be called to serve in another country. The fact that some are called to specialize and are called to very specific areas of ministry does not negate the fact that all of us, as the church of God, are to be sent in mission.

It is significant that in Matthew's Gospel the call of the first four disciples leads immediately to Jesus' word that he would make them fishers of men and women (Matthew 4:19). Likewise, in Mark 3.13ff., Jesus calls the twelve not only to be with him in intimate relationship, but also to be sent out to preach with authority even over demonic powers. The danger remains that we often find it easier to care for aquariums than to go out into the oceans to catch new fish. Or, to change the metaphor, it is easier to comb the wool of the sheep in the sheepfold than to go out onto the mountains to search for the lost sheep.

Notes
1. For further study of the findings of this key church council, see W. M. Abbott (ed.), *The Documents of Vatican II* (Geoffrey Chapman, 1966).

2. G. Gutiérrez, *A Theology of Liberation* (SCM, 1974).
3. See N. Goodall, *Uppsala '68 Speaks: Section Reports of the 4th Assembly of the WCC* (World Council of Churches and New York Friendship Press, 1968).
4. The papers of Lausanne I are published in J. D.Douglas (ed.), *Let the Earth Hear His Voice* (Minneapolis: World Wide Publications, 1975).
5. For further exposition of Matthew 28 see M. Goldsmith, *Matthew and Mission: The Gospel Through Jewish Eyes* (Paternoster, 2001).
6. For a more detailed study of the biblical basis of mission and the Jew–Gentile issue in the early church, see M. Goldsmith, *Good News for All Nations: Mission at the Heart of the New Testament* (Hodder, 2002); and A. J. Köstenberger, *Salvation to the Ends of the Earth: A Biblical Theology of Mission* (Apollos, 2001).

1 Why Christ, not Krishna?

Why should I believe in Christ, not Krishna, Buddha or Muhammad? Aren't you arrogant to think you have the truth and to expect everyone else to believe what you believe? Isn't so-called 'truth' just a question of personal preference and choice? Is there any objective standard for truth or morality? And, to talk of mission, aren't you intolerant when you want to thrust your religion down other people's throats?

Such questions and the attitudes behind them not only undermine all Christian witness and mission, but also present major obstacles to people coming to faith in Christ. They form perhaps the major objection to the gospel in British and other European universities and among non-Christian graduates. Gerald McDermott asserts: 'Arguably, the church's greatest challenge ... will be the problem of the scandal of particularity.'[1] Postmodern thinking rejects 'particularity', the limiting of God's saving grace and love to any one group of people or community. Of course, as Christians, we also object to the methodology of 'thrusting the gospel down people's throats'; people have a nasty way of regurgitating in such circumstances! But behind the emotive expression lies the serious question of truth and Christians' responsibility to share that good news lovingly and humbly with our neighbour. Such questions of pluralism, and whether God's revelation and truth are narrowly limited to Christians, are cutting the very roots of Christian mission both in our home countries and overseas.

No place for truth

One day I was talking with an agnostic British businessman in his late thirties. At one stage I mentioned the word 'truth' and he immediately interrupted me. 'Truth!' he said. 'What an interesting word!' After a pause for reflection, he added, 'I don't think I've heard that word since I was a boy.'

When I suggested that all business surely requires truth and therefore the possibility that people can trust each other, he said strongly, 'No, I would never trust anyone in business.'

Some while later I met a Japanese businessman in Tokyo airport. We were both travelling to London (but he was going first class!). I politely asked him how long he would be staying in London. 'About an hour,' he replied, to my amazement. 'Then I fly back to Tokyo.'

I asked him why he was flying all the way to London if he was planning to have only an hour there before returning.

'I have to sign a contract.'

I asked whether it could not be signed electronically.

'This is a large contract,' he said. 'We couldn't trust just electronic signatures or even doing it by post.'

I realized that lack of truth and therefore of trustworthiness was resulting in a top businessman having to fly from Tokyo to London and back first class. What an expense, and what a waste of time as well as energy!

Truth is vitally important even in practical economic matters, let alone in questions of faith. As Christians we have to show by our lives the reality of truth and trustworthiness as followers of the one who claims to be *the* truth (John 14:6). And we need to defend the fact of truth in our apologetics.[2]

It is noteworthy that Jesus repeatedly calls the Holy Spirit 'the Spirit of truth' (John 14:17; 15:26; 16:13). In contrast, Satan is shown to be 'a liar and the father of lies' (John 8:44). Whereas Jesus is, in his fundamental nature, 'the truth' (John 14:6), no truth is found in Satan, and lies are 'his native language'. On the other hand, Jesus not only *is* the truth, but inevitably, he therefore also *tells* the truth (John 8:45). We are not surprised, therefore, that the Christian gospel is commonly called 'the truth' (e.g. Romans 1:25; 3:7; 2 Corinthians 6:7, etc.). As followers of Christ, we are called not only to live lives of truth and trustworthiness, but also to express that inward nature of truth in our speech. In the context of coming to know Christ, in whom is the truth (Ephesians 4:21), we are instructed to put off the old life of deceitfulness and 'falsehood' and 'speak truthfully to [our] neighbour' (4:25). Otherwise, we shall 'give the devil a foothold' (4:27). Knowing Jesus Christ, we know the truth. As his followers, we are to exhibit truth in our lives and speak truth. And through Christ the gospel we believe and proclaim is itself the truth. We notice that the New Testament is talking not of '*a* truth', but of '*the* truth'.

Living in the ethnic mix

In Britain, the question of our attitude to other faiths is still relatively new. Back in the 1950s, when I was a student, we Jews were almost the only ethnic minority in Britain, and we formed the only major non-Christian community. Historically speaking, fifty years is not a long time, but it already seems like a different world. Today, our cities have large and influential ethnic-minority communities. About 30% of the resident population of London is not British ethnically – and that figure does not include tourists, business people, students or other temporary visitors to London.

Because rubbing shoulders with people of other faiths is relatively new to Christians in Britain and other European countries, the church is still struggling to find right biblical and practical answers. It is easy to become emotive in one's response to this, historically speaking, new situation. But actually the Bible has much to teach us, for in the Old Testament the people of God lived in the midst of a variety of peoples who followed their own traditional religions. In some matters (such as some elements of the sacrificial system and the concept of a covenant), they were influenced by these surrounding religions and adapted elements from them into their worship of Yahweh. All such adaptation can run the risk of corrupting the true worship of God, but at the same time it adds to the richness of our faith and also prevents God's people becoming an irrelevant ghetto. And in questions of idolatry no compromise was permitted with the Baalim and other gods. So Elijah forced the people of Israel to make a clear decision whether they would follow Yahweh as Lord, or Baal (1 Kings 18:21). He would not permit them to compromise and allow both to be true. They should no longer 'waver between two opinions'. Likewise, in the New Testament, the church was surrounded by other religious systems as practised by the highly sophisticated Romans and Greeks. Greek philosophy certainly influenced the theological expressions of the church (for instance, in the formulation of the doctrine of the Trinity), but Christians willingly suffered in order to resist compromise with idolatry. Even at the cost of their lives, they absolutely refused to bow down to pagan deities or to statues of the emperor.

On the one hand, some today feel threatened by the multitudes of ethnic-minority people in their cities, and react negatively with a view that other faiths are demonic and totally evil. On the other hand, some feel guilty about Britain's history of imperialistic colonialism and our contemporary forms of racism and economic exploitation, with all their concomitant evils. They long for a humble tolerance that will not be critical towards other faiths, other cultures or their followers. But such open-hearted tolerance can lead to naïve untruth which fails to note the sin and error in other faiths and which may therefore be weak biblically and theologically – what some have called 'wishy-washy theology'.

So how, as Christians, should we view other faiths? It is sometimes said that there are three basic approaches: pluralism, inclusivism and exclusivism.[3]

Pluralism

'I don't drink coffee with intolerant people,' he declared, as he turned his back on me.

We had been talking happily together before the rather pluralistic ministers' conference began. I was to be the speaker on the topic, 'What about other faiths? Christianity and pluralism', and in the brochure I was described as a Jewish Christian. He therefore assumed that I had been converted from Judaism. Believing that Jews have their own way to God and should not be converted to the Christian faith, he objected to my presence. He assumed that conversion from one faith to another involved an arrogant intolerance towards one's previous religion. So he would not drink coffee with me! The obvious reply was, 'Who is being intolerant? I will drink coffee with anyone.'

Pluralism may be described as being tolerant of tolerance, but gravely intolerant of anything or anyone deemed to be intolerant. If I had quickly assured him that all religions are equally good and are all on the same road towards God, he would cheerfully have drunk coffee with me. But any form of assured faith in an absolute truth is intolerable to pluralists. For them, the only absolute truth is that there is no absolute truth.

Perhaps the leading advocates of religious pluralism are John Hick of Birmingham and the Roman Catholic theologian Paul Knitter of Chicago.[4] They have written a variety of books on the subject, both individually and together. They envisage an Ultimate Absolute, towards which each of the faiths, with their founders and scriptures, is moving. This Ultimate Absolute may also be called the Idea or even the Ideal – terms used in the Hindu *Vedas* to describe the indescribable, the infinite and unknowable Brahman, who is neither personal nor impersonal. Judaists, Muslims, Christians and the followers of tribal religions may call this Absolute 'God' and think of it as personal. Buddhists may call it 'Brahma', and normally describe it as neither personal nor impersonal. Many Hindus use the terms 'Brahman', 'Om', and so on, but may also not consider it personal. Confucians believe in an impersonal 'Heaven', while Taoists seek an equally impersonal 'Tao'/Way. Actually, for the pluralist, the Absolute remains beyond all human descriptions. It/he/she cannot be known or described. For students of Hinduism, this philosophy is reminiscent of the classical Hindu belief that Brahman is the great Neti-Neti, 'Not This, Not This'. Brahman is beyond description and can finally be understood only negatively as 'Not This'.

Islamic theology faces the same dilemma concerning the transcendence of Allah. Al-Ghazzali (1059–1111), who, with his Aristotelian theology, influenced Thomas Aquinas and the Jewish Maimonides, affirmed that Allah is describable only in negatives. Thus the description of Allah as one (the Tawhid Allah) merely means that he is not many; likewise the Qur'anic mercy of Allah merely means that he is not unmerciful.

Christian theology, too, has a parallel debate. Particularly in the Russian Orthodox Church, apophatic theology affirmed that God is so gloriously holy that he is unattainable to mere humans. He remains in glorious splendour, the one whom no-one can see and then continue to live. But Orthodox theology balanced this with its cataphatic theology, which noted that, because of the incarnation of Christ, God is also knowable. Paul himself brings the two together in Colossians 1:15, with the profound observation that Christ is 'the image of the invisible God'; God is indeed essentially 'invisible', but through the incarnate Christ – God's image – we mere humans can know God.

Pluralists believe that all religions and their followers are searching for the Absolute, but never attain to it. This religious approach has become very fashionable in western societies. It is now politically correct to be searching, to be on a pilgrimage or 'on the way'. But it is considered arrogant and unacceptable to affirm that one has found the true way or arrived at the final place of pilgrimage. We can only parody the words of Jesus and describe religious pluralism by saying, 'Seek and you shall [not] find' (Luke 11:9).

Mission as dialogue

What then does mission consist of, for such pluralists? The key word is 'dialogue'. But the word is not used in the biblical sense of the Greek terms from which the word derives. In the post-resurrection Acts of the Apostles, Luke carefully changes the words he uses for 'dialogue'. In the Gospel of Luke, the words used (*dialogizomai* and *dialogismos*) convey a sense of doubting uncertainty (e.g. Luke 1:29; 3:15; 5:21–22; 20:14). But in Acts the word he uses for 'dialogue' (*dialegomai*) describes discussion with the specific aim of leading the other persons to faith in Jesus Christ (Acts 17:2, 17; 18:4, 19; 19:8–9; 20:7–9; 24:12, 25). In Acts and in the Epistles, 'dialogue' never means mere debate in order to learn and understand the other person's views. Nor does it signify any lack of assured faith. It always involves definite witness to truth with the aim of conversion to Christ.

For pluralists, mission does not seek the conversion of people from one faith to another; that is considered intolerant. They look, rather, for us all to encourage each other to strive forwards in our different belief systems. Thus the Buddhist may encourage the Taoist to be a better Taoist, while the Muslim will encourage the Christian to be a better Christian.

Such an approach automatically denies any final divine revelation and the uniqueness of the incarnation, atoning death and resurrection of Jesus. All truth is thought to be subjective, good for the believer but lacking any absolute validity for all humanity. Thus Jesus' affirmation that he is 'the way and the truth and the life. No-one comes to the Father except through me' (John 14:6) or Peter's declaration that 'salvation is found in no-one else, for there is no other name under heaven given to men by which we must be saved' (Acts 4:12) are likened to a child's declaration, 'I have the best mother in the world.' For the child, its mother may indeed be the best in the world, but this is obviously not objectively true; she is not the best mother for other people. Likewise the pluralists obscure the absolute truth of Jesus' affirmation that he is the unique way to the Father. They consider that John's recording of this saying reflects his love for Jesus. For John, Jesus is the one true way, truth and life. For John, Jesus is the unique way to the Father. But the pluralists affirm that this saying remains true only for Jesus' followers, not for other people.

Such pluralist belief reflects the life of the supermarket society. 'I like chocolate biscuits,' exclaims one person. Others may declare their preference for other types of biscuit, but no-one should be exclusive and deny others their particular likes and dislikes. It is just a matter of personal choice. Actually, one sort of biscuit is equally good as other types; likewise the pluralist will affirm that one person's faith is just as valid and true (or invalid and untrue) as any other.

It almost goes without saying that this extremely popular current view of religion undermines all active evangelism. It cuts away the very roots from which the tree of Christian mission grows. As Christians, we believe in the finality of God's revelation in Jesus Christ as the incarnate Word. Jesus alone is the Word which was with God from the beginning, and indeed was God, the Word which in due time became flesh (John 1:14) and dwelt among us. He alone 'has ever seen God' and he alone 'has made him known' (John 1:18). And it is the Bible as God's written Word (2 Timothy 3:16) that makes us 'wise for salvation through faith in Christ Jesus' (2 Timothy 3:15). We believe we have a unique saving message to declare to a bankrupt world.

Inclusivism

The best-known advocate of the inclusivist position is the highly popular Roman Catholic theologian Hans Küng.[5] But inclusivism has also become the normally accepted view among the majority of Roman Catholic scholars and missionaries.

Hans Küng does not think in terms of an 'Ultimate Absolute' or an indescribable 'Idea' or 'Ideal'. Like all Roman Catholics, he clearly believes in a personal God. All religious faiths aim upwards towards God, he believes, and all religious believers will finally come to him in salvation. As is often the case with Roman Catholic thinkers, the emphasis lies heavily on the present and future tenses in his understanding of our being saved. But the assured confidence of a salvation which has already been granted to us is sadly lacking. True biblical faith needs to affirm the fact that we already have God's gracious gift of salvation. Thus John's Gospel assures all believers in Jesus Christ that they have already received eternal life, using a present tense (e.g. John 3:36). But at the same time we must never forget the continuous process of 'being saved', whereby we grow in that salvation and God continually saves us from our sin. And then we rejoice in the assured reality of the future tense, that we shall ultimately be saved, with the fullness of God's gift of eternal life, and with him in all eternity.

Of course, Küng would maintain that Roman Catholics are further up the slope towards salvation and God, because they are said to have the true means of grace, the true sacraments in the true church, with the true teaching of the magisterium. Not far behind the Roman Catholics would come the so-called 'separated brethren' (a term popularized by the second Vatican Council), the other Christian churches – Protestant and Orthodox. Roman Catholics would consider that these lack the true church and sacraments, but they have much in common with the faith of the Catholic Church. They therefore attain a considerable measure of salvation.

Behind them come other monotheists, Muslims and Judaists in particular. Sadly, they lack the Trinity and thus the incarnate Saviour and the Holy Spirit. But they have a true knowledge of the one God through God's revelation in the Hebrew Scriptures and the Qur'an. After the monotheists, and somewhat lower than them on the climb towards God and ultimate salvation, come the other faith systems which demonstrate true religious zeal and ethical standards. They lack not only the Trinity, but also the church with its teaching, sacraments and other means of grace. Nevertheless, all are on the way towards God. Indeed, Karl Rahner in his theological-dictionary article on 'Hell', conjectures that hell exists as a reality, but probably no-one will be there! How one could wish that this were true! But the Bible is more realistic, and shows the tragic truth of human sin and unbelief under the holy judgment of God.

It may be noted that inclusivism clearly tends towards a belief in universalism, in which all people are on the way to salvation. The biblical contrasts between light and darkness, faith and unbelief, truth and untruth, goodness and evil, are downplayed. In their inclusive emphasis on universal salvation, the realities of God's absolute holiness, which cannot tolerate sin, are largely lacking. But biblical Christians cannot escape the clear New Testament teaching that those who believe in Jesus Christ have eternal life, while 'whoever rejects the Son will not see life, for God's wrath remains on him' (John 3:36).

When we come to the question of revelation, Küng and other inclusivists would believe not only in the Bible as God's revealed Word, but also that, in a lesser way, the scriptures of other faiths reveal God and his will. So other religions not only are forms of the human search for God, but also have in themselves some degree of divine revelation. The perfect revelation lies in Jesus Christ, the incarnate Word of God, and in the Bible as God's written Word. But God also reveals himself and his will in a lesser way, they would affirm, through the scriptures of other faiths. This approach fails to deal adequately with the evident contradictions between the teachings of the Bible and those of other religions' scriptures. Non-Christian religious scriptures are not only inadequate and lacking the fullness of God's revelation (though they may indeed contain much wisdom and truth); they are also fundamentally contradictory to the Christian revelation in Christ and the Bible in many of their beliefs. As Bible-based Christians, we can, then, only reject them as divine revelation, however much we may observe elements of truth and wisdom within them.

Mission as unconditional love

What about the inclusivists' approach to Christian mission? Again, 'dialogue' is a key word, for they believe that all are on the way of salvation and all have something of God's true revelation. Therefore, they rightly maintain, we can with tolerance seek truth in and from each other. And yet they may also believe that it can remain desirable for people to move upwards towards God and so be converted to a faith which is nearer to a perfect knowledge of God and of his salvation. It may therefore be helpful for a Muslim to become a Christian or for a Protestant to become a Roman Catholic. But such conversion is never essential for salvation and so there is no urgency for evangelism or conversion.

This inclusivist view is common not only in the Roman Catholic Church, but also among those who may be termed 'liberal evangelicals'. In their humility, they seek to avoid all criticism of and controversy with other faiths. And in their desire to love unconditionally, they tend to avoid the apparently negative doctrines of sin and judgment. Inclusivism prevails in many Christian churches, both Protestant and Roman Catholic. But again, it undermines an assured witness to Jesus Christ and zeal for evangelism. One can hardly imagine the apostles in the early church advocating either the pluralist or the inclusivist position. Their strong affirmation of Christian truths excluded all easy acceptance of the surrounding religious philosophies and practices. In Athens, Paul used the local belief in an 'unknown God' as the introduction to his preaching of Christ (Acts 17:23), but he proceeded to declare to the Athenians the one true 'God who made the world and everything in it'. He went on to denounce all idolatry, the worship of gods made of gold, silver or stone. This he denounced as 'ignorance', and called on the people to repent – and some, indeed, did come to believe (Acts 17:34). Finally, he warned of the judgment to come through Jesus, whom the Father had raised from the dead.

The apostles strongly denied any 'other gospel' (Galatians 1:9), one which is not 'by the grace of Christ' (Galatians 1:6). With strong language they denounced any 'deceivers, who do not acknowledge Jesus Christ as coming in the flesh' (2 John 7) as 'the deceiver and the antichrist'. John goes on to urge his readers to 'continue in the teaching of Christ', which he defines as 'walking in the truth', and to 'love one another', which means walking 'in obedience to [Christ's] commands' (2 John 4–6).

To be positive, however, inclusivists may have a clear faith in the living God of the Bible together with a definite belief in the fundamental truths of traditional Christian theology – the incarnation, atoning death, resurrection, ascension and second coming of Jesus Christ, within the overarching truth of the Trinity. But the exclusive uniqueness of these truths may be watered down. Evangelicals may rejoice in the positive truth of what inclusivists hold, but may disagree with their failure to note the sin and untruth in other faiths plus the downplaying of God's holy judgment, which can undermine passion for evangelism. Other, more social and developmental, aspects of mission may be emphasized rather than the call to evangelism.

Exclusivism

As is also true of pluralists and inclusivists, so too the exclusivist position ranges along a spectrum from extreme conservatism to a far less rigid belief system. Fundamentally, exclusivists believe that there can be no revelation outside the Word of God in Jesus Christ and the Bible. Likewise, they hold that salvation can be gained only by grace through specific faith in the death and resurrection of Jesus Christ.

In each of the three movements revelation and salvation lie at the heart of the debate.

Revelation

Is God's self-revelation found only in Jesus Christ and the Bible? Or can followers of other faiths also know something of God and his truth? The answer to such questions will partly determine whether truth can be found in other faiths. I say 'partly' because some knowledge of God's nature and will may remain within human tradition from before the advent of sin into human history. Despite long centuries of human corruption, truth and goodness may linger within us.

Throughout the history of Protestant theology, Christians have always believed in 'general revelation'. In Roman Catholic theology, this has been known as 'natural revelation'. It teaches that a remnant of God's creational image and likeness has remained in his creation, and particularly in humanity. This means that something of God can be seen in nature, and particularly in our fellow human beings (cf. Romans 1:19, 20). Sadly, however, the whole creation is joined to humanity in our descent into sin, so that our knowledge of God through nature is corrupted. Similarly, we have to confess that our human eyes are dimmed by sin and do not see clearly (cf. 1 Corinthians 13:12). Thus the revelation itself is imperfect, as are those who observe the revelation within creation.

But we look forward to the glorious climax of history when we shall come into the full presence of the Lord with all our imperfections washed away (Revelation 7:14–17). Only then shall we enter into a full and perfect apprehension of God's revelation. Meanwhile, even God's redeemed people still have imperfect sight. Even with the indwelling Holy Spirit to lead us step by step into all truth, our understanding remains clouded by imperfection and we have an inadequate grasp of the glories of the Lord. The unredeemed and followers of other faiths are likely to suffer even more from the lack of the Holy Spirit of truth.

The corrupted nature of our human appreciation of God's revelation in nature may be illustrated by an extreme story told of Hitler. It is said that he stood on the veranda of his beautiful centre in Berchtesgaden and looked out over the magnificent Austrian Alps. A pretty stream wound its way through the meadows and woods in the foreground, while the beauty of the snow-capped mountains formed a splendid backdrop. Handsome deer further enlivened the beauty of the scenery. But Hitler's only comment was, 'If nature can be so cruel, why should not I be, too?'

While other people might see the beauty of the scenery, Hitler's corrupted eyes saw only nature's cruelty. He certainly did not see the glory of God there. Of course, he was partly right. It is true that nature is cruel in its fallen state. Trees compete with each other for light, with the result that some die. Stags fight each other for supremacy. Each autumn, leaves die and fall to the ground. Birds devour worms and insects. Cruelty and beauty coexist together in nature. Something of

God and his perfection can be seen in nature all around us, but the revelation is now imperfect. Indeed, it not only shows the glory of God, but also the fallen nature of the world and humanity.

Within us as human beings, too, goodness and evil, truth and untruth, struggle together. In Romans 7, Paul sees the flesh and the spirit struggling together within us, so 'nothing good lives in me' despite the fact that 'I have the desire to do what is good' (Romans 7:18). The remnant image of God in us is at all points corrupted by sin. But it can equally well be said that the evil and untruth in us are mitigated by the influence of that same remnant image of God. Unbelievers are therefore never totally demonic, and redeemed Christians are never perfect or without error.

Other religions are therefore a mixture of good and evil, truth and untruth. It would be naïve to glorify them as true revelations of God and his will. But it would also be wrong to condemn them as totally demonic, evil and untrue. They contain much that we as Christians will agree with and rejoice in, but there is also much that will require the atoning work of Jesus Christ in order to bring salvation. From a mission perspective, therefore, we shall find much in other faiths and in their followers which can be seen as a bridge to the full revelation of God in Christ, much that can be used as a foundation upon which to build the true edifice of the good news of Jesus Christ. We shall also be challenged by them and have much to learn from them. But at the same time we shall be called to proclaim the glories of salvation and new life in the gospel of Christ. 'Dialogue' and gospel preaching will go together.

Salvation

In the past, many evangelical missionaries were motivated by the thought of multitudes of the unevangelized facing the judgment of a holy God (e.g. Romans 2:5; Revelation 20:15; 21:8). They had nightmares in which they saw thousands of lemmings running towards the edge of a cliff without anyone warning them of the danger. They calculated how many people per hour were entering a Christless eternity. Hudson Taylor was moved by the thought of the multitudes of unbelieving Chinese facing a Christless eternity. Amy Carmichael had a dream in which she saw people casually enjoying a picnic while multitudes were hurtling towards their death. So they were themselves moved to spend their lives in evangelistic mission and to encourage others to share the same passion.

Can no-one be saved, then, without specific faith in Jesus Christ? This question met a definite negative answer in the past, but now people are querying whether the answer is quite so simple.

The Bible clearly shows that no-one can be saved through his or her own meritorious deeds or religious sincerity and zeal, for 'all have sinned and fall short of the glory of God' (Romans 3:23). There is no-one, Jew or Gentile, who can claim to be adequately righteous for God, who is so holy that he cannot even 'look on evil' (Habakkuk 1:13; Romans 3:9–20). So we are never going to point to the sincere religious faith to be found in other religions and suggest that this will lead to salvation. And salvation comes exclusively through the work of Jesus Christ on the cross and in his resurrection. We cannot believe, therefore, that other religions in themselves are the means of salvation.

Our relationship as sinners to God is by grace alone. We can never deserve his acceptance of us. That much is clear. But the question remains whether God in his infinite grace could not apply the saving work of Christ to some people who *would* have believed, if only they had heard the good news of Christ in an adequate way. God knows our hearts, and he knows who would believe if they really heard the gospel. Of course, the word 'adequate' is impossible to define, but God remains the perfect and just judge. I sometimes wonder about some fellow Jews who have suffered horrendously at the hands of Christians in Nazi death camps. Their experience makes it almost impossibly hard for them to accept a faith which they associate with such fearful evil. Does God see their hearts and make allowance? What does the word 'adequate' mean for such folk? Happily, we can remain assured that judgment and therefore salvation remain firmly in God's hands. And God will always be just in his judgments.

Sadly, we have to admit that probably only a small minority humbly seek salvation with repentant hearts. And it remains the responsibility of all Christians to preach Jesus Christ to Jew and Gentile alike, to all people of every background everywhere. But our motive is not only that people may be saved from the wrath and judgment of God. Salvation includes the whole spectrum of God's gracious working on our behalf. In the Gospels the word 'save' is used for Jesus' miracles of physical healing, deliverance from demons and rescuing from storms. Mission wants all people everywhere to enter into the fullness of God's abundant grace and generous love, both for this life on earth and for eternity.

The threat to mission

An aggressively 'tolerant' pluralism threatens Christian mission, particularly in Britain and the rest of Europe. Already we hear ominous reports. A Scandinavian Bible school has been fined for dismissing a member of staff on moral grounds, because she was living with someone who was not her husband. Such 'discrimination' on the basis of sexual practice is now illegal there. A British pastor has received a warning from the police that he should remove a poster from his church notice board. Its message that 'Jesus is the only way' might offend the local Sikh community. It may soon be illegal to say anything that implies anything negative about another faith.

Will churches and Bible and theological colleges in Britain and in Europe generally have to defy the law if they want to employ only committed Christians? This will probably relate particularly to the employment of people for administrative and practical work. The European Union social laws disallow any 'discrimination' on the basis of sexual practice or orientation, gender, religion or age. The time seems to be approaching when Christian leaders will face prison or fines if they remain faithful to their Christian principles, insisting on employing only Christians whose lives match their biblical profession. One wonders how many will stand their ground even against the law. It has been easy to pray for Christians in communist and other countries who have suffered for their faith, but we do not expect this in western Europe. Are we ready for it? Perhaps we need to teach our churches more adequately about suffering for the faith of Christ, following in the footsteps of the Suffering Servant.

The pluralism debate impinges very much on Christian school-teachers, as also on social workers and people in the medical professions. Can social workers and those in the medical profession encourage people to use eastern religious practices such as yoga and Asian forms of meditation? How should Christian teachers relate their faith to school assemblies and to the teaching of religious education? Is it right to show one's Christian convictions in such contexts? Can a Christian teacher introduce the festivals of other religions with their worship practices into the life of a school? Churches have also to ask whether they should allow other religious communities to use their hall for meetings which include non-Christian worship. All of us may sometimes face the issue of multifaith meetings in our local cathedral or other prominent locations. If we stand rigidly in opposition, we can appear intolerant and thus mar the graciousness of our witness. If we are tolerant, we may seem to affirm the prevailing pluralist view that all religions are equally good.

We may expect growing opposition to the Christian message of the uniqueness of Jesus Christ as the one Saviour and Lord for all the world. A clear and definite witness may not be considered acceptable.

The cutting edge to this mission debate at present is in the area of evangelism among Jews. As we have seen, many liberal Christians query whether it is right to evangelize Jews, believing that they have their own way to God and to salvation without faith in Jesus Christ. Such liberal Christians even oppose evangelism by the Jewish mission, Jews for Jesus, among their own people. This opposition stems from cultural as well as theological reasons. Culturally, they object to the very Jewish forms of communication, which are direct and robust. Some British Christians would wish to impose more 'English' patterns of evangelism, in which words like 'perhaps', 'rather' and 'somewhat' predominate. Sadly, even the Archbishop of Canterbury's office has made it clear in a letter to Jews for Jesus that it opposes such controversially up-front evangelism of Jews. But Jewish Christians, particularly, will reject such unconscious cultural imperialism, which seems to assume that Jews should practise a more British and less robust evangelistic methodology.

But the opposition is not just cultural. It is also philosophical or theological. The prevailing pluralism strongly objects to any evangelism among people of other faiths, and particularly among Jews. The debate about the evangelization of Jews is therefore just the thin end of the wedge. If it can be shown that Jewish evangelism is wrong, then that can be extended to witness among Muslims, who are also monotheistic. And then the question will be raised: should we evangelize Hindus and others? If Jews do not need Jesus Christ for their salvation and relationship to God, do not other religions also have their own ways of salvation apart from Jesus Christ? This challenge to mission stares us in the face, and it will increase as the twenty-first century develops, with its growing multicultural, multi-ethnic and multi-religious societies.[6]

Discussion starters

1. Which beliefs do you consider to be unique to the Christian faith?
2. Which aspects of life in Christ would you wish to underline in your witness to a Muslim, a Buddhist, a Judaist and a Hindu?
3. How can we maintain our faith in the unique and absolute truth of the Christian faith without appearing arrogant and therefore unacceptable to our pluralist neighbours?

Notes

1. G. McDermott, *Can Evangelicals Learn from World Religions?* (IVP, 2000).
2. For further thinking on the topic of absolute truth, see H. Netland, *Dissonant Voices: Religious Pluralism and the Question of Truth* (Eerdmans, 1991).
3. For a good explanation of the pluralist, inclusivist and exclusivist positions see C. Wright, *Thinking Clearly About the Uniqueness of Jesus* (Monarch, 1997).
4. See J. Hick, *The Myth of God Incarnate* (SCM, 1993), or *The Rainbow of Faiths: Critical Dialogues on Religious Pluralism* (SCM, 1995); J. Hick and P. Knitter, *The Myth of Christian Uniqueness* (SCM, 1988); P. Knitter, *No Other Name? A Critical Survey of Christian Attitudes towards the World Religions* (SCM, 1985).
5. Hans Küng has written various very useful books relating to the different world religions. For his overall thinking on the Christian attitude to other faiths, see his *Christianity Among World Religions* (T. & T. Clark, 1986).
6. For further reading on the subject of the Christian attitude to other faiths, see M. Goldsmith, *What About Other Faiths?* (Hodder, 2002); and C. Wright, *Thinking Clearly About the Uniqueness of Jesus* (Monarch, 1997).

2 What a small world

How good it is, as Christians, to be reminded that not only did God love his own people, Israel, with their land, but he reaches out in love to the whole world, which he created and for which Jesus died. In John 1:9–10, John uses the word 'world' four times to underline the width of God's love – not just for Israel, but for *all the world*. John's use of the word 'world' has special significance. It is clearly employed in the context of the fact of creation (cf. John 1:3, 10), but John changes the word used in the Genesis account. In Genesis 1:1, God created the heavens and the 'earth'. The Hebrew for 'earth' is *eretz*, which, in New Testament times and still today, is used for the 'land' of Israel. But John is not wanting to limit the relevance of Jesus' coming to just Israel, so he carefully uses the wider term 'world'. To show that he has purposely and significantly changed the Genesis term, he uses 'world' four times.

Jesus has come not only for Israel, but for the whole world. Indeed, John notes with tragic pathos that Jesus' own Jewish people have largely refused to receive him (John 1:11), but the door is now open for 'all' who receive and believe in him to become the children of God (John 1:12). In Old Testament times the Jews were the children of God, for the Lord himself declared to Pharaoh through Moses, 'Israel is my firstborn son' (Exodus 4:22). But now the Gentiles, too, can become what they were not before, the children of God.

John further stresses the universality of God's purposes in Christ by declaring that the Word became 'flesh' (John 1:14), a wide term which relates to all humanity. So both Jews and Gentiles are welcomed into the family of God.

This global vision climaxes in the great, end-time vision of the international multitudes before the throne of the Lord (Revelation 7). The vision starts with the 144,000 from the tribes of Israel (Revelation 7:4). This symbolic number consists of 12 × 12 × 1,000, the twelve tribes of Israel × the twelve apostles × 1,000. In Jewish thought, 1,000 stands for a large, but not infinite, number. Multitudes of Old and New Testament believers stand before the throne, but not everyone is saved. The large number remains limited. But we look forward to multitudes of Jews and Gentiles worshipping the Lamb of God:

'Salvation belongs to our God,
who sits on the throne,
and to the Lamb.'
(Revelation 7:10)

The global village

For many years people have been talking of the world as a 'global village'. How remote other continents seemed in the past! But that is no longer true today. Relatively cheap, convenient and rapid travel has changed the whole perception of the world.

Back in the sixteenth and seventeenth centuries, travel was fearfully slow, dangerous and expensive. The Jesuits sent some great pioneer missionaries to India, China and Japan. Robert de Nobili followed in the footsteps of Francis Xavier, planting churches which have continued even to our time.[1] Matteo Ricci[2] ventured to China, where he became famous as a Confucian Christian scholar, while Alessandro Valignano headed up the dangerous ministry in Japan and wrote his two-volume book on mission principles and practices for that area.[3]

Their journeys to Asia from Europe defy the imagination for us now. To get to Macao in China took them at least two years, stopping in Goa and Malacca. And the sea journey was both expensive and horrendously difficult. Pirates threatened, and the small sailing ships were at the mercy of storms or of being becalmed. In those days, too, Europeans did not understand hygiene at all, so they never washed, and on the ships they crowded into the lower decks, where they slept and ate. The same overcrowded, stiflingly hot living quarters were also used for toilet purposes. Travelling slowly through the windless heat of tropical climates in such appalling conditions took its toll, and many died *en route* to the Far East. Clean water for washing and drinking was in short supply. A flushable toilet or a little deodorant and fresh-air spray would not have come amiss!

My wife Elizabeth's great-grandfather sailed round the Cape of Good Hope in South Africa to work in India as a missionary in 1846.[4] By his time, sailing ships were more advanced and he was able to reach India in only four months. This made the call to mission just a little easier. When Elizabeth and I went to Singapore in 1960, the Suez Canal had long been open and ships travelled more quickly. So it took us only three weeks to reach Singapore – to the amazement of Elizabeth's old father, who had needed many weeks when he went to China as a missionary in 1913.

Now, in the twenty-first century, Elizabeth and I have the privilege of a travelling ministry in which we are invited to speak in a different country once each month, on average. Without air travel this would be quite impossible. How easy it is now to flit from London to Africa or Asia or the Americas! And the cost of air tickets is relatively small, so missions and churches feel able to afford to invite a foreign speaker. As we shall see in a later chapter, the ease and cheapness of travel also allows short-term mission and brief mission trips.

As a result of modern travel opportunities, the whole world has been forced to interrelate more closely. It is no longer possible for one country or area to remain isolated from others. We are all impacted by what happens elsewhere in the world. Even a hermit nation like North Korea can no longer hide behind doctrinaire walls. It has to face the impact of influences from America and also the rest of Asia. Likewise, the formerly very closed country of Saudi Arabia now has multitudes of foreigners working within its borders. Westerners play a leading role in the higher echelons of its oil industry and in medical, educational and other professional aspects of society. Indians, Egyptians and others do much of the blue-collar work, while Bangladeshis, Sri Lankans and black Africans add their muscle-power in manual labour. With their oil money has come prosperity. Mobile phones and easy internet access join the television with international news and programmes. These bring the wider world right into the sitting-room, even in formerly isolated parts of the world. As a result, even Saudi Arabia now faces the challenges of contemporary life and radical demands for greater democracy. People no longer assume that a chauvinistic, royal-family Islamic dictatorship is the only possible system, even for a strictly Muslim nation.

The effects of globalization are here to stay and can only increase as the twenty-first century unfolds in the coming decades. Mission in all our countries cannot avoid the consequences. What happens in one country's churches affects the life and witness of other churches around the world. If the church is to relate relevantly to the modern world, it must log on to globalization.

Globalization or tribalism?

It is no longer a surprise to find a large centre in Singapore supporting Manchester United and selling their merchandise. All over the world, people support Manchester United, Liverpool or Arsenal. Pop singers and film stars are famous the world over and everyone knows their faces. Western television dramas and soaps fascinate their viewers in every country. The same teeshirts and contemporary dress fads adorn bodies of every colour in every continent. People all over the world drive the same cars, use the same washing machines and depend on the same computer programs. Outwardly it seems that globalization has won the day.

Actually, however, as we shall see, an undergirding of the local culture remains beneath the surface. Globalized African youngsters still remain very African. Beneath their westernized veneer, their way of thinking, their relationships and their worldview cling firmly to their particular background. This is equally true for Europeans, Asians and indeed all people everywhere.

I read a well-researched article in a leading journal on the subject of British businessmen living and working in East Asian cities. To my great surprise, it claimed that Singapore was the most difficult Asian city for such British businessmen to come to terms with. Having lived there happily for some years, I found this incredible, until I read the article more fully. It said that cities like Seoul, Bangkok and Tokyo force the foreigner to adapt culturally, because their Asian-ness stares us in the face. Singapore, however, appears entirely westernized and culturally modern and tolerant. It lulls Europeans into a comfortable unaware-ness, in which they fail to adjust culturally. Local people remain friendly and polite, but relationships never go deeper, and business contacts often somehow fail to develop. This can lead to frustration. While people may look very globalized or even westernized, actually their traditional background and values still cling on tenaciously.

There is also a reaction against the unifying effect of globalization. A fierce local identity rears its head in nationalistic and sometimes violent opposition. In many parts of the world, minority peoples are rebelling against larger nations, demanding their independence. Thus, while the European Union enlarges and we are encouraged more and more to become European citizens rather than just British or French, at the same time there is a growing emphasis on regional identity. Local parliaments are established in Scotland, Wales and Northern Ireland. Likewise, the Basques and Catalans in Spain insist on regional autonomy.

The same is true of other continents. The Organization for African Unity unites many African nations and seeks to bring into being a pan-African trade area and political co-responsibility. But at the same time, nations are divided along strong traditional tribal lines, and even the church feels the baleful influence of tribal rivalries. The Association for South East Asian Nations helps to bring unity in economic and security issues in Southeast Asia, but ethnic animosities rage in the Philippines and Indonesia. The Muslim peoples in Mindanao, the southern-most island of the Philippines, continue to use violence in seeking independence from the Catholic Philippines. Rebellious Pattani Malays fight for independence, or at least autonomy, in South Thailand. Aceh rebels continue to fight the Indonesian army for independence even after the horrors of the 2004 Boxing Day tsunami. All over the world such tribalisms coexist with the internationalizing effects of globalization.

Inevitably, all this affects the mission of God's people both in Europe and elsewhere. The church has to identify with local sensibilities and yet at the same time relate across ethnic divides to the transnational movements.

The combination of globalization and the local search for a more personalized identity needs to be reflected in our Christian concept of the church. Before the Reformation, people believed in the one international church, the one body of Christ – although actually it was already divided into the western Catholic Church and the eastern family of Orthodox churches. At the Reformation, the concept of the church was narrowed down to national churches – the Church of England, of Germany, of Norway, and so on. This process was taken a step further with the new development of denominations, and then still further with the emphasis on the local church or congregation, and an even greater narrowing down into cell churches. In today's world we need to recover the New Testament teaching on the one body of Christ worldwide, while still enjoying the local church with its more intimate identity and fellowship.

In 1 Corinthians 12 Paul maintains a careful balance between the smaller unity of the individual and the larger body of Christ. To each individual Christian 'the manifestation of the Spirit is given' (1 Corinthians 12:7), but this is never for mere selfish enjoyment. The gifts of the Holy Spirit are 'for the common good'. Individual Christians, with their differing gifts, stand together, therefore, as united members of the one body (1 Corinthians 12:12ff.), which is formed from Jews and Greeks, slaves and free (1 Corinthians 12:13). The one Holy Spirit indwells people of varying ethnic background, as also of different social status. In Christ, all such barriers of division are broken down in the one church of God. Love flows across borders in the global church. As Christians, we are all children of the same heavenly Father, united in faith in the one Saviour, Christ, and indwelt by the one Holy Spirit. We dare not allow western individualism to keep us from a true knowledge of our unity in the worldwide church. Our differences remain – we are still Jews or Gentiles, men or women, free or slave – but our unity shatters all worldly pride and status.

Andrew Walls [5] helpfully reminds us that the concept of the church as the body of Christ is not only spatial but also temporal. It includes not only all Christians everywhere, but also God's people throughout all generations. Postmodern globalization tends to be unduly influenced by existentialism, with its lack of interest in anything but the present. The past and the future have lost interest for many today. Immediate gratification and results alone concern them. But in mission we have to buck this trend, for God often works slowly. The 400 years of divine silence between the prophet Malachi and the coming of John the Baptist must have tested people's faith. Many Christian workers in Europe today, as also in some Muslim and Buddhist societies, face uphill struggles with little apparent fruitfulness. The words of Habakkuk may encourage us:

'Though it linger, wait for it;
  it will certainly come and will not delay.'
(Habakkuk 2:3)

The relationship of globalization to the teaching of the New Testament needs to be kept to the fore in all church-planting mission, both in Europe and elsewhere.

What sort of churches, with what relationships, are we planting?

Ethnic movements

Stanstead Abbotts, where we live, is hardly a metropolis. We are just a small village, north of London. Some years ago I was given an American postcard showing the skyline of a large city with huge skyscrapers and high-rise blocks along the shore, with their lights reflected in the water. The picture was accompanied by the words, 'Every village dreams of becoming a big city.' To us in Stanstead Abbotts, this seems more a nightmare than a dream!

And yet globalization affects us, too, with the movement of peoples from country to country. Even in our small village we have various families from different ethnic backgrounds. And we enjoy the international food offered in Chinese, Indian and Italian restaurants.

In our village, most people who came to Britain from overseas did so either because they had married British citizens or as so-called 'economic migrants'. None came to Britain for more traumatic reasons.

International business and trade demand that many professionals have to live and work in other countries. Sometimes downsizing and consequent unemployment forces people to move elsewhere even when that proves detrimental to marriage and family life. Sometimes people are eager to work in wealthier countries in order to earn larger salaries, to save for their future or to support families back home.

The world today is also facing huge movements of peoples to escape injustice, war and violence, oppression or natural disasters. Many millions of refugees flood over the borders from Myanmar, Sudan and Somalia, Iraq and Iran, Afghanistan, the Democratic Republic of Congo, the former Yugoslavia and other troubled regions of the world. Although we have survived half a century of peace in terms of world wars since 1945, multitudes of relatively minor wars have erupted in various places. Each of these pushes whole segments of the local population over their borders to escape violence and devastation. Refugee camps spring up like mushrooms with lines of Red Cross tents in the midst of fearful shortages of water, food and hygiene. Television has made us almost immune to the sight of such appalling trauma, with the wailing of the bereaved, the swollen stomachs of the starving and the flies roaming freely on bodies too weak to remove them.

A relatively new phenomenon has shocked us. The trade in human beings snatches large numbers away from their homes and native lands to work as virtual slaves in wealthier places. Even children are transported from their own countries to work in sweat shops, producing cheap goods, or to work on agricultural estates to feed our supermarkets. Young girls are smuggled into the wealthy, sex-hungry countries of the West to feed the sex trade. Others are kept in their own countries to satisfy sex tourism, but they, too, are virtual slaves in situations of terrible oppression.

The needs of refugees and oppressed people all over the world, including our own country, challenge the Christian church in its mission. And mission must relate to the multi-ethnic situation in almost every country.

Cultural globalization

A young man told me that he was wondering whether God might be calling him to full-time mission work in Africa. He was very English in his particular youth-culture way. Earrings hung from his ears, tattoos adorned his arms, his unshaven face bristled beneath his shaggy hair, and his T-shirt shouted a quotation from a modern song. Would he have the self-discipline to learn an African language and adapt to the culture there? Later, I bumped into him in a large city in Asia. I noticed how brilliantly he fitted in with the globalized local young men, the sort of people more traditional missionaries may find it hard to relate to. Many in that city could also speak English, so there was no problem in communication. Like him, they watched the latest soaps and listened to the same music. They had much in common. With the spread of a common global culture, mission recruitment must change.

And yet those same young men can struggle if their backgrounds are more traditional. How can people relate the new international culture to the old patterns drummed into them by family and school throughout their youth?

We were walking through the plaza at the foot of the superb twin Petronas towers in Kuala Lumpur, the Malaysian capital. Crowds of young people thronged the food stalls. Young men and women walked together in an uninhibited proximity which would have scandalized their more conservative Muslim forefathers. I saw a Muslim Malay girl with a strongly Muslim head-covering, which normally denotes someone who is conservative in their faith. But then I observed that she was wearing a tight-fitting mini-skirt, revealing acres of bare flesh. What struggles was she facing between her traditional Muslim background and her new, modern culture? How did such struggles affect her Muslim faith? How can we communicate Christ to her in a way which relates to her cultural and religious struggles?

In the melting-pot of rapidly changing postmodern culture in the great cities of the world, it is important for Christian workers to be culturally flexible. It may be helpful to have teams of Christian workers from various ethnic and national backgrounds. We can no longer afford to have rigid workers who export their particular culture or Christian tradition.

Elizabeth and I belonged to an international mission whose members brought with them a wide range of backgrounds. When I first applied to the Overseas Missionary Fellowship (OMF), the Anglican home director interviewed me, asking how I would feel as an Anglican in an interdenominational mission. I hastened to assure him that I was no dyed-in-the-wool Anglican and was happy to fit in with other expressions of the Christian faith.

He smiled and replied, 'You have given the wrong answer!' He then explained that OMF is an interdenominational mission, not non-denominational. 'We want all our members to be fully themselves and to contribute to the whole fellowship the positive values of their particular Christian background with its beliefs and practices. We don't want a lowest-common-denominator approach to the life and work of our mission.'

In the postmodern context of multicultural societies, we need to be demonstrating, as Christian workers, the reality of mixed teams who can be fully themselves and yet work in unity and loving harmony. Each member should contribute the richness of his or her own tradition.

Economic globalization

It has been said that, when the oil minister of Saudi Arabia smiles, the world smiles with him. But when he frowns, all the world shivers in its economic boots.

It is not just the supply and price of oil that influence the lives of us all in every part of the world. All trade is now internationalized. Our cheap prices in the large supermarkets depend on their being able to squeeze the farmers into selling their produce with minimum profit. So farmers, both in our home country and overseas, find it hard to make ends meet, and many go out of business. Because of this, we in Europe have subsidized our agricultural exports to other countries and so given more business to our own farmers. But our subsidized agricultural products have undercut subsistence farmers in Africa and Latin America, so they cannot sell their produce. This in turn contributes to the fearful poverty and even starvation many experience in some nations.

Talk of globalization immediately brings to mind the enormous power today of the huge multinational companies. Some of these have larger budgets than many nations, and wield greater power. The bottom line for all these companies is financial profit. Because of this, the temptation to exploit local people hovers over them. Horror stories abound of such companies raping the environment in order to get cheap materials, treating local workers like slaves and ignoring the welfare and prosperity of society. As Christians, we have to acknowledge the economic success of such exploitative enterprises. But because of our love for our neighbour, we are called to work to change attitudes.

Thus one evangelical Anglican bishop in South America showed the international mining company in his area that humane treatment of workers would make it less likely that the local government would nationalize their work. If such nationalization took place, they would lose their whole investment in the country. So they agreed to give good housing and education to their workers and families. Good health facilities followed. And the mining was done with an eye to the environment and ecology. Local people then associated the benevolence of the foreign international company with the church and the good news of Jesus Christ.

So it can often be true that our social and spiritual ministries may work together like the two cutting edges of a pair of scissors.

Global economics reign, not just in agriculture, but in every area of enterprise. Salaries in India are generally much lower than in Europe, so call-centre work and other computerized jobs can be done more cheaply there. Many magazines go to India for their typesetting, and even their printing may be done in Hong Kong rather than in Europe. The rapid economic development of China and India, with their vast populations of 1,300 and 1,000 million respectively, causes a shortage of steel and other raw materials. This has accelerated steep price rises. Inevitably, this affects employment opportunities and economic developments generally both in Europe and elsewhere.

Mission and global economics

How does all this relate to the work of mission in our age? Of course, love for our neighbour should move us to be willing to change our lifestyles. We have to be concerned for a right use of resources and a fair price for all farmers in selling their produce. How far should world economic issues affect our shopping? Missions have alerted people to the gross economic inequalities in our world. Urgent calls have been issued to support such movements as fair trade.[6] Mission today, particularly, involves matters of economic self-help, assisting local people to set up micro-businesses to give employment and finance without having to depend on handouts.

The mission of God's church in every country depends more and more now on world economics. Thus the British church has had to face the employment insecurity of its members, as the old pattern of life-long jobs has gone out of the window. Many Christians now live with one-year job contracts and the constant threat of losing their job. Such insecurity inevitably hits the amount in the offering plate on a Sunday. Increasing numbers of workers face times when they are away from their family because of having to visit branches of their firm overseas. International trade forces people to travel, with consequent strain on their marriages and their relationship with their children. Both in evangelism and in pastoral care, the mission of the church needs to relate to such contemporary issues. Otherwise we do not scratch where people itch.

For non-Christian travelling business people, the reality of the Christian church worldwide is good news. Many years ago I sat next to a non-Christian South African businessman on a flight to Cape Town. He told me that in his work he had to visit that city every three months, but he found it terribly lonely. No-one would welcome him at the airport and he would stay at the hotel on his own, have his dinner on his own, go to bed on his own, have his breakfast on his own and get a taxi to the factory on his own.

Anticipating my first visit to Cape Town, I told him, 'I shall be met by a sister of mine and shall stay with her and her family.' I proceeded to tell him how in visits to Kabul, Buenos Aires, Nairobi and other cities I had stayed with other brothers or sisters.

His eyes widened in amazement. 'It must be brilliant to belong to such a large family all over the world.' Only then did I reveal to him what the family was.

For a lonely travelling businessman (or preacher!) the international church is indeed good news. Rose Dowsett, in her book *The Great Commission*,[7] rejoices that she had been 'born into a worldwide family, with global privileges'. She continues with the further implication that such privileges also carry 'global responsibilities'.

Travelling business people have untold opportunities to encourage local Christians wherever they go. They also have the chance to give

New Testaments as presents to those who invite them to dinner. With the introductory words, 'Would you graciously accept the gift of a copy of my Holy Book?', surprisingly, almost nobody will refuse. Christian professionals overseas are meeting people who may never otherwise hear the good news of Jesus Christ, so they are God's chosen messengers for mission.

Of course, it is also true that economic globalization carries with it the responsibility of sharing financially with those in need, not only in our own country, but also across the world.[8]

Globalization and the environment

'Our lakes are no longer suffering from bad acid rain, so fish are beginning to return,' our Norwegian friend remarked.

We felt a sense of relief. On previous visits to Norway, people had sometimes commented on acid rain that was affecting the lakes and their supply of fish. It was commonly believed that the acid rain came across the North Sea from Britain. Norwegians (probably correctly?) accused us in Britain of allowing our motor traffic and industry to pollute the atmosphere to such an extent that it affected them too.

Many of us remember with horror the explosion in Chernobyl in 1986, with its tragic consequences. These still continue in Ukraine, where the country is classified into regions according to their distance away from Chernobyl.

I well remember teaching at a missions training course for Ukrainian Pentecostal mission candidates in Region 2. Every morning the students came to class recounting what skin diseases had developed overnight, particularly in their children. Much discussion followed as to what creams might alleviate the symptoms. One morning a student came with a big smile all over her face. Yes, her sister had had a baby and it was without physical disability. Hers was apparently the only baby born whole and without handicap at that time in the large maternity hospital of the city. Even after some years, Chernobyl was leaving its mark. And its baleful consequences reached out across Europe, even infecting sheep in Wales.

Misuse of the environment not only affects the immediate neighbourhood, but stretches its ugly tentacles into other countries too. We live in a globalized world in which we all depend considerably on each other. We shall look further at the importance of ecology and the environment in mission when we discuss the holistic nature of mission.

Global problems

As we have seen, none of us today can live in isolation from the wider world. What happens in one part of the world can impact us all.

For example, the worldwide epidemic of Aids is thought to have started in apparent insignificance in what was, to us Europeans, a remote part of Africa. It has now spread into every country and threatens all our societies with ever-increasing ferocity. Unlike most epidemics, it hits particularly young adults, who form the major part of a nation's workforce. The massive social tragedy of sickness, suffering and death is therefore compounded by its economic consequences. While Aids has been controlled to some extent in the wealthy nations of the West, it multiplies like wildfire in Africa, Asia and Eastern Europe. The already prevailing poverty of those parts of the world is now exacerbated by this pandemic.

Christian mission workers are increasingly now on the frontline of the battle against Aids. Many are involved in educational work, teaching about Aids and how to avoid it. In their teaching, Christians also stress the compassion of Christ towards all who suffer. With greater understanding, people learn not to fear any contact with Aids sufferers, and not to shun them, as is the common reaction. Jesus gave us a beautiful model in the way he related to people with leprosy and other sicknesses. He even reached out his hand and touched a leper (Matthew 8:3) as he healed him. And he evidently visited the home of Simon the Leper (Matthew 26:6). He would often touch the untouchables with his hands of love, showing them in practice the love of God.

Christian workers face a tension between, on the one hand, the secular emphasis on so-called 'safe' sex and, on the other, Christian moral standards, which advocate celibacy outside marriage. For biblical Christians, the practice of homosexuality or sex outside marriage goes against God's values of holiness. It is now commonly recognized that Aids will never be defeated just by advocating condoms and safe sex – which also have been shown to be deficient and not entirely 'safe'. Defying God's biblical standards reaps a fearful harvest. But non-Christians feel that Christian standards of sexual morality are impossible in today's world, and that therefore the only hope is the spread of condoms, with good teaching on how to be careful sexually. Perhaps the answer lies in a balance between the two: strong Christian teaching about saying 'no' outside marriage plus teaching on 'safe' sex. Uganda has tried this double approach with considerable success, reducing its former epidemic-proportion problem to something more manageable.

Battle rages between governments and those companies which manufacture antiviral drugs to halt Aids in its development. Sadly, such drugs are very expensive, as also are condoms in poorer societies. Drug companies need to recoup the cost of their research, for otherwise they will not continue to search for future drugs to conquer this terrible illness. But governments in developing societies demand that our present medications should be priced so that their people can afford them. This problem relates not only to Aids, but also to malaria and other major diseases.

A recent newsletter from Gambia reminded me of another problem. A missionary doctor wrote: 'How can a health system that is failing to control malaria (which needs two-to-four-day courses of fairly cheap drugs) and TB (which needs just six months' treatment costing about £8) hope to administer a programme of drugs which have to be taken every day for life to avoid the widespread development of resistance?'[9] The same problem has arisen in Central Asia and elsewhere. It is common in the fight against disease. With leprosy, too, I remember facing this issue many years ago as a missionary in South Thailand. At that time anti-leprosy drugs had to be taken regularly for several years if healing was to be complete. People in a rural area found that almost impossible to understand, and the drugs began to lose their efficacy.[10]

Other epidemics have also shown a growing tendency to have worldwide impact. Asian flu has been followed by SARS. A problem with a few chickens in Hong Kong or China impacts world tourism and the whole air industry suffers. This in turn affects international economics which concern us all.

Likewise, political developments in one part of the world cause problems to us all. Suicide bombers in Washington and New York on 11 September 2001 changed the whole course of world history. Violence in the tiny country of Israel and among Palestinians stirs emotions everywhere, although numbers are relatively small. Poverty in Eastern Europe or Africa can lead to a destabilizing influx of asylum-seekers in other countries. War, injustice or oppressive systems of government can have similar consequences, with refugees flooding into neighbouring countries and the West.

Secular commentators sometimes fail to note that religious issues can also have wide international consequences. But the massive evangelical success in USA and its influence even on presidential elections will inevitably influence American decisions in every area of life. No-one can ignore what America, as the sole superpower, believes and practises, whether we like it or not.

Similarly, the world should watch carefully the struggle within Islam, between the so-called 'moderates' and the Islamists ('funda-mentalists' or 'extremists'). Much hangs on the outcome of this theological debate, which hinges on the question of how the Qur'an is to be interpreted. Do the later revelations, which are aggressively militant, abrogate the more friendly and peaceful verses which were revealed earlier in Mecca? Theology is not just an ivory-tower activity in this case.

In the next chapter we shall see that the Christian church has also become a major global movement, so what happens to Christians in one country has worldwide significance for the church and its mission to the world.[11]

Discussion starters

1. Discuss in your group how far globalization affects your own culture, and then think of what impact this makes on your Christian faith.
2. How far should we adapt our lifestyle in the light of global injustices and environmental abuse?
3. Should we as Christians be more active in public protest and political action?
4. How far do your life and faith reflect a blinkered 'tribalism'? Do you have a world vision in your Christian faith?

Notes

1. For the life of Robert de Nobili see V. Cronin, *A Pearl to India* (Darton, Longman & Todd, 1966).

2. For the life of Matteo Ricci see V. Cronin, *The Wise Man from the West* (Collins, 1955, 1984).

3. J. F. Schutte (ed.), *Valignano's Mission Principles for Japan* (Institute of Jesuit Sources, 1980).

4. See Elizabeth Goldsmith's family saga, *Roots and Wings: Five Generations and Their Influence* (OM Publishing and Paternoster, 1998).

5. A. F. Walls, *The Cross-cultural Process in Christian History* (Orbis, 2002).

6. For practical help on changing our lifestyle as Christians to relate to such problems, see R. Valerio, *L is for Lifestyle* (IVP, 2004).

7. R. Dowsett, *The Great Commission*, Thinking Clearly series (Monarch, 2001), p. 10.

8. There is a flood of new books now on globalization and economics, but a helpful way in may be found in P. Heslam (ed.), *Globalization and the Good* (SPCK, 2004).

9. Dr James Erskine's newsletter of August 2004.

10. For a simple but practical introduction to a Christian approach to the Aids problem see Dr P. Dixon, *AIDS and You* (OM Publishing, ACET International Alliance and Kingsway, 2002).

11. For an overall understanding of globalization and mission see R. Tiplady (ed.), *One World or Many? The Impact of Globalization on Mission* (William Carey Library, 2003).

3 A new centre of gravity

From time to time in the history of the church, God surprises everyone with a major change of direction.[1] We see this even in the Bible. In the Old Testament, Israel was God's people and Gentiles were really accepted only if they joined themselves to Israel as proselytes or God-fearers. But in the Acts of the Apostles, we see the Jewish foundations of the Christian faith quickly spreading out into Gentile circles. Although Jesus and the first apostles were Jews and the Bible was written by Jews, the church became increasingly a Gentile movement. Jerusalem had to share her key position with Antioch and Alexandria.

Peter was moved to accept this formerly inconceivable change by the shocking vision of all sorts of animals let down on a sheet before his eyes. 'Kill and eat' was God's command, although many of those animals must have broken the kosher laws – pigs, crabs, worms . . . No wonder Peter resisted. 'Surely not, Lord!' (Acts 10:13–14). Peter was already somewhat prepared for a life which was no longer kosher, for he was staying in the house of a tanner, which was against Jewish law. To eat such animals was abhorrent, nevertheless. But God was preparing him for the radical step of accepting the Gentile Cornelius and his household into faith in Jesus the Messiah. Luke dedicates almost two whole chapters to the story of Cornelius' conversion, for it ushers in the radically new stage of history in which the church would no longer remain purely Jewish.

Paul, also, did not initially find it easy to preach to Gentiles. But in Antioch of Pisidia, the opposition of the Jews and the open hearts of the Gentiles convinced him that God was moving in this new way. He supported his crucial declaration, 'We now turn to the Gentiles', with a quotation from Isaiah:

'I have made you a light for the Gentiles,
    that you may bring salvation to the ends of the earth.'
(Acts 13:47)

The East–West divide

Eastern Orthodox Christians look back to the year 1054 as another turning-point in church history. In that year, the whole of the western Catholic church split off (as they would see it) from the true apostolic church. To them, this event begins a whole new period in church history.

Already, in the ninth century, the great Orthodox patriarch Photius had so disagreed with Pope Nicholas I that the universal church had nearly broken into two sections. From that time on, the western and eastern churches drifted further and further apart until the process climaxed in 1054. Humbertus, the hot-headed papal legate to Constantinople, strode up to the high altar in the great cathedral church of St Sophia. There he affixed a papal bull excommunicating the Orthodox patriarch Cerularius. Hardly a tactful piece of diplomacy! In return, the eastern church cut the western churches off their diptychs, the official Orthodox prayer lists. In effect, they thus excommunicated the Roman church. This incident changed the whole course of church history and remains strongly in the minds of Orthodox Christians.

Western Protestants will parallel this with Martin Luther's nailing his Ninety-five Theses to the door of the Wittenberg church. Or perhaps they will think of Luther's defiant words of faith, 'Here I stand; I can do no other.' For western Christians, the Reformation signals the most radical change in the history of the church, after which the Spirit of God has moved in new directions.

Christianity spreads through Europe

But perhaps the shift of direction that most closely parallels our situation today happened around AD 400. We can imagine the feelings of the typical Roman centurion at that time. Christianity was centred on Rome, with the civilizing influence of the Roman Empire. But pagan tribes were sweeping in from the north, destroying and pillaging wherever they went. Even Rome was finally sacked, and it seemed that the very foundations of Christianity and civilization were being shattered. The typical centurion must have wondered whether he was living in a post-Christian world or whether perhaps the second coming of Christ was now imminent. Barbarism and paganism seemed unstoppable. Where was God, and what was he doing in the face of such chaos and destruction?

The words of Habakkuk must have seemed fearfully appropriate: 'How long, O Lord, must I call for help, but you do not listen? Or cry out to you, "Violence!" but you do not save?' (Habakkuk 1:2). Our centurion will surely have nodded his head in agreement as he noted Habakkuk's sad description of Israel with the words 'violence', 'injustice', 'wrong', 'destruction', 'strife', 'conflict'. Indeed, at that time in Rome, Habakkuk's condemnation of Israel fitted Rome like a glove:

> . . . the law is paralysed,
>> and justice never prevails.
> The wicked hem in the righteous,
>> so that justice is perverted.
> (Habakkuk 1:2–4)

But actually God was moving by his Spirit:

> 'Look at the nations and watch –
>> and be utterly amazed.
> For I am going to do something in your days
>> that you would not believe,
>> even if you were told.'
> (Habakkuk 1:5)

Our proud Roman would indeed have found it hard to believe that those wild tribes from central and northern Europe would eventually be converted to the Christian faith and become for centuries the very heart of the church. He would hardly have believed that, in the future, people would even accuse Christianity of being a western religion because of the central role in world mission played by the tribes of northern and western Europe.

God's Spirit is still moving

Today, however, the Spirit of God has moved again – and perhaps some can hardly believe what they hear, thus paralleling Habakkuk again. For many years, some of us have been aware that the churches of Africa, Asia and Latin America have been growing not only numerically, but also in maturity and spiritual vitality. More recently, it has become clear that the centre of gravity in the Christian church has shifted; it is the churches of the South which are now the heart of the Christian faith. They form the majority of active Christians and are growing in every way. Meanwhile, the churches of Europe are, at best, static.

Judging by statistics from the different countries, it would seem that there are now more practising Anglicans in Nigeria than in the United States, Canada, Britain, Australia and New Zealand put together. Likewise, there are probably more active Presbyterians in South Korea, as also in Indonesia, than in all Europe. This is equally true of Lutherans, where the great Toba Batak churches of North Sumatra, Indonesia, have more active members than Germany, Switzerland and Scandinavia together. Baptists and Pentecostals in Brazil would outnumber their equivalents in Europe.

The one striking exception to this remarkable development is the United States. Modernity and even postmodernity have not undermined the strength of the American Christian church. By European standards, an amazingly large proportion of Americans are still regularly in church on a Sunday.

Of course, the size and wealth of the American church have enormous implications for Christian mission. These churches supply large numbers of workers overseas and they dominate the world church financially. It is American books and therefore their mission principles which prevail all over the world. American evangelical churches tend to be strongly activist and pragmatic, so Christian mission worldwide often reflects these characteristics. Conservative evangelical churches in the USA communicate brilliantly, with relevant and attractive slogans, which then determine the whole direction of mission and become the current vocabulary to describe the task of worldwide mission today. Later, we shall examine more carefully such slogan expressions as 'cell churches', 'hidden or unreached people groups' and 'adopt a people'.

All change in Europe

How hard it must have been for Jewish Christians in the early centuries of church history to see 'their' church overrun by new Gentile Christians. Inevitably, those Gentiles introduced their forms of church life and leadership, worship, biblical understanding and theology. The Jewish Christians, with their traditional background of good biblical knowledge, must have felt dismayed as they watched the Gentile Christian leaders. Did they consider them rather naïve, untaught and spiritually immature? Did they resent the fact that, as Jews, they had lost the power to control the beliefs and practices of the church? Did they feel alienated by the biblical studies and theological debates of the Gentile churches?

Such temptations hover around our present situation as our European Christian leaders begin to experience a parallel loss of overall control in the worldwide church. This has become very apparent in the Anglican controversy about the practice of homosexuality. Already, in 1998, it was the African bishops, with the help of their brother bishops from Latin America and Asia, who won the day at the Lambeth Conference of bishops. Traditionally, the 'southern' bishops had always followed in the wake of their western leaders. But now they used their numerical and theological superiority to insist on a conservative biblical statement which rejected the practice of homosexuality.

This has caused some petulant reactions by one or two liberal bishops in Britain and the USA. One American bishop actually described the African bishops as theologically naïve and only one step out of animism! It was then discovered that earned theological doctorates abounded among African bishops. By contrast, American bishops often had only honorary doctorates.

The Anglican Episcopal Church in America has been determined to follow its own desires, standing out against traditional Anglican teaching and the theological agreement fixed at Lambeth. Some dioceses in the Canadian and British Anglican churches were not far behind in opposing this shift of power from the 'North' to the 'South', with its firm stand on moral and theological issues.

But no church can stand against the sovereign moving of the Holy Spirit in history without serious decline.

From the rest to the West!

Mission was sometimes described as coming 'from the West to the rest'. Europe was considered to be a Christian continent which had the biblical responsibility to share the blessings of God with the 'heathen' overseas. It never entered people's heads that the time might come when the old slogan would be reversed – mission might become 'from the rest to the West'!

We sometimes forget that the former heartlands of Christianity in the Middle East – Turkey and the Mediterranean lands of southern Europe and North Africa – have for many years been thought of as 'mission fields'. In the sovereignty of God, central and northern Europe also now cry out for cross-cultural mission workers from the more vibrant churches of the 'south'.

Some years ago, I was asked to share in discussions between two largely British missionary societies about a possible merger. Sadly, these discussions proved abortive, but they were influential in our thinking as we saw a new pattern for the future of mission. We thought and debated much about what sort of mission society might be appropriate for the twenty-first century, so that the suggested merger should not just continue the old patterns. We wanted to start a totally new mission. We quickly realized that almost all the countries in which our two missions were working had a higher proportion of Christians per head of population than we in Britain had. How should a missionary society relate to this fact?

A new slogan

We agreed that we had to bring into reality a newer missionary slogan – that mission is 'from everywhere to everywhere'. We no longer wanted to remain as a European mission sending only white missionaries to other countries. We wanted to be truly international and inter-ethnic, encouraging Christian workers to join us from all continents in order to work cross-culturally in other continents. So Asians might go to Africa, Africans to Europe, Europeans to Latin America, Latin Americans to the Middle East and so on. Such cross-fertilization will bring international benefit, enhancing the life and growth of God's people. It always enriches a church to learn to give. As Jesus said, 'It is more blessed to give than to receive' (Acts 20:35).

At the conclusion of a conference for Christian workers from the North Caucasus, the little group of ex-Muslim believers from Grozny in Chechnya came to me with a big smile and handed me an envelope, with the words, 'We want to thank you for your ministry to us.' The envelope contained $15, a large sum of money for them. Their smile revealed how they were experiencing the joy of the Lord in giving. They had received spiritual food in the conference and now they wanted to share what they had.

Blessing will come both in receiving and giving in mission. If poorer churches continually hold out their hands to ask for money from Europe or America, their spiritual life will suffer. All churches need to give as well as receive.

Within this vision, we saw the need of Europe. British churches struggle to express a dynamic and lively spirituality without losing their biblical depth and theological strength. We find it hard to do effective evangelism and to plant churches which will continue into the long term with spiritual and biblical life. Surely the churches of Latin America, Africa and Asia, with their abundant gifting and experience in these matters, will have much to give us. We in Europe need missionaries from other continents. Happily, they are beginning to come.

While, at first, most foreign missionaries to Britain worked only among ethnic minorities, now a growing number have joined us in the hard and often discouraging work of evangelistic mission to the ethnic British. Of course, we also need people from overseas to help us in our outreach among the large numbers of ethnic-minority people. The crowds of overseas students challenge us with a wide-open door for witness. Large communities of Pakistanis, Bengalis and Arabs, and a host of other peoples, present us with enormous opportunities for Christian service and outreach. But the majority of people in Britain remain the ethnic British population, with its millions of unchurched and unbelieving people. Perhaps our co-workers from overseas will help us to become more effective in outreach in the hard areas of British life. Our churches tend to be relatively strong in small towns and suburbs, but we seem to face an uphill struggle in rural villages and in urban-priority areas in inner cities and among large blocks of flats.

National churches everywhere

In the past, it was assumed that missionaries were going out from the strong and vibrant churches of the West to evangelize people who had never heard the gospel of Jesus Christ. Today, we have to face the fact that there are national churches in virtually every country. We must not just ignore this reality. Mission should now always be done with the agreement, and under the leadership, of the local churches. No longer have we the right to go it alone. We need to co-operate with our national brothers and sisters.

Of course, the size and strength of churches overseas will vary considerably. Some countries have large Christian populations, while others range from medium-sized churches to the rather small. In some countries, the Christian church includes old, traditional denominations like ours in Europe. In others, there are only small, struggling, new churches, which have been planted quite recently. In some countries, the Christian faith is well accepted as part of society, while in others it is badly persecuted. There are also underground churches in some countries. The nature of the church in a country will influence missionaries' relationships and co-operation with it.

In this post-colonial age, any form of paternalistic pride may well be resented. No longer, as western Christians, can we come to others with any sense of superiority. The fearful weakness of our own churches must induce genuine humility, while at the same time we recognize also the growing strength of national churches worldwide.

Jesus said that he sends us in the same way that the Father sent him (John 20:21). Jesus came not to be served, but to serve and to give his life, with all the suffering that this would involve (Mark 10:45). All mission workers, as disciples of Christ, are called to follow him. A church leader in China said to us, 'The missionaries gave us a model of suffering for Christ and we have followed in their footsteps.'

In following the Suffering Servant, we are to break out of the safe comfort zones of security, daring to shed our status and pride. As expatriate workers within another church, we have to remember how gracious they are to allow us to work with them in their country, among their people, in the fellowship of their church. Our task under their leadership is to promote the life and welfare of God's church in their country. We are to come as servants, not as the experts who condescend to give our expertise and spiritual ministry to them. As Anne Ruck states concerning the work of the Overseas Missionary Fellowship in Indonesia,[2] their purpose was to 'be the servants of the local existing ... churches and work for *their* renewal and outreach'. She further quotes the former OMF leader in Indonesia: 'They work not only *with* Indonesians but *under* Indonesian leadership.' We shall consider what that can mean in a future chapter.

Who is the boss?

Let us suppose that an African or Indian missionary society or church wanted to send one of its workers to minister in, through and under a large English church in London or Manchester. We may presume that the missionary's English would be fluent, but probably laced with a strong African or Indian accent. Never having previously lived in England, the newcomer would be somewhat lacking in understanding of how English people tick. We may imagine the reactions of the English church leaders if this foreign missionary just turned up without consulting them at all, and then announced that he or she would like to preach at least once a month, take the lead in the church's youth work and teach groups of Christians how to evangelize and plant new churches!

Any foreign missionaries coming to work in Britain would have to prove their worth to the British church before being invited to share in the life and work of the church, fitting into the needs of that church or congregation. It would be up to the church leaders to choose the areas of ministry in which to invite the foreign mission worker to help.

Let me give an example of this. A young Chinese from the church we pastored in Malaysia came to London for further studies. He was shocked to discover that there was no active Christian witness in his college, so he obtained from the bursar a list of all 2,000 students. He then systematically visited and witnessed to all of them in his first year, and established a Christian Union with some twenty-five members by the end of that year. Meanwhile, he was attending a local church, believing that Christians should attend the church on their doorstep rather than commuting to something stronger and more lively. This particular church had just a few old people and no pastor. It was obvious that its days were numbered and it might soon close.

Our friend was gradually accepted in the church, and, after a while, he was asked to take a lead in various activities, even to preach and lead services. When he finished his studies, they asked him to stay on and pastor their church, but they could not afford to pay him. So he got a teaching job to support himself while pastoring this little church. Gradually, it came to life and became self-supporting and able to continue effectively without him. As a result of this experience, he felt that God was calling him to stay in England and bring dead churches to life.

Back in the 1960s, the leaders of the Church of Christ in Nigeria (COCIN)[3] began to feel that they should carry the responsibility of pastoring their missionaries from Britain. They therefore sent their vice-chairman to All Nations Christian College to study British missionaries' backgrounds and cultures and see what they might find difficult in Nigeria. The leaders of COCIN also received the candidate papers of any new missionary wanting to work with their churches. But they found that they did not appreciate the significance of much that was said in those papers. Yet it was they who determined whether an applicant should be accepted or not.

This was a radical change from former times when the missionary society's candidates committee in the West would determine the acceptability of a candidate.

For me, it was fascinating constantly to be asked by him why our British students reacted to certain things in the way they did! Why did they find this thing difficult? Why did they relate to another student in a particular way? Why did they enjoy certain aspects of their studies more than other parts? Questions flowed; answers perhaps less so!

Even smaller and weaker churches are now reacting against the way foreign workers have ridden roughshod over them, ignored their presence in their own land or assumed that, as foreign Christian workers, they have the right to do what they want. On a visit to a Muslim country I discovered that even the small, struggling Christian groups and churches there were unhappy about the work of many overseas Christian workers. They were willing to accept into their fellowship only a very few, who had proved themselves and who were humble enough not to dominate their teaching and witness. Of course, this was proving very frustrating to some new workers who had inadequate language but were still new to the local culture. Many of them were longing for fellowship with local Christians, but found themselves not yet accepted. Such new missionaries needed to exercise considerable patience and understanding.

The strength of national churches all over the world will increasingly affect our approach to cross-cultural mission in other countries, and to the way we receive as well as the way we send people.

Not *our* gift or calling

Christian conferences love to include a seminar on 'How to discover your gifts'. Having been a tutor at a mission training college, it has been a privilege to watch students beginning to find out what sort of ministries God has gifted them for. And what joy we all find in using these God-given gifts in his service and for his glory! If we do not discover what natural talents and spiritual gifts we have, we can easily become a square peg in a round hole. Paul therefore reminds Timothy to 'fan into flame the gift of God, which is in you'; and he asserts that God's gift has come to him 'through the laying on of my hands' (2 Timothy 1:6). Christians who are more mature have the immense privilege and responsibility of helping younger workers to develop their gifts.

It is wonderfully true that we gain deeply satisfying fulfilment as we serve in accordance with the gifts God has given us. Christian ministry is not just a dreary round of sacrifice and duty, but rather a joyful expression of our loving gratitude to the Lord in ways which bring deep satisfaction. Rejoicing happiness and glorious self-fulfilment can come to us in the service of the Lord.

But a selfish desire for our own fulfilment and self-satisfaction can only lead to disaster. It is those who dare to lose their lives for Jesus' sake who will actually find them (Matthew 10:39). It is noteworthy that Matthew locates this principle towards the end of a chapter devoted to mission. If we insist on exercising the gifts we think we have in order to gain satisfaction, we shall lose the very happiness and fulfilment we are searching for. It is in taking up the cross (Matthew 10:38) that we gain the fullness of life. What a paradox! But what a beautiful truth for Christian workers!

How does this work out in mission practice?

Some years ago I observed a large group of young western Christians ministering in a South American city. On the Sunday they fanned out across the city, with small teams in a variety of local churches. One of them preached, one gave a testimony and the whole team would sing a few modern songs with a guitar. It seemed that they were only thinking of the ministry they wanted to have and they enjoyed, rather than asking themselves what the South American churches actually needed. South American Christians generally are much more gifted in evangelistic preaching than we are in the West. They give brilliant testimonies, and their singing makes ours sound woefully inadequate. As western Christians, we don't have much to contribute in South America in those areas of ministry.

But many of the Latin American churches lack good Bible teaching and are fearfully weak in their theology. Because their teaching is often paper-thin and inadequate, many churches lose large numbers of their people after they have been Christians for a while. The churches can be likened to a bath with both taps full on, but with the plug out. Water flows wonderfully into the bathtub, but much is being lost. So it is in many Latin American churches. Multitudes get converted and join the churches; usually, more join the church than leave it, so the churches continue to grow. But inadequate teaching results in many people feeling dissatisfied and finally outgrowing the church. It would have been good, therefore, if the visiting teams had encouraged some of their members with Bible-teaching ability to share in that way in the various churches.

It is often the case that western churches are relatively good in Bible teaching, pastoral care and administration, but weak in vibrant biblical worship, evangelism and church-planting. African and Latin American churches may prove strong where we are weak, but weak where we are strong. In every situation, we have to ask ourselves what gifts the local churches can impart to us and what weaknesses need to be addressed. Then we can honestly face the question of whether and how we might be able to contribute usefully to their churches.

The New Testament stresses that the church is the body of Christ (e.g. 1 Corinthians 12). The different members have differing gifts and abilities. In the body, we all need each other. In giving to others, we are in no position to be proud. While it remains true that we have gifts to contribute to them, it is equally true that they have much to give to us. Every church in every part of the world has both strengths and weaknesses. Let us humbly share our strengths with others and be hungry to learn from them too.

For example, Jewish Christians very much need the depth and mature experience of the Gentile churches, with their long history of biblical study and theology. Also, the Gentile churches have developed helpful structures of leadership and oversight. Most Jewish Christians are relatively young believers, and need this input. But they may also have a few insights to contribute to the Gentile churches.

Christians of different backgrounds would benefit from humbly interacting together, learning from and giving to each other.

We need each other

This principle of ministry within the international church is equally true of the churches within any one country, and also between the individual Christian members of a single congregation.

Between churches

What a diversity we have within the British church! And, of course, that is equally true of the churches within any other country. Traditional denominational churches differ considerably from some of the new charismatic churches. The character of a Baptist church differs somewhat from an Anglican. More conservative evangelical churches have different strengths and weaknesses from strongly charismatic churches, although they may belong to the same denomination. But, in the total body of Christ in the nation, we need each other and have much to give to and learn from one another.

In our day, as we have seen, the church of God in many of our countries is also multi-ethnic. Some 12% of all church people in Britain are of an ethnic-minority background. They are a very considerable part of the body of Christ in this country, as also in many others. Ethnic churches also have varied strengths to contribute to the whole. In many British cities we have large black Pentecostal churches, dynamic Chinese and Korean churches, with their pragmatic Confucian background, and messianic fellowships, with their particular Jewish understanding of the Bible and worship. There is always a danger that, just as various ethnically British churches fail to work together and contribute their strengths to each other, so also the different ethnic churches may form cultural ghettos with no relationship to other Christians. Often, too, they show no interest in witness among people who do not share their cultural or ethnic background.

Between individual Christians

Men and women, young and older, highly educated and less academic, wonderfully practical or artistic members and those who lack such gifts – what a rich diversity we have in our churches!

Congregational leaders need to make sure that all their members feel free to offer their gifts to the whole church. Leaders especially need Barnabas' gift of encouragement (Acts 4:36) to inspire and mobilize every Christian in the congregation. What would church history have looked like if Barnabas had not brought Paul to the first apostles (Acts 9:27) and thus opened the door for his future ministry? Would Mark ever have been restored to acceptance among the early Christians if Barnabas had not taken Mark with him to Cyprus when Paul was strongly rejecting him? If Barnabas had not encouraged, inspired and mobilized Mark, we might have had only three Gospels instead of four!

Throughout the ages and in every part of the world, the church will be deficient if it does not use the full range of gifts available in the various members of the church. The art of delegation must have priority in the ministry of all church leaders. Sadly, we have to confess that many of us believe in delegation, but lack the necessary skills to put our beliefs into practice. And sometimes the traditional rules of our denomination hinder or even prevent lay leadership in our congregations. Perhaps the growing shortage of ministers in the countries of western Europe may force our denominational leaders to question the traditional roles of clergy and laity. For example, we have to ask whether it is biblical that only ordained people can administer baptism and the Lord's supper.

Having worked in Indonesia at a time when the average minister was responsible for twelve congregations, I feel that the British church has much to learn from Indonesia in our current situation. Their ministers were more like bishops, overseeing the work in their various churches. But the responsibility and decision-making authority lay in the hands of the local elders. The traditional role of Bible women as church leaders in the Chinese church surely has much to contribute to our churches in Europe. With the increasing shortage of clergy it is generally acknowledged that the church needs to make greater use of the laity.

But such delegation must always allow decision-making authority to be devolved, so that ordinary Christians are not merely servants of the clergy, but have full scope to lead the church. The Latin American Pentecostal pattern of developing gifts of evangelism and church-planting among ordinary, less educated Christians could surely help the British church. Lay leaders must be given the opportunity to gain experience in all forms of ministry and must be trained effectively for this.

Indonesian, Chinese, Latin American and other churches have much experience to share with the European churches. As we have seen, we all need to learn from each other. No longer is the European church to be only giving and not receiving. No longer are the churches of former 'mission-field' countries to remain as those who only receive.

Mission is now truly from everywhere to everywhere, from every church to every church.

Discussion starters

1. What more could we do in our church or our student or work Christian Union to mobilize every member for active witness and mission?
2. What strengths do you see within the churches of your own country? How can we therefore contribute more relevantly to the church worldwide?
3. What weaknesses do you see within the churches of your own country? How can we learn from other ethnic churches in our own country or from the church worldwide?

Notes

1. For further study of changing 'paradigm shifts' in mission history, see D. Bosch, *Transforming Mission: Paradigm Shifts in Mission Theology* (Orbis, 1991).
2. A. Ruck, *God Made It Grow: OMF Indonesia – The First 50 Years* (OMF International, 2003).
3. COCIN is one of the largest denominations in Nigeria, working largely in the north. It was founded by the Sudan United Mission (now Action Partners).

4 Not all missionaries have big noses

God often calls unlikely people to unexpected mission tasks. Jonah is a supreme example of this. What an unlikely person to be given the task of preaching to the city of Nineveh! He shows himself to have been reluctant to obey the call of God and rebelliously unhappy when God showed mercy to the repentant people of Nineveh. He tried hard to run away from God's clear call, and later moaned grumpily under his shelter (Jonah 4:1ff.). He evidently resisted the fact that God's grace was being offered, not only to Israel, but also to the Gentile people of Nineveh.

In the New Testament, too, God called unexpected people to engage in his mission. In Matthew's Gospel, the sole witnesses of the resurrection were two women, and they were told by Jesus to preach this message to the other disciples (28:10).[1] In those days of male chauvinism, women were not the obvious instruments for God to use in his mission. Matthew points out that there were two of them, thus fulfilling the Jewish law in which witness is acceptable only if there are two people bearing witness (Deuteronomy 19:15). Likewise, God used the Ethiopian eunuch as his witness to bring the gospel to his native Ethiopia. It must have seemed highly unlikely to orthodox Jews of that time that God would use a eunuch, a black African, as his missionary. But God's ways are higher than ours (Isaiah 55:8–9).

For many people around the world, the very word 'missionary' conjures up a picture of a western man or woman with white skin, body hair on arms and legs, tall and big-built, with a large nose. In days gone by, a sharp distinction was formed between a 'missionary' and other Christian workers. Pastors, Bible teachers or evangelists were often local people, but 'missionaries' were by definition foreigners.

In Europe, too, 'missionaries' were people who went out from Europe or other western nations to work in other parts of the world. European Christian workers who stayed within the confines of Europe were counted as pastors or evangelists, but not usually as missionaries. Missions working from one country to another within Europe have tried with a measure of success to disprove this. Their workers are also called 'missionaries'.

But those of us who have stayed in our own country and culture have never been thought of as 'missionaries' unless we worked for specific missionary societies such as the London City Mission. We may be working in evangelism and church-planting, in Bible teaching or pastoral ministry, but no-one will use the term 'missionary' to describe us. Even staff workers with organizations such as Scripture Union, or student ministries such as the Universities and Colleges Christian Fellowship, will not generally be recognized as 'missionaries'. And if a worker comes from Asia or Africa to work among our people here in Britain, we still do not think of him or her as a 'missionary'. Traditionally, missionaries have been white people who work cross-culturally abroad.

Of course, no biblical basis can be found for such ideas. They have grown up with history, without being challenged biblically.

In our day, however, such ideas no longer fit our situation. We have already observed that mission today is from everywhere to everywhere. All churches in every part of the world are called equally to get involved in mission, both in their own country, among their own people, and abroad in other countries all over the world.

We have also observed that, in most countries today, the church of God consists of people of many different ethnic backgrounds. British missionaries will no longer all have white skins and big noses. British Chinese and Koreans will join with British Afro-Caribbeans, and with British people of West African extraction, in going overseas to share the good news of Jesus Christ. Likewise, white South Africans may join with white-skinned Latin Americans to bring the gospel to us in Europe, as also to other parts of the world.

Radical change

I have watched these changes taking place in my adult lifetime, a relatively short period of church history. It was only in 1965 that the Overseas Missionary Fellowship (OMF), the mission I worked with, changed its policy. Previously, it had accepted only Caucasian applicants, believing that Asians, Africans and Latin Americans should work within their own, very needy, countries. The mission did not want to rob such nations of their best workers. They also saw dangers in the possibility of Christians from poorer countries joining a western mission and being supported by foreign money. In 1965, however, our mission leaders realized that this approach was no longer acceptable in the context of growing national churches in Asia and elsewhere. They therefore determined to open their doors to applicants of any and all ethnic backgrounds. Today, a growing proportion of the mission's membership is Asian, and considerable financial and prayer support also comes from Asia.

A few years ago, my wife Elizabeth was invited to be the speaker at a conference for expatriate Christian workers in a North African country.

'Well, how did it go?' I asked when meeting her at Heathrow Airport.

Her smile expressed how she had really enjoyed her ministry, although her words modestly downplayed her excitement.

'Tell me more!' I continued.

She began to describe the conference. She underlined the fact that 10% of those present had been from South America.

'That's remarkable! It's amazing that Latin Americans of all people should be called to work among Muslims,' I exclaimed. 'There are so few Muslims in South America. Most Christians there have never even met a Muslim, and have so little understanding of Islam.'

She responded with confidence. 'Well, that's the work of the Holy Spirit! He seems to be giving believers in South America a vision for the Muslim world.'

And she was right!

A few years ago, when I was preaching in his country, our Korean friend asked me, 'Would you be willing to speak at our mission prayer meeting this Saturday evening? It will be in the Seoul Olympic Gymnastics stadium.'

I assumed that he meant a small back room in the stadium complex. Coming from Britain, I could hardly imagine a Saturday evening missionary prayer meeting attracting sufficient people for a stadium. But I was wrong. Although the stadium holds 20,000 people, it was completely full, with about 1,000 people standing at the back.

The open times of prayer followed the Korean pattern in which everyone prayed loudly and all together. Emotion flowed, with people beating their breasts and tears flooding down their cheeks. Elizabeth was reminded of the book of Revelation, where the voice of 'one like a Son of Man' thundered 'like the sound of many waters' (Revelation 1:15, NRSV). I felt some sympathy for God, in that he could hardly resist answering such importunate prayer! A serious appeal for commitment to long-term mission overseas, whatever the sacrifice involved, triggered a rush to the centre of the stadium, with at least 5,000 young adults responding to the appeal.

There are now more long-term Christian missionaries from South Korea than from all Europe, including Britain. On a recent visit to Mongolia, we found that 60% of all missionaries there came from South Korea. When we talked with Christian workers in Myanmar (formerly Burma), they said that about half of all expatriate Christian workers were Korean. Korean missionaries are beginning to evangelize in Britain and other countries of Europe, too. For example, a Korean former theological student has been working with steady fruitfulness for many years now with a Baptist church in London.

Money matters

The sending of missionaries to other countries has been closely linked to the need for considerable financial support. It is so expensive to send missionaries overseas that African churches face enormous difficulty in this. This is sad, for many of the African churches are large and dynamic. If they were released into worldwide mission, they could have a big influence on the whole development of God's church.

Although it is rare to meet an African missionary in Latin America, Asia or the heartlands of Islam, African churches do have a vision for witness in other African countries. Thus the powerful churches of Nigeria are sending workers across the border to Chad, up into Gambia and to other countries of West Africa. Their experience of relating to their Muslim fellow countrymen gives them much that they can contribute elsewhere in Africa.

The churches of East Africa, too, are often very large and strong. At least 50% of the total population of many East African countries is actively Christian, and the East African Revival has influenced the region deeply during these past fifty years. Much good work is being done among the unevangelized peoples of that region, and some Christians from there are moving across borders into other areas of the continent.

Here in Britain, African Christians are forming some of the largest churches. Together with the black churches, they can also be a natural bridge for the Christian faith to cross over from the largely white churches to other ethnic-minority communities. For example, it will prove easier for them to witness among our Pakistani and Bengali Muslim neighbours, who often find it difficult to accept the Christian faith from white lips and lives.

I found it deeply moving to meet an East African missionary at a mission conference in Britain. He and his young family were working in a very rough housing estate on the edge of Manchester. He shared with us all how they had a visit on their first day there from two muscular he-men with tattoos showing above their vests. Their square heads with close-cropped hair exuded violence and hostility.

'Don't think you're coming to our estate,' they snarled. 'You'd better get out of here fast, before we beat you up.'

As the young missionary looked at his small children and his attractive wife, he knew that neither he nor they were streetwise. They really didn't know how a rough English housing estate functions, or how one can relate to people in such an unevangelized and un-Christian context. Could they really trust their Lord for protection in the face of such a violent society? They also found that there were no other Christians or even churchgoers on the estate to give them support or fellowship. There was nothing on which to build in their desire to plant a church on that estate. The call to mission in Britain challenged their faith to its uttermost.

It turned out that the two he-men lived next door in the home of their elderly alcoholic mother. Gradually, after the missionaries' frequent visits to the mother, the two men were reconciled to the idea of having an active black Christian family next door. In fact, after a while, the mother professed faith in Christ, and her two sons appointed themselves the missionaries' protectors.

Then came the question of whether to baptize the mother.

She had become a believer, but her faith stumbled forward with many a fall back into alcoholism and sin. The missionaries rightly asserted that baptism is not a sign of sanctification, but of initial faith. And yet they wondered what was wise. Would it be helpful for any future witness if the only baptized believer was still an alcoholic? What sort of testimony would it bring if the only local Christian was seen to be blind drunk? They began to find that mission to Britain presented them with questions they had never asked in the relatively moral context from which they came in East Africa.

Mission from the poor to the rich?

We sometimes fail to see the significance of what happened in New Testament times. Jesus came into the world in a back-end corner of the great Roman Empire. Israel was by no means the heart of the world at that time. Culturally, educationally and politically, it was a somewhat remote little place, to which failed leaders were sent to cool their heels. No up-and-coming ruler would want to be exiled to Israel, where they would hardly be noticed by the top people in Rome.

It is therefore from the relatively backward and poor Israel that the Christian gospel began to reach out into the wealthier parts of the empire. How could those first Christians dare to suggest that their faith should be accepted by people all over the civilized world?

The early mission of the New Testament church extended into the centres of wealth and culture. We can imagine the reactions of people in Athens, Corinth and Rome itself. These were the homelands of Greek philosophy, with great men like Plato, Aristotle and Socrates.

Surely they had nothing to receive from the Cypriot Barnabas, or Paul of Tarsus, with their Israel-based religion! These men came from their relatively unsophisticated homelands to the world's centres of education and philosophy.

Likewise, they came from relatively poor backgrounds to cities which oozed wealth and sophistication. But the history of Christian mission has pushed us into a corner where the reverse is true. For several centuries, Europe was the core of the Christian faith, and it was from these shores that the gospel spread out to the rest of the world. But it happened that Europe was also supreme in education and economic development. This meant that mission went hand in hand with education and wealth, becoming dependent on them.

Missionaries needed to be well educated, preferably with white-collar professional skills. And they would need to be supported financially by their sending churches. This pattern became so fixed that, for a long time, it remained unquestioned. Still today, it is assumed that missionaries should be supported by their sending churches rather than by the receiving church. This inevitably inhibits poorer churches from sending missionaries all over the world. To change this would be revolutionary. But it is not the only biblically acceptable pattern.

The only example we have in the New Testament of Paul being supported financially comes in Philippians 4. Evidently, the church he had started in Philippi sent him money several times when he was planting the church in Thessalonica (Philippians 4:16). If no-one supported him, he earned his living by making tents. He must have lived at the level of other people, as he stayed often in their homes. Could that be a model for us today?

Might it be good for European or American missionaries to live at the same level as local people in the country where they work? That would stop all danger of paternalism. Some immediately cry that this is impossible for health reasons, and that we from richer countries are not accustomed to such suffering. But our mission might prosper if we were supported by the national churches where we serve and if we lived like them. And if there is no national church to support us, we could then work to earn our living like other people. Likewise, if missionaries are called to work in poorer situations where the church could not support them, they would again need to earn money by working.

If missionaries were supported by the receiving church rather than by the sending church, this would allow the poorer churches of the world to engage in international mission outside their own continent. The spiritually impoverished but financially wealthy churches of Europe would then receive and support more dynamic workers from Africa, Eastern Europe or China. In this way we would release personnel from the large and energetic churches in poorer countries.

In China, there is a significant movement of Christians who believe they are called to take the gospel westwards through Central Asia back to Jerusalem. This 'Back to Jerusalem' movement in China is already challenging us with the problems of missionaries from rural and less educated churches. They feel the call to go to the Muslim populations *en route* from China to Jerusalem. But it is not easy, without sufficient education, to learn other languages and to relate the gospel effectively to Muslims. In fact, they have been criticized for their lack of cross-cultural understanding, and so far have failed to make any significant impression in witness among the Muslims of northwest China. Having suffered terribly for their faith during the long years of the Cultural Revolution, and coming from unsophisticated homes, they are not worried by shortage of money or a low-income lifestyle.

They thus have advantages and disadvantages. But will they prove to be forerunners of a new style of international mission, in which the majority of cross-cultural workers will come from poorer backgrounds and will not be supported by their home churches?

Multinational missions?

Both from Europe and from other areas of the world, there are one-nation and also multinational missions. For example, Elizabeth and I lecture each year at the training school of the Norwegian Normisjon. This is a purely Scandinavian mission organization. As a result, it faces none of the difficulties of an international mission where members from different countries have to get used to the cultures of their fellow missionaries. In the latter situation, it is often said laughingly, but very seriously, that it is relatively easy to identify with the culture of the people among whom they are working; what is really troublesome is adapting to fellow mission workers from other nationalities.

Most Norwegian Christians are Lutheran by background, so it comes as quite a shock to mingle with Christians from other denominations. Their theology of baptism and the Lord's supper remains strongly Lutheran. But many evangelicals from other countries hold rather loosely to any particular denominational theology of the sacraments. Christians from different nations may have very different beliefs concerning mission practice. Many American workers are very pragmatic, while Scandinavian Christians tend to be much more theologically orientated in their approach, not only to what they believe, but also to how they engage in mission. Such differences have to be carefully worked through if Christian workers are to share as a team together.

In international missions or developmental organizations, a common language will have to be agreed as the means of communication among workers. Very often, the English language becomes accepted as the lingua franca. But this can cause heartache among some. For example, we have watched some Korean mission workers struggling with learning English as a prerequisite for joining a missionary society; and yet their goal is to work in Mongolia or Myanmar, where they will then also have to learn a local language, or even two. Some Swedes have worked in North Africa. For their official work they have to do all government reports in French, but the common people speak Arabic. The language of communication in their international aid society was English, so they ended up having to be fluent in three languages apart from their own Swedish. Happily, this has now been changed, and all communication within that organization, their conferences and other meetings, will be in Arabic. In francophone West Africa, too, the same problem causes heartache. Overseas workers have to learn English, French and a local language or two. In such situations, of course, their children grow up with a major advantage over one-culture youngsters, for they speak at least two languages fluently.

Back in the late 1960s, Elizabeth and I were in charge of the initial training in language and culture for new Overseas Missionary Fellowship workers. We had the privilege of welcoming the very first Asian members of our mission. While OMF proudly asserted that it was international, it had in reality, at that stage, not yet adapted to having Asian workers in our midst – although, as a mission, we were working exclusively in Asia, so our workers had to adapt to Asian cultures in their work. But, together within the mission, we formed a very western organization. The means of communication within the mission fitted western backgrounds. Our orientation centre, as indeed all our centres, was very western. Those first Asian members suffered accordingly. They felt so lonely when asked to sleep in single bedrooms. The quietness which westerners enjoyed at that time felt eerie to our Asian friends. And the food was definitely alien to some.

Yes, there are difficulties in forming any organization along fully international lines. And those of us who are just a tiny minority within the total membership have to acknowledge that, of course, we don't have the right to impose our views on the majority. For example, throughout my time at All Nations Christian College I was the only Jew on the staff, so it was inevitable that the culture of staff interaction should be Gentile.

But a team consisting of just one people has weaknesses too. Because it does not have to adapt within the team, it often finds it harder to fit in with the cultures and worldviews of the people amongst whom its members minister. They often do not notice that things from their own background belong only to their culture and may not be appropriate elsewhere. For example, our Norwegian friends love to have their national flag prominent inside or even outside their home. In Norway or Sweden this small demonstration of national pride is enjoyed, but in newly independent post-colonial countries such nationalism among Europeans is often offensive.

Training for mission

After preaching in a lively church in Manila, it was a privilege to meet the government cabinet minister responsible for overseas workers from the Philippines to other countries. It was an opportunity, too, to check my statistics. I had previously been informed that some three million Filipinos work overseas at any one time, and that approximately 10% of these are committed evangelical Christians.

'Actually, we in the government are not confident exactly how many Filipinos work overseas,' she replied to my questions. 'But normally we reckon it is between three and seven million, so your statistic is probably on the conservative side. But we also think that probably about 10% are evangelical Christians, so you are approximately right in that.'

A little piece of mental arithmetic revealed that there are therefore a minimum of 300,000 evangelical Christian 'tentmakers' from the Philippines. They do not generally go with mission as their primary motive, for they are largely in search of work and money. But the potential for mission is enormous, if this multitude of Christians can be helped to witness in the countries where they are working.

Most wealthy and influential families in the Muslim Middle East have Filipina girls working for them as nannies and domestic servants. Many of these girls have fearful experiences of oppression, misuse and even abuse. But as Christians they can have considerable influence in training the family's children, in praying for family members who are sick and in the daily testimony of their living and working. From time to time we hear of Muslims who have been impressed and even converted through a Filipina's witness. These girls are able to bring the good news of Jesus Christ into homes which might never otherwise have any chance of hearing about him.

Filipina girls are serving in wealthy homes, not only in the Middle East, but also in many countries of Asia. In thinking of them, one is reminded of the wealthy and powerful Naaman (2 Kings 5). It was an apparently insignificant little Hebrew girl who pointed him to the Jewish prophet, through whom he then received God's healing. The glory may go to the prophet, who was God's more obvious instrument in this healing miracle. But the prophet's ministry could never have taken place without the initial witness of that unknown Hebrew girl. Likewise, the Filipina women will never be counted in Californian statistics, nor will their stories be told in missionary books and magazines. They are God's anonymous missionaries.

'What would the Philippines government think if a mission started training days or weekends for Filipinos who are planning to go overseas for work?' I asked.

'We would be absolutely delighted, and would very happily support such training financially as well as encouraging people to attend.'

I pictured a typical training course, with teaching on how to live and work in another culture. Perhaps there would also be particular seminars for those going to Muslim countries or families. They would need specific teaching on how to react and defend themselves effectively in situations of oppression and abuse. In the afternoons there could be optional seminars for committed Christians on how to maintain one's spiritual life and how to witness for Christ.

A few Filipino Christians and expatriate missionaries do now have the vision for such training, but it is still on a very small scale. There is a danger that people working in the Philippines have other priorities and may fail to see the strategic nature of such missionary training. All of us are tempted to be interested only in work within our own area of concern rather than sharing God's vision for the whole world. And missionaries are not above such temptation. Their vision can become blinkered, and they can lose interest in anything other than the task for which they came initially.

But it is not only Filipinos who stand in need of missionary training. We have already noted the growing tide of missionary activity coming out from the churches of the Two-thirds World. The Latin American, African, South Korean and other Asian missionary movements are growing apace. They will surely be the predominant Christian influence around the world in the future.

Their missionary candidates need effective cross-cultural training. Sadly, many of the theological seminaries and Bible schools in those parts of the world are merely following the curricula, teaching methods and forms of training which they have observed in America, Australasia or Europe. Most of these training establishments are preparing people more for pastoral ministries within the church than for cross-cultural evangelism and church-planting. Often, their patterns of Bible teaching are not geared to cross-cultural situations, failing to motivate church members for outreach and witness. They may stress our personal relationship with God through Jesus Christ to the neglect of an emphasis on mission.

For example, one church preached through Acts, Sunday by Sunday, with considerable emphasis on the work of the Holy Spirit in people's lives and on the worship and fellowship of the early church. But they failed to underline the mission outreach of the church. Likewise, teaching on the Trinity may fail to help people to relate this to non-Christians such as their Muslim or Jewish neighbours. Such forms of biblical teaching may actually stifle the growth of the church rather than stimulate it.

In most African, Asian and Latin American churches, there is still a paucity of older, experienced missionaries who have returned to their home country after long years of service overseas and can now train future workers. Even within the very large South Korean mission movement, there is still a shortage of such people to train mission candidates. Of course, numbers of experienced ex-missionaries are growing, and the time will come when they will not need our assistance as much as at present. But meanwhile the door is wide open for western missionaries to play a very significant role in missionary training in such countries and under local national leadership.

In western countries, too, we face a desperate need for training of Christian leaders in mission. Traditionally, our churches have been centres of pastoral care and biblical teaching. This stems from the assumption in previous years that our countries were Christian and therefore no longer needed mission-minded churches – except for the sending of workers overseas and then for supporting these missionaries.

Today our countries have slipped away from the Christian faith and our churches have become little islands in the midst of a non-Christian or even anti-Christian sea. But our theological colleges and Bible colleges are still training people largely for Bible teaching and pastoral ministries. Theological teaching often still fails to relate the truths of the gospel to communication among people of other faiths or no faith. How can we so change the whole structure and life of our churches as to turn them into missionary centres, with evangelism at the very heart of the church's life and purpose? How can we train, motivate and inspire our church members to become effective missionaries in their neighbourhoods and workplaces? Christian leaders in America, Europe and Australasia also need mission training, so that they can train their church members in the task of mission in their own neighbourhoods.

Christians need help in discerning what questions people are asking in life. And then they must be stimulated to find suitable answers, so that their witness will scratch where people itch. Discussion groups with enquiring non-Christians, as in the Alpha courses, will help church members to relate the gospel relevantly to their neighbours. Perhaps people can also be encouraged to ask the basic question: what might make the gospel sound like 'good news' in the ears of their neighbours? Many of our church members – sadly, also some of our pastors and leaders – have little experience in the basic mission task of leading people to saving faith in Christ and then discipling them. Quite simple teaching in the fundamentals of evangelism is required, so that the whole church is mobilized for mission locally.

Building a support base

Over the past two centuries, much hard work has been done in missionary deputation within the churches of the West. As a result, we have good numbers of Christians who understand the basics of mission overseas. Many respond with enthusiasm to God's call to support mission work overseas, both in prayer and in finance. They also know that we need to send more workers for the tasks of worldwide evangelism, teaching the national church and developing social and relief ministries. In the West, we have a good support base for those who go overseas in mission.

This may not always be the case in areas of the world where overseas mission is a relatively new calling. For example, we have already observed how overseas mission vision is growing in many of the Latin American countries. They are sending increasing numbers of their people to serve outside their own continent. Missionaries from Latin America may abound in dynamic evangelistic zeal with lively worship and prayer. Those who come from the very Latin churches of Brazil, Chile and Argentina often bring with them an experience of the power of the Holy Spirit and a great expectation of highly fruitful evangelism and church-planting. This is very different from workers who come from the more Indian-background and dour cultures of the Andean republics of Peru, Colombia, Ecuador and Bolivia.

But both the churches from the Andean republics and the more Latin-background churches generally lack a real understanding of how to support their workers overseas. They often make extravagant promises of prayer and financial support, but this can vanish like the morning mist after a year or two. Some Latin American mission workers overseas have therefore found that their support has dried up. Not only are they unsupported in prayer; they are no longer receiving the money they need to live on. As a result, some have returned to their home countries discouraged and disillusioned.

There is a real need for wide deputation work in their home churches to teach Christians how to support their missionaries. Until there is a broad base of mission interest, understanding and support within the churches, their workers will continue to face difficulties and unnecessary hardship overseas. In this context it is not insignificant that Paul stresses the need for ongoing and steadfast prayer (e.g. Colossians 1:9; 4:2), not just an immediate response of prayer. It is not easy to go on praying year after year for Christian workers overseas. But they need the support of such faithful prayer, which does not give up. Good communication, with frequent emails and pictures, will help, but the need for faithfulness in persevering prayer remains a challenge.

In the South Korean churches, there is often a need for realistic teaching about the realities of much mission work overseas. Because the churches in South Korea have been dynamic and large, it is sometimes hard for them to appreciate the difficulties and frustrations which their missionaries may face.

A Korean single lady missionary in a Muslim country in Central Asia shared her problem with us. She had been in the country for about six months and was still working hard to learn the language. Every week her pastor at home phoned her to ask whether she had planted a new church that week and how many people she had led to Christ. It was encouraging that her pastor was so interested in her and felt his responsibility towards her. But the pressure he put on her was unbearable. A foreign single woman in a Muslim context does not usually plant churches in her first few months! And until she can speak the language well, she may not even lead many to faith in the Lord.

Many South Korean Christians visit overseas situations to encourage and help their missionaries. They usually come in quite large teams and are treated with generous care by those missionaries. Their choir-singing and preaching is often much appreciated, but they may not see the realities of the daily routine in spiritually unresponsive situations.

Something parallel may occur with western church leaders who visit their church members working overseas.

Conclusion

With the growth of the church worldwide and the increasing passion for international mission in Africa, Asia and Latin America, we have entered a challenging and exciting new era. And when the massive church in China begins to reach out effectively into other parts of the world, God will surely glorify the name of his Son in even greater measure. We can look forward with tremendous joy to the coming years. This confidence encourages us, as John Wesley said in his *Journals*, to 'bend our backs to second the work of the blessed Holy Spirit'. As Christians it is our amazing privilege to be Christ's fellow workers.

Discussion starters

1. What training does a Christian need in preparation for effective cross-cultural mission?
2. Europe has become a needy 'mission field'. How can our churches be helped to restructure in order to meet the needs of mission locally, rather than just the pastoral and teaching needs of their congregations?
3. The western churches hold considerable financial strength and professional expertise in their hands. What dangers do you see in this? How can we use these gifts in a true way? How can poorer churches in other parts of the world engage more fully in world mission?

Note

1. In Matthew 28:7 the angel told the two women to 'go and tell', using an ordinary word for 'tell', with no deeper significance. But in 28:10, Jesus changes the verb for 'tell' (*apangeilate*), using a word which includes the concept of proclamation.

5 No bypassing the locals

'Never again will we have foreign missionaries in our churches!'

The leaders of the Karo Batak Protestant Church in North Sumatra, Indonesia, were determined that missionaries should never regain power over their church. The gospel had first been brought to that area by Dutch missionaries in the days of Dutch colonialism, and it had been assumed that leadership should lie in the hands of the foreign workers. Surely no local Christian could attain to the missionaries' level of education and training! Then, after the Second World War, Indonesia gained its independence following a ferocious war against the colonial power. Suddenly all missionaries were thrown out, and all links with Holland were cut.

As the missionaries hurried to the port to leave the country, they were aware that the Karo Batak church would be left without any ordained ministers. Hastily, therefore, they laid hands on four local, semi-trained Bible teachers.

When the Dutch still ruled, 93% of the church's budget had come from Holland. Then suddenly the source of supply was broken and the church had to survive without overseas finance. But local Christians were poor and not accustomed to giving sacrificially. Why should they suffer in order to give 10 cents to the church, when Dutch Christians could cheerfully give $100 without any sacrifice?

Suddenly the church had its independence and had to learn to stand on its own feet. At first it wobbled badly, unable to pay its workers or repair its buildings. Standards of teaching failed to satisfy the spiritually hungry people. Yet the church grew numerically, from 5,000 to 20,000 members in the following ten years. And it changed from being very Dutch in character, developing an authentic Karo Batak culture.

Gradually the church grew stronger and learned to walk with confidence. But the fear remained that they might one day again come under the power of some outside group. Therefore they determined never again to have missionaries in their midst.

In 1960, the leaders noticed an Overseas Missionary Fellowship couple working under another denomination in the large city of Medan. As OMF workers, they did not bring foreign money into the church, and they worked under the national leadership, living simply in a home just like a local pastor.

'We could perhaps invite overseas workers to help us if they would live and work like that,' the Karo Batak leaders decided.

As a result, my wife and I as new missionaries were asked to serve in the Karo Batak church.

The church laid down three conditions for our coming:

1. *Money*. Money always has strings attached. Power lies in the hands of donors. So we were told that we should not bring any foreign money into the church. They allowed us to give an offering on a Sunday, but it should not be more than a typical Indonesian teacher would give – and that was very little indeed! (Sadly, in more recent years the church has succumbed to the lure of western riches.)

2. *Housing*. The earlier Dutch missionaries had lived in comparatively splendid homes, but the church was determined that we must live at their level. They therefore said that we must live in the house they would choose for us. It turned out to be a simple shop-front house, with one room downstairs and an outside staircase to the single room upstairs. There was no kitchen, so we put our simple paraffin cooker under the staircase and against the wall which separated us from the house next door. Out the back was a cement cistern for water and a hole in the ground for the toilet. There was no running water or

electricity. And the wood was not of the best quality, so people could look through the holes in the walls to watch our every move. At least our neighbours could not understand our language, so it did not matter that they heard everything we said. In this we had the advantage!

Because people felt at home in our simple home, they felt free to drop in for a visit in large numbers. The house stood directly on the street, with no garden, so it required no courage to venture in. Of course, the fleas followed the example of our other visitors in making themselves very much at home with us!

As Elizabeth has described in her life-story,[1] water was a continual problem. It came most mornings for about half an hour at six o'clock. We normally staggered to the front of the queue twice each morning, allowing us four buckets of water with which to wash, clean the house, do the laundry and cooking and so on. In the dry season, if the town pump broke down, there just was no water. Miracles were not just a boost to faith, they were sometimes essential for daily living.

3. *Don't dominate!* The third condition for our coming was that we should not speak at any church meeting unless we were asked to do so. We could not venture our opinion in administrative discussions unless asked. Likewise, we could not preach or teach unless they invited us. The local leadership knew that Europeans tend to speak too strongly and too quickly, thus dominating discussions. They were also afraid that we would do our own thing in ministry rather than serving the church. They were aware, too, that if we took the lead in ministry, it could give the Christian gospel a western image. In much of Asia, the greatest obstacle to the gospel is that people think it is a foreign European or American faith.

We were forced to learn this very soon after our arrival there. Needing some relaxation, we cycled out to a local village, where we were quickly surrounded by an eager crowd of local people. Questions flowed. Who were these white foreigners and why had they come to our village? This led on naturally to many questions about the Christian faith. The gospel had never been preached in this village, and yet the people were hungry to hear about Christ. Finally, the head of the village school invited us to come regularly to their village and promised that at least 300–400 people would become Christians.

We were excited. I had previously worked in South Thailand among Muslims. There had been no converts at all there. The thought now of 300–400 people turning to the Lord thrilled us. On returning to our town, we told some of our local friends about our visit to Lingga.

They poured cold water on our excitement.

'If we want to do evangelism and plant a church there, we'll do it. You are only missionaries. You don't lead anything.'

And that was a condition of our being in their churches. But how frustrating!

Several months passed before a local elder finally decided to organize church-planting in Lingga, and his team duly planted a dynamic and growing church, which now numbers at least 1,000 members.

In the past, missionaries had led all the evangelism and church-planting. Local Christians felt that they were incapable of such ministry. If we had led the work in Lingga, it would have reinforced the idea that mission depends on foreign workers. It would actually have stifled the development of local evangelistic church-planting. As it was, they led the work themselves, and this became a model for widespread church-planting in the following years. So we learned the important mission principle that overseas workers should normally work *under*, *in* and *with* the local churches.

Then the church began to invite us for a wide variety of ministries, but always subject to their leadership. They asked us to start a youth meeting, a village evangelism training course, teaching in various weekly cell groups, hospital evangelism, Sunday school teachers' training, and visits to their seventy-five congregations for preaching, teaching and training. There was also an open door for teaching religion in local schools and colleges, so each week we were asked to teach the Christian faith to about 1,000 students. But if we were not invited to a particular church, we could not go.

Learning from mistakes

Sadly, we have also observed the negative aspect of this principle. Sometimes our use of computers makes it appear that mission depends on such modern equipment. Likewise, we can give the impression that evangelism requires the 'Jesus Film', with all the necessary electricity, projector and so forth. In this way the local church becomes dependent on outside help if it is to engage in evangelistic outreach.

After we had worked in North Sumatra for some while, we learned that a distant relative of Elizabeth had also worked there. After some years living and witnessing in a neighbouring town to ours, he had returned to his home country disillusioned and fruitless. We were amazed. How could he remain fruitless in his ministry in the midst of a mass movement to Christ?

We asked our local Christian friends. They showed us where he had lived, but evidently knew nothing of his preaching. 'He was a Jehovah's Witness or some such sect,' they affirmed. We assured them that actually he was a committed evangelical Christian. They refused to believe us, because, they declared with confidence, he did not show the marks of being a true Christian. He showed no sign of loving other Christians and thus sharing fellowship with them. And he never attended the local churches, whereas the Bible clearly tells us not to forsake meeting together (Hebrews 10:25).

It turned out that he had been very conservative in his views and so did not approve of churches which were members of the ecumenical Council of Churches. He also reacted against Christians who smoked and occasionally drank beer, who practised infant baptism and worshipped using liturgy. Such churches and Christians he dismissed as 'liberal'. But was he right? It was true that there was much nominalism in those churches, but the former Dutch missionaries had laid strongly biblical foundations. We felt that the churches there were like a well-laid fire which just needed a match to set it alight. In God's grace we were allowed to be one such match. It was right to work within those churches.

Another example relates to mission in Britain. I was at an international missions conference in Chicago. An American mission leader came across to where I was drinking coffee with other delegates. 'You must come from Britain,' he declared, with amazing perceptiveness, as he heard my accent. 'You must know our missionaries to Britain.'

I duly asked him where they were working and in what sort of ministry.

'They are in a church-planting ministry,' he explained.

I asked him which churches they were working with, but he

restated the fact that they were in church-planting and so had no connection with existing churches.

My antennae bristled.

I later asked various people about these American missionaries, but it was a considerable time before I found anyone who knew of them. As members of an excellent and, in many countries, well-known mission, they were attempting to plant a church of their particular denomination. But in Britain we didn't have that type of church, so people easily assumed it must be some new sect. After some years, they gathered a little group of five people around them, but finally their headquarters withdrew them from work in Britain. They were not showing fruit for their labours.

How sad! If they had worked with a British church, they could have helped to train local believers in church-planting, started a daughter church which would be genuinely British, and left something ongoing behind them when they returned to America. British Christians are not naturally gifted in church-planting, and these American missionaries could have given the British church something really useful for God's glory. Of course, the churches they planted would not have been of their denomination, but whose kingdom are we trying to build?

Finding the right church base

When presented with this approach to mission, some inevitably ask how one determines which local church one should work with. It is not only missionaries going overseas who need to consider this question. It applies equally to Christians moving from one place to another within their own country. What church should we serve in? In this I am assuming that we do not attend a particular church merely for our own spiritual gratification, but specifically in order to serve.

There are three possible approaches.

Gravitate towards the type of church we know

We can decide to work with a church which relates well with our particular background. Those of us with a more charismatic experience will then work with definitely charismatic churches. More Reformed Christians will try to find a parallel church which is

Reformed. Anglicans will seek out an Anglican church, Baptists a Baptist church, Pentecostals a Pentecostal church and so on.

This approach makes life and work easier, but may not necessarily be strategically wise. Sometimes, although the sort of church we belonged to before may be significant in the whole scene of Christian mission in our country or area, somewhere else it may prove to be in a side-stream. In mission, we want to influence widely and so to be in the main bloodstream of the area or country, not irrelevantly in a minor vein.

Work with the church where we live

Secondly, we can decide to work with whichever church happens to be the nearest to where we find housing. It is of course good, if possible, to belong to our immediately local church rather than to commute to another town or to the other side of a city. Living in a village in England, we sometimes feel sad to see so many committed Christians commuting from our village to churches in nearby towns. Inevitably, their witness in the village becomes diminished, and the village church is robbed of their input. The town churches have so many people to serve, whereas a village church struggles, having fewer gifted Christians.

But often we may find that the church nearest our home may not prove to be the best centre for mission locally. Some may therefore feel it better to throw their energies into a church further away, which has more potential for mission.

Look for the significant church

So we can work with churches of our particular background or with a church in our local geographical area. But thirdly, we may look strategically at what sort of church is significant for mission in our area or country. Sometimes a denomination which is central in one country may prove quite insignificant in another. For example, the Anglican church is vitally important in England, but in Indonesia or South Korea most people will never have heard of it. In our time in Indonesia, there was one Anglican parish of Java and Sumatra, which was 1,500 miles from end to end and had a population of 120 million! In those countries it is the Reformed or Presbyterian churches which play a central role in the work of God's Spirit.

Wait patiently

It is not easy to work under the leadership of a local church which is not already alive in the Spirit and outward-looking evangelistically. Particularly in our postmodern world, we all expect God to work today, not just tomorrow. In our contemporary culture we find it hard to wait patiently for God to act, and so to develop a mission approach which aims more for an ongoing work in the future than for obvious fruitfulness in the present.

The Japanese theologian Kosuke Koyama has written a book called *Three Mile an Hour God*, in which he compares God with the slow, trudging walk of a water-buffalo cart rather than with a fast jet plane. As twenty-first-century Christians, we find it hard to continue steadfastly when God is not evidently at work. How would we have got on if we had been alive during the 400 years of divine silence between the prophet Malachi and the coming of John the Baptist? The blank page between the end of the Old Testament and the start of the New represents those centuries when God seemed to twiddle his thumbs in inactivity. If we had been God (which fortunately we never were), we would assuredly have brought the Messiah into the world much earlier; but the time would not have been ripe, and his coming might have been abortive.

In mission we often need to exercise Godlike patience. This is particularly true of Christian witness in modern Europe, where the message of Jesus Christ often falls on deaf ears and spiritually hardened hearts. Living in a small village, Elizabeth and I have become very aware of this. The comparison with the fruitfulness of evangelism in Indonesia is striking.

Gifted, well-trained Christians are often tempted to feel that they can themselves achieve the desired fruit in God's mission. Of course, we quickly acknowledge that by ourselves we cannot do anything (John 15:5), and so look to the Lord to bless our ministry. But we can still forget that, apart from the local body of believers, we may also fail to achieve lasting fruit.

In Indonesia, too, it would have been easy to lose patience with the local church as spiritually lifeless and without vision. But we have to ask ourselves whether we truly believe in the Holy Spirit's ability and desire to revive his church. If the local church in all our countries comes alive, and large numbers of Christians catch the vision of dynamic mission, there will then be no shortage of workers for God's harvest fields! If millions of Christians in Indonesia, China, Brazil, sub-Saharan Africa, the United States and all our other countries in every continent burn with holy zeal for mission, what a harvest God will reap!

Let us pray and work with that aim in mind. Such a vision can inspire us as we work and wait for its fulfilment. Working within existing churches may be God's means of mobilizing his people for mission.

In Singapore and Malaysia, many of the churches consist of Chinese and Indian Christians. The Chinese and the Muslim Malays are culturally miles apart, and they often dislike each other. But can the Holy Spirit break down such ethnic bias and use Chinese Christians in witness among their Malay neighbours? It may appear easier and quicker for us as foreign Christian workers to do the work of evangelism ourselves. But in the long term, this approach may prove ineffective. It may be better to work within the Chinese churches, seeking to inspire and mobilize them for outreach among the Malays. Surely God has the gracious power to break down any ethnic or cultural barrier to enable a loving and powerful witness. And again and again he is doing precisely that!

Beware propaganda

Some contemporary mission propaganda divides Christian workers into two camps. Those who 'maintain the status quo' by merely working within already existing churches are not 'true missionaries'. Those who are moving beyond the boundaries of existing churches in order to bring the gospel to the unevangelized are said to be the ones we should commend and support.

I am often amazed at how easily so many Christians buy into such glib statements without discernment. As we have seen, evangelistic mission should be done not only by Christian workers coming from outside, but also, and especially, by local believers. Teaching, training, inspiring and mobilizing the church for mission may prove much more effective in the long run than doing the evangelistic work ourselves. I have observed that this is true even in evangelism among Jews. While many do come to faith through the witness of missions like Jews for Jesus, a good proportion also come to faith in Jesus through the living testimony of local Gentile believers and churches.

Mission propaganda, like political or other forms of propaganda, thrives on simple, easily understood slogans. Such slogans always contain a heady mixture of truth and untruth, so we have to discern their positives as well as their negatives.

Mission thinking today has been bombarded with terms such as 'unreached peoples' and 'hidden peoples', stressing the missionary imperative of bringing the good news of Jesus Christ to those who have never heard. Related to these is the geographical '10/40 window', the area lying between 10° and 40° north. Most of the least evangelized peoples live in this part of the world, so, again, the expression is underlining the call to evangelistic mission.

These expressions have undoubtedly motivated individual Christians, churches and whole missionary societies to a renewed passion for pioneer evangelism. With the current emphasis on holistic mission and social ministries, we need to be reminded of Christ's call to go into all the world with the good news of his salvation. After an initial church-planting stage of mission, it is easy so to concentrate on teaching and discipling the church that we lose the vision for further fresh outreach. So one can only rejoice in the positive impact of these slogans, with their easily understood message, challenging us to reach out to new geographical areas and to new ethnic peoples.

It is also undoubtedly true that we have in the past concentrated on some areas of the world to the neglect of others. And the neglected parts of the world are often those that seem to be hardest against the gospel and most difficult to penetrate with the good news of the cross and resurrection. So it has been with the geographical box described by the neat formula 'the 10/40 window', which covers the heart of the Muslim world and central Asia. As a result, there has been a new desire among many Christians to reach out to these neglected parts of the world. This has meshed in, too, with the emphasis today on mission among Muslims. We can only rejoice in the positive outcomes of these powerful slogans. The Holy Spirit has undoubtedly used them to further the gospel of Christ.

But there are also dangers which we need to be aware of.

First, mission teaching which has issued from the Center for World Mission in Pasadena, California, has misunderstood the biblical term 'peoples', seeing it as denoting a multiplicity of 'people groups'. But the word 'peoples' in the New Testament is the normal word for 'Gentiles', as distinct from Israel and the Jews. This misinterpretation inevitably leads to a misuse of Scripture, which is always dangerous for Christians. It leads to a failure to see the biblical emphasis on the fact that, although the church is rooted in Israel, it now also incorporates Gentiles into the tree of Israel (see Romans 11). Thus, not only is evangelistic mission among Jews neglected, but also the biblical emphasis on the universality of the gospel is sidetracked. The incorrect interpretation fails to perceive the struggle the very early Jewish church had, not only in reaching out to Gentiles, but also in developing harmonious relationships of love within the now ethnically mixed church.

A biblical example

The first church council in Jerusalem (see Acts 15) struggled with such issues. It stemmed from a culturally and religiously Jewish background, but quickly widened to include converts from among the Greeks and Hellenists. They may sometimes have developed separate house churches, but still they belonged to the one body of Christ and the one church. Before conversion, they had never eaten together, for Jewish food laws prohibited such social intercourse. The Gentile practice of offering food to idols also placed an insuperable barrier against table fellowship. But as Christians they ate together in each other's homes, sharing bread and wine together in memory of the Lord's sacrificial death (Acts 2:46).

Such cross-cultural and inter-ethnic fellowship placed enormous strains on the church. The Jerusalem council met to determine how such fellowship could be maintained and how far either side needed to compromise their previous customs. Should Gentile Christians submit to the Jewish laws? Or should Jewish Christians compromise in their religious practice? Church-planting among formerly unevangelized ethnic groups is just the beginning. Mission includes the resolution of all sorts of issues which emerge as the church faces new cultural and religious backgrounds and needs to form loving relationships between people from different traditions.

The 'unreached peoples' emphasis seems to define mission as just evangelism and church-planting. But, in the Bible, mission involves a wide variety of ministries. These include evangelism, but we must not so underline evangelism as to neglect other aspects of mission. It is clear from his letters not only that Paul, the great missionary evangelist, evangelized and planted churches among both Jews and Gentiles, but also that he worked to lead these churches into loving fellowship and holiness. God requires us not only to evangelize but also to minister within churches to bring them to holy maturity. Christ himself so loved his church that he desired to present it to himself 'as a radiant church, without stain or wrinkle or any other blemish, but holy and blameless' (Ephesians 5:27).

On the assumption that Christian workers have themselves been called to mission, Matthew 28:20 would seem to demand that we so work within churches that all Christians also hear God's call to mission. God's commands to us are to be passed on to others within his church. We therefore need to be careful that our Bible teaching and preaching do not just fill Christians full of biblical knowledge, turning them into over-full sponges which never overflow to water the world. Our teaching and preaching must have practical out-workings in evangelistic outreach and mission, in holy living and in loving relationships.

The '10/40 window' approach has a further danger, namely that areas outside that particular geographical box may be downplayed. Thus one or two missions have withdrawn all their workers from countries which happen to lie outside the 10/40 window. Sometimes these have even been countries with large Muslim, Hindu or Buddhist populations which desperately need the good news of Jesus Christ. And their churches may need help in teaching and training so that they can more effectively fulfil their mission. Uncritical adherence to a slogan can have sad consequences.

Another current slogan is 'Adopt a people'. Lists of unevangelized peoples are circulated, so that churches or individuals can choose a people to adopt. They then concentrate prayer and missionary vision on that particular people. Again, God has used this movement to stimulate prayer and evangelistic missionary vision. But dangers also abound. The very term 'adopt' assumes a certain paternalism. Normally, people only adopt children, so there is a presumption in the very term 'adopt' that these peoples are somehow less advanced than we. If more mature people are to be adopted, they must certainly be consulted, and the choice must be theirs. I never heard of a church asking an unevangelized people whether it actually wanted to be 'adopted'!

When my wife Elizabeth was a young missionary, she was informed by our mission that a Christian lady in Singapore had decided to adopt her as her missionary. Elizabeth was duly invited to tea, and walked up the long drive to a large, old colonial house. Here a young English-woman welcomed her, asked her to sit down and served tea in the old colonial style. She then informed Elizabeth that she would be supporting her. Elizabeth felt an assumption of superiority which irked her, although of course she welcomed the support in prayer and finance. There was no feeling of mutual giving and receiving.

The overarching emphasis on particular 'peoples' or ethnic groups can lead to a blinkered vision, in which we so concentrate on one 'people' that we lose interest in the wider world. In this way we may also foster a narrow tribalism among those whom we disciple.

In all of these mission movements, with their brilliantly com-municating slogans, it is assumed that we, whoever 'we' may be, will do the work of evangelism. They do not seem to take into consideration the existence of national churches or the need to consult and co-operate with them. And they certainly do not talk in terms of submission to national churches, working *under* their leader-ship. Such movements hardly relate to Paul's deep concern for his fellow Christians in the various churches. Thus Paul writes to the Thessalonians: 'Night and day we pray most earnestly that we may see you again and supply what is lacking in your faith' (1 Thessalonians 3:10).

All churches, in every country all over the world, demonstrate weaknesses in their faith. This inevitably hampers their mission and witness to their own people locally, to ethnic minorities around them and to other countries and nations. God calls us to mission in order to 'supply what is lacking' – the same word as is used in Matthew 4:21 for 'preparing' their nets. God longs for his church to be in a fit shape, so that his people are ready for fishing. As Christians, we are called to be 'fishers of men and women'. Beautifying the fish tank or aquarium must always be inseparably linked to the outgoing task of fishing in the oceans of the world.

Discussion starters

1. If you moved to another town, how would you decide which church to belong to?
2. Is your church strong, both in evangelism and in the teaching and training of its members? What can we do to ensure a full ministry in our church?
3. Discuss the positives and negatives of current mission slogans.

Note

1. E. Goldsmith, *God Can Be Trusted* (OM Publishing, 1996).

6 No pith helmets in a concrete jungle

When I was visiting Manila, my host drove me through the crowded streets to where the meeting was due to take place. He had been back in Manila six months after home assignment in Britain.

'I have still not managed to get my car above second gear,' he laughed ruefully. 'The traffic is so fearful, I just never get up into third or fourth gear – except on Good Friday, when people in this very superstitious country think Jesus is dead and therefore cannot protect them on the roads. That day everyone stays at home, so one can drive through the city in fifth gear!'

My friend was perhaps exaggerating slightly in order to make a point. The infrastructure in many cities around the world cannot cope with the huge growth of population and traffic. I have memories of being stuck in a traffic jam in a South American city with eight lanes of traffic in each direction. As our car stood unmoving, I had the chance to stand on the bonnet and count the lanes of traffic. In Seoul, South Korea, we have often suffered jet lag, got up at two or three in the morning and looked out of the window to see the slow-moving traffic in all directions.

Mission today has to take into account the trend to urbanization. Already, twenty or thirty years ago, we used to comment on urbanization as an issue for Christian mission, but it has accelerated in more recent years and is likely to continue to grow into the future.

So how does the Bible view cities? There is an ambivalence.

On the one hand, cities are places where sin and evil reign. The first mention of cities in Genesis reveals that, while Abraham lived in the wide countryside of Canaan, Lot 'lived among the cities of the plain and pitched his tents near Sodom' (Genesis 13:12). In Sodom, wickedness prevailed and its people 'were sinning greatly against the LORD' (Genesis 13:13). Israel's ideal was rather to 'live in safety, each man under his own vine and fig-tree' (1 Kings 4:25). On the other hand, it was in cities that people found shelter in times of danger or attack. People accused of murder could run to cities of refuge (Numbers 35:6ff.). And Israel's life and pride were centred on the city of Jerusalem, the place where God had chosen to dwell. It is striking that the worship of God is located in a man-made temple in a city.

The end-time picture of glory concludes with this world having 'passed away' and being replaced by a new heaven and a new earth in the form of 'the new Jerusalem' (Revelation 21:1–3). Whereas the earthly, old Jerusalem had been spoiled by the sinfulness of God's people, the new Jerusalem is like a beautifully dressed bride, and in it God dwells perfectly with us (Revelation 21:3). Revelation pictures the ideal city of Jerusalem remaining in heaven with God until the final climax of history, when it 'comes down' to earth (Revelation 3:12; 21:2, 10). And the sinfulness of Israel is replaced by the 'holy' character of the city (Revelation 21:2). The Bible does not overlook the pervasive evil of city life, with all its depersonalization, greedy materialism and crime. But it holds firmly to the ideal of the city as the place where God should be present and where holiness should rule, with the lovely image of the beautifully dressed bride. That is God's purpose for the future, and must also be our purpose in Christian mission.

So, despite the rural idyll in the dreams of the Israelites, God sanctifies the city with its human constructions. And the story of Jonah further demonstrates that God has purposes of grace and salvation even for a heathen city with all its sinfulness.

Europeans find it hard to picture the size of cities in Asia and Latin America, feeling more at home in the relatively smaller African cities.

But even an African capital city like Bamako in Mali will have at least a million people. Cities like São Paolo or Mexico City in Latin America, or Beijing, Bangkok, Manila, Jakarta, Seoul and Tokyo, make a mere London or Paris seem quite unpopulated. They have perhaps twice the population of any European city. Even so-called 'smaller' cities may be two or three times the size of Birmingham.

Some years ago, in Northern Ireland, I shared the platform with a woman working in Java, Indonesia. When she spoke, she described how, after getting off the plane in the capital city of Jakarta, she would take a bus up through the rice fields and mountains towards the city of Bandung, where she lived and worked. She described passing *en route* through 'the small town' of Bogor. When it was my turn to speak, I explained that 'the small town' of Bogor had the same population as Belfast – and that was some years ago. Now, Bogor would be much larger than a 'small town' like Belfast. Population statistics for cities in Africa, Asia and Latin America fall out of date so quickly; so we shall not attempt to give such statistics in this book, as they would be out of date before it was finally published.

Tough city living

Particularly for westerners, it is not easy to live in such huge, over-crowded cities. The constant noise disturbs us, and we find it hard to have to jostle with crowds every time we leave our flats. In cities we have to protect our homes with all sorts of security devices, for burglary is common. And on the streets we are constantly alert for pick-pockets, muggers and even terrorists. As Christian workers, too, we are baffled to know where to begin in any sort of effective outreach which will touch, not just a few individuals here and there, but the multitudes. Coming from individualistic cultures, we tend always to relate our gospel to individuals. But Jesus did not only show his love to particular people; he also looked on the multitudes and had compassion on the crowds (e.g. Matthew 9:36; 14:14).

In a crowded city, people face very real isolation, anonymity and loneliness. They may never even see their neighbours in their high-rise block of flats. Within the European Union, it has been discovered that the primary problem people feel they face in life is loneliness. We might have expected people to think of financial, housing or work-related issues as their main problem, but actually loneliness heads the list by a long way. Christian workers, too, are not immune from this fundamental problem in cities.

If the gospel is to attract lonely people, it must demonstrate the reality of Christian relationships of love. As Christians, we seek to follow the model of Jesus himself, who related in love, humble service and unity within the Trinity. In our study and teaching of Christology, we should no longer be restricted to the traditional divisions of the person and work of Christ, but should add the relationships of Christ.[1]

In the Gospels, Jesus makes a point of eating with various people. He gives us a model of enjoying fellowship and companionship over food. In this way he demonstrates his love for them and draws them into a close relationship with himself and with each other. Perhaps we need to add a biblical theology of food to our systematic theology!

Very few western Christian workers stem from inner cities or from a background in high-rise flats. Most of us were brought up in suburbs, small towns or the countryside. The call to minister in the loneliness, violence and bustle of the inner city or in the anonymity of blocks of high-rise flats will involve very real sacrifice. Those who have families also have to think of what it will mean for their wife or husband and any children.

It is clear that Christian mission must increasingly be located in cities. That is where most people live, and it is city people who will also determine the future of people in rural or tribal areas. City people hold the trump cards.

But mission in big cities is far from romantic. In Britain today, prestige attaches to Christian workers who respond to the call to urban priority areas, but for mission overseas there remains a certain romanticism whereby tribal and unsophisticated rural areas attract. One wonders whether this may also sometimes reflect a certain unconscious paternalism, in which we can sense our superiority over such less developed situations. But in this century God is surely calling us to develop a hard-nosed realism in our mission strategies, both in the West and in other continents.

Adopting the right approach

When God calls us to mission in an urban situation, we need to discover the social structures in order to understand and relate meaningfully to the people of our city. In western cities, most people want to live on the outskirts, in the leafier suburban areas, while the inner city may rot away into disrepair. Yet there may also be areas in the very heart of the city which become millionaire paradises, with sumptuous penthouse flats. The middle classes will, however, generally commute to work in the city, while residing some distance away in pleasant suburbs.

In such cities the church flourishes in the suburbs, but struggles to gain more than a toehold among the poor and the very wealthy in the heart of the city. This may also affect denominational styles of the church. Pentecostals may have more appeal to the poor and less educated in the heart of the city and in the high-rise blocks of flats, while more traditional churches relate more easily to the middle classes. Our styles of worship and communication need to take into account such considerations. Thus one missionary in South America has planted a middle-class church which is very traditionally Anglican, with liturgy, robes and well-groomed hair. But he has also planted some Anglican churches in shanty towns. Here, informal guitars have replaced organ and liturgy, while jeans and casual clothing make people feel at ease. This is in line with Archbishop Cranmer, who, in crafting the Anglican *Book of Common Prayer*, insisted that church services must be understandable by the common people.

In many Latin American countries, multitudes flood into the cities from the rural areas. On arrival, most of them are destitute, with little money or educational qualifications with which to gain employment. They generally start urban life in a squatter settlement on the edge of the city, but, as they gain work and money, they move further and further towards the centre. The richer you are, the closer you live to the centre. And the very heart of the city is reserved for the super-rich. Of course, there may sometimes be shanty-town pockets even in close proximity to the richer sections of the city.

Mission workers often live in middle-class areas, commuting into the shanty towns to do church-planting ministry. This may not always be welcome.

'We don't want people like you,' declared one shanty-town civic leader, bitterly. 'We are fed up with people who come in their cars from their smart homes to visit us. With your Christian songs you entertain our people, who have no work and are bored and so enjoy any entertainment. Then you get back into your cars, drive home and have a shower to wash off our dirt.'

Incarnational mission is required, and Jesus gave us the model. He did not come to earth in a heavenly spacesuit with an oxygen tube to heaven. No, he lived as one of us, getting his hands dirty and suffering with us. It is that sort of sacrificial, incarnational mission which is needed in our cities worldwide – including America and Europe.

Many Asian and African cities can be thought of as glorified villages. Each area of the city contains interrelated people of the same background. People of one tribe or village all come and live together in the same area of the city. Sometimes a street may house one particular extended family, with cousins and second cousins living close by. To some extent this may also be seen in larger western cities, with ethnic minorities forming their own ghettos. Thus, if I drive into London, I pass through Greek Cypriot, Chassidic Jewish, Afro-Caribbean and Pakistani areas, one after the other. Together they all form the one city, but actually the various sections of the city are almost entirely independent of each other and they do not mix. In language and culture they remain distinct. The mission of the church cannot ignore this.

Of course, we have to look into the future, too. Will such ghettos be able to maintain their separate identities? Or will the next generations become increasingly adapted to the host country? When I was a new missionary, I lived in the big city of Medan in North Sumatra, Indonesia. In those days each ethnic group lived in its own area, spoke its own language and followed its own culture. But now, the next generation has become much more definitely Indonesian. Indonesian education and media have wide and deep influence. And people mix freely at school and work with people of other ethnic backgrounds. Here they all speak Indonesian, the national language. So, gradually, wider influences impact on succeeding generations.

How then should mission look in such situations? How far should we develop churches along ethnic lines? Or should we concentrate on ethnically and culturally mixed churches?

Alternatively, should we attempt to run on both tracks simultaneously? Perhaps churches should start homogeneous midweek meetings, with their various members gathering separately according to their race, culture and age. On Sundays they could then all meet together to demonstrate their unity in Christ. The older generation may require narrowly ethnic gatherings, while the younger generation may be attracted to something wider.

Onnuri church in Seoul has run along the lines of having separate congregations for different ethnic backgrounds, but all belong to the one church and are under the same overall leadership. In London, Kensington Temple has developed a different approach. They have various ethnic cell groups, but on Sundays they all meet together as one fellowship in Christ.

Reaching students

Students form a large and influential segment of a city's population. Outside the western world, young people hunger and thirst for education. It is the route to a better life, with good jobs, money, decent homes and health. Without it, the prospects for an easier life remain bleak. So colleges and universities abound with students pressing to get in. Thus Yogyakarta in Indonesia has some seventy universities, some of good quality and state-accredited, others private and often of lower standard.

In my generation in Britain, a high proportion of Christian leaders first came to know the Lord through the ministry of their university Christian Union. The Universities and Colleges Christian Fellowship (at that time called the Inter-Varsity Fellowship) played a central role in the life and growth of the church throughout our country. Still today, together with other student ministries, it turns out quality Christian leaders for mission both in Britain and abroad. Overseas, too, the International Fellowship of Evangelical Students, Navigators and Campus Crusade reach out to the student world.

As Christian workers, it is strategic that we get involved in such ministries and encourage student witness as best we can. We can become advisers to the leaders of student groups and offer hospitality to their members. An open home for students rapidly becomes a magnet, attracting students to come and eat, talk, play games, read and ask questions. In some countries, it may be helpful to rent a home near a university and have a small hostel for students from outside the city. Unsophisticated rural students are particularly vulnerable morally when they first taste the freedom and bright lights of student life in a big city. Living in a Christian hostel or home may save them from disaster. Even regular visits by day may give stable roots for life in the shifting sands of student and city life.

If our city has a more liberal theological seminary or theological faculty at the university, it is strategic for a Christian worker to invite theological students to come and discuss their essay assignments and their lectures. We may also be able to recommend more biblical study books to balance the liberal input they are getting from their teachers. These theological students will become leaders in God's church. How helpful for them to have someone to pray and discuss with – someone, too, who will give them a model of a Christian life and home!

Back in communist times in Poland, all theological students in training for church ministry had to attend a Marxist-orientated theological faculty. Here they were indoctrinated into atheistic Marxist philosophy and political thought. Only after two years of such indoctrination were they allowed to do any biblical or theological courses. Many students lost their faith during those two years. But one pastor in Warsaw had a daily breakfast meeting in his home for theological students. Each morning he dealt with the issues the students were facing in their studies and answered them biblically. And his times of devotional prayer and Bible study encouraged the students to remain strong in their love for the Lord.

My daughter studied theology at Cambridge University. Here she was sometimes faced with aggressively liberal teaching. Like many other theological students, she was deeply grateful for the encouragement and help she was given at the evangelical study centre, Tyndale House.

Penetrating high-rise flats

As a young new missionary I stood one day in the heart of an Asian new housing estate. The high-rise flats stretched up into the sky, one next to another. Around me crowds of Chinese swirled. No-one even noticed me at all. I realized in a new way the challenge of evangelizing such crowds of people, all living cheek by jowl anonymously in their flats. These were those crowds on whom Jesus would have compassion.

There was no space in the housing estate for a traditional church building. Of course, one could invite people from the flats to go to a church outside the estate somewhere, but the pressing need was for churches within the estate as a living presence for Christ. I began to dream of Singapore churches planting a church in every block of flats. That would require church people moving into the area and opening their flats for churches to meet in – 'flat churches'! In more recent years, Christians have begun to talk of 'cell churches'. In a housing estate of this sort, this seems to be the only possible answer.

Cell churches allow the flexibility to start meetings in more and more locations. As the cells increase, they can divide and multiply. We may start with just one cell in a whole estate, but hopefully this will multiply and subdivide until there is a light for the gospel in every block of flats, perhaps even on every floor of every block.

Cell churches do, however, have their weaknesses. Inevitably, they have only a very few people from which to develop leadership. Their leaders may therefore be inadequately taught and may become little dictators over their small flock, and they can easily hive off into extreme teaching. Such cell churches require good oversight and leadership training from a central mother church. With limited resources of personnel, this is not an easy problem to overcome, but the central leadership will need to work hard to train good leaders and provide them with good teaching materials.

Sometimes in a block of flats it may be possible to start a kindergarten. As the children grow up in a Christian environment, they will feel a natural attraction to the Christian faith. And the Christian teachers will develop ongoing relationships with both the children and their parents in an everyday situation. In the loneliness of high-rise blocks, such relationships meet a fundamental social need and people will be thankful for it.

As we think of high-rise blocks of flats, inevitably we are once again faced with the question of reaching crowds with the gospel, not just a few individuals. Literature and media play a vital role in this, and will be discussed in our next chapter.

Embracing ethnic minorities

We have already observed that the population of a city may consist of many different ethnic or tribal groupings which have their own homelands in various parts of the country. Thus Medan in North Sumatra included people from the various Batak tribes, Javanese, Sundanese and a host of other ethnic groups. But today that is not only true of different peoples or tribes from within the country. Now people from all over the world congregate in our bigger cities. Even a formerly largely monocultural city like Seoul in South Korea now has growing numbers of Africans, Europeans and other Asians. In London, Elizabeth and I often look at our fellow passengers on the Underground and feel that we are almost the only white, English-speaking people on the train. I am ethnically Jewish, so perhaps she is unique in being English! And even her blood is mixed with Norwegian and American.

Mission today has to take into consideration this inter-ethnic mix in our cities. Thus the church we have associated with in Seoul has not only its main Korean congregations, but also English, French, Filipino and Arabic ones. Chinese and Japanese also abound there. In London there are messianic Jewish fellowships, many Korean and Chinese churches, large black and West African churches, Indonesian, Spanish, Arabic and a multitude of other ethnic churches. In city churches the main Sunday services are often held in the national language and seek to attract people of all ethnic backgrounds, while they hold midweek homogeneous groups for the various peoples and cultures.

It is clearly helpful if the different ethnic and cultural groupings can both have separate meetings and also meet together sometimes. We all benefit from fellowship with people of our own language or culture, with whom we can have teaching and worship that relate to our background. Elizabeth often comments on how enlivened I seem after an all-Jewish meeting. In such homogeneous groupings it is also easier to make non-Christians or new converts feel at ease, as they do not have to cross cultural barriers.

On the other hand, we all have much to gain from other peoples. No homogeneous fellowship should dare to say of another, 'I don't need you!' (1 Corinthians 12:21). Paul's picture of the different members of the body needing each other relates to whole churches needing one another, as well as to individuals.

Some years ago I suggested in a talk that the British church could learn a lot from Indonesian Christians. Afterwards I received an angry letter from an English Christian leader, in which he said: 'We have *no* (I repeat *no*) need of *any* (I repeat *any*) help from *any* (I repeat *any*) Christians overseas!' He was reacting to people who talk extravagantly about God's work overseas and imply that God would do the same in Britain if only we did things exactly as they do in South Korea or the United States.

The visitor-friendly approach of Willow Creek Church in the USA is extremely effective, but culturally American, in its welcome of new people. For other countries, different tokens of welcome may be more appropriate. Some Christians want to emulate the success of the South Korean Full Gospel Church, said to be the largest single church in the world. But the topside-down authority structures may fit a Confucian-background Korean church better than churches in other cultural contexts.

It is true that overseas models never fit exactly elsewhere, and their patterns of Christian life need adaptation before they can be applied. Nevertheless, all of us have much to learn from other Christians of different ethnic or cultural background. This applies equally to congregations of different age brackets. A youth church desperately needs the maturity and wise experience of older Christians, while older Christians will stultify without the youthful enthusiasm and vision of younger believers. We need each other.

Including overseas students

Tens of thousands of overseas students flood into our colleges and universities. This is true, not only in the West, but equally of many African, Asian and Latin American institutions. Some come for their final secondary-school years, others for primary degrees, and yet others for higher qualifications and postgraduate studies. One current phenomenon is the massive growth of Chinese scholars coming from the huge population of mainland China.

When students are away from the pressures of their family, their society and even their government, they often manifest a new openness to the gospel. Their time overseas opens the door for them to explore other faiths and philosophies, which might be frowned upon in their home country. Particularly if they come to study in a nominally Christian country, it will seem natural for them to learn more about the Christian faith. Opportunities abound for sharing the gospel lovingly and humbly, but clearly, with them. Such students may appear ordinary and not specially significant while still studying, but the MA and doctoral students, especially, will almost certainly become key leaders in their home countries in coming years. It is doubly strategic, therefore, that they gain a good impression of Christians and, even better, that they should become believers in Jesus Christ. Their influence in the future can be of tremendous significance.

Unfortunately, research done by Friends International, a mission working among overseas students, has shown that the great majority of overseas students in Britain never have a meaningful conversation with a British student and never see the inside of a British home. Such inhospitable and uncaring lovelessness can only impact overseas students negatively. It is encouraging that such student movements as the UCCF and Friends International have developed hospitality schemes, through which British Christians are invited to open their homes to an overseas student. In this way, lifelong friendships can evolve and the gospel may easily be shared in a natural and unforced manner.

Many overseas students will have had some contact with Christians before, so we may be able to build on that foundation. For example, I was asked to be the speaker for an overseas students' conference in England. I was talking one day with a Turkish post-doctoral student, who shared with me that he was still a Muslim despite attending this Christian conference. I asked him why, as a Muslim, he had come to a Christian conference.

'When I was doing my first degree in Izmir, I observed the students in my hostel. To my surprise I saw that the Christians were no worse than the Muslims. This challenged me, because my grandmother had told me that Christians are grossly immoral and idolatrous with a belief in three gods,' he explained.

Seeing the Christian students and comparing them with Muslims, he had decided that Christianity might be just as good as Islam, or at least no worse. So in curiosity he had taken the opportunity to come to a Christian conference. He wanted to know more about the Christian faith. He was not thinking at all of conversion; merely of learning and understanding. But his curiosity may entice him further than he intended.

In relating as Christians to students from abroad, it is helpful to know something of the religious background of their countries. With students from some countries (e.g. many Muslim countries, or Buddhist countries like Thailand and Sri Lanka), we need much patience and much prayer, knowing that they are likely to be very resistant to the gospel of Christ. On the other hand, students from some other countries (e.g. Iran) are likely to be wide open to the gospel. Others, from sub-Saharan Africa and some other countries, probably come from Christian backgrounds, but need fellowship and encouragement to grow in love and faith.

In today's world, many Christians have travelled overseas and gained some experience of a foreign country. Short-term mission has also become a popular option for many. Such knowledge and experience of an overseas country gives us a natural rapport with students or other ethnic minority people from that part of the world. And longer-term missionaries who have to return to their home country can continue their overseas ministry, still using their language and cultural understanding. Thus most of Friends International's workers were formerly missionaries overseas. One missionary who had worked with a mountain tribe in North Thailand returned to America and found there were more people from that tribe in Los Angeles than had remained in Thailand. Back in the 1950s, while still in England, I was taught a tribal language by a post-doctoral student from that remote hill tribe. Opportunities abound!

Improved education

Standards of education have skyrocketed all over the world. In Africa, Asia and Latin America it has become common for every young person to have at least primary education. Increasing numbers go on to secondary and even tertiary education. Colleges and universities multiply. In the West, too, more and more young people go on to university and graduate with degrees. Fifty years ago, only a very few, clearly gifted, students would progress to an MA, but now an MA and even a doctorate have become much more usual.

The growth of educational levels must influence mission. The educational level of Christian workers and missionaries overseas needs to be much higher than in the past. And standards of biblical teaching and preaching will need to satisfy more educated minds.

In Latin America, many young Pentecostals go on now to higher education, while their pastors often remain biblically and theologically untrained. Emotionally lively but biblically weak preaching no longer satisfies, and many leave the church. When I talk with university students in Britain, many tell me that they attend two churches on a Sunday – one for the lively worship and the other for its biblical teaching. How sad if dynamic, Spirit-filled worship that is culturally relevant cannot be joined together with quality biblical exposition and teaching.

Educational institutions have moved to centre stage for Christian mission. Even the government in Britain has recognized that faith schools achieve better results than other schools. Christian teachers, in both Christian and in secular schools, play a vital role in the outreach of the church, demonstrating to their students the reality of Jesus Christ and life in him. Students will be influenced by teachers and university lecturers who unashamedly, but wisely and discreetly, confess their faith in their teaching.

Good news for the poor

The Bible paints an ideal picture of cities as places of refuge and security. Even the ultimate glory of heaven is described as a city, the new Jerusalem, shining with the glory of God, 'and its brilliance was like that of a very precious jewel, like a jasper, clear as crystal' (Revelation 21:11). Sadly, we live today in a fallen world, in which cities have become places of lonely disorientation, crime, poverty and godless opulence.

Quoting Isaiah 61, Jesus declares his mission statement in Luke 4. The direct consequence of the Lord's Spirit being upon him was that he would preach good news to the poor (Luke 4:18). So it must be with us, too, as those who follow Jesus and walk in his footsteps. For our ministries, we need the reality of the Holy Spirit upon us. And his infilling must inevitably lead to a passionate concern to preach good news to the poor.

Jesus' quotation from Isaiah has a double emphasis. First, it underlines the anointing of the Spirit in preaching and proclaiming. Secondly, it stresses a call to the poor, prisoners, the blind and the oppressed. Many writers emphasize the primary call of the gospel to the poor and oppressed, but fail to note the threefold call to preach and proclaim. Service among the poor should not exclude verbal preaching, but our proclamation of the good news of Jesus Christ relates directly to those in need.

How relevant these words are for work in large cities! Cities always contain an underside of poverty. Christian workers dare not turn a blind eye to the unemployed, the homeless, street children, sex workers – those who Karl Marx called the *Lumpenproletariat*, those nameless ones who apparently don't count in the ongoing life of the city.

Such people not only need handouts of charity. They long also for such personal recognition that they begin to feel they have value and dignity. Christians can help in getting them started in mini-enterprises to provide them with work and money. Some overseas missionaries are now very much involved in such work. They may help people form a viable business plan and then lend them a small amount of money with which to get started.

In a recent visit to Myanmar, the need for such micro-businesses became evident to us. An unemployment rate of 60% means that most Christians, as well as Buddhists, have no work, and so the churches are desperately short of financial support. If Christians can be helped to develop micro-businesses, they can then give to the church, which will then become much less dependent on overseas aid.

This has been done with good effect in the North Caucasus and other places where poverty prevails. European, American or Korean Christians have used their professional skills to assist people to develop cottage industries, producing leather goods or knitted garments. In China and parts of Africa, farmers are being loaned a few sheep or goats, helping them develop better-quality stock. At least one church in the north of England has helped unemployed people to get their feet onto the first step of the ladder towards starting a small business. One church in Toxteth trains unemployed people in how to present themselves favourably at interviews, so that employers are more likely to offer them work. Skills in plumbing or carpentry are being taught to fill the great need in Britain for people who can do such practical jobs in the home. Many people are too busy to do such work themselves and require outside assistance.

Work among cities' criminal underclass and among sex workers sometimes carries political overtones. We have to ask who runs such criminal activities and who profits from them. Where I worked in South Thailand, the local Muslim imam ran all criminal activities – so when someone stole our cycle, we asked him to arrange for it to be returned! He apologized and, sure enough, the bike turned up that afternoon, propped against our house. He headed up all the local drug trade, prostitution rackets and cross-border smuggling. How vital in that context that our Christian message should proclaim that, in biblical faith, religion and ethics go hand in hand.

In Myanmar it is the Army political leaders who are responsible for all the corruption which has turned their country from high education and prosperity to deep poverty and suffering. Persecution and oppression of Christians stems from the military government's realization that, unlike Buddhism in Myanmar, Christians are con-cerned for truth and justice in this world as well as in eternity. Most Christians also belong to the tribal minorities, who are rebelling against the oppressive Burmese military regime. Faith, politics and justice issues mix inexorably together with ethnic overtones.

In one South American city, an Anglican missionary couple started work among prostitutes. A few began to find other employment and therefore freedom, while at the same time coming to faith in Jesus Christ. Then, one evening, the missionaries had three strong he-men visit one after the other.

'We come from the army, from the police, from the city govern-ment. Leave our girls alone or else there will be violence!' they growled.

Without changing the whole city power structures, work among prostitutes would be virtually impossible. The Christian gospel relates to social and political structures as well as to personal salvation and relationship with the living God.

Discussion starters

1. Our cities are a far cry from the biblical picture of the heavenly Jerusalem or the Cities of Refuge. What can we do to meet the problems of city life today?
2. What more could we do to evangelize students in our university or town? What about overseas students?
3. How can evangelism best be done in high-rise flats?
4. Could our professional skills be used for mission in our area or overseas?

Note

1. See M. Goldsmith, *Jesus and His Relationships* (Paternoster, 2000).

7 Let the airwaves bring good news

In his first letter, John declares that he proclaims what he has personally seen, heard and touched. The aim of this preached message, he says, is 'that you also may have fellowship with us' (1 John 1:3). Our Christian fellowship of love, he implies, is so sweet and beautiful that it motivates us to preach Christ to you in the hope that you will enjoy those loving relationships with us. John declares that fellowship with us is the motive for preaching Jesus Christ to a world of fractured relationships. Our fellowship is good news for a lost world.

In his conclusion to the section (1 John 1:4), John declares that he is writing these things 'to make our joy complete'. Some New Testament manuscripts have '*your* joy'. But if *they* join *us*, *their* joy will indeed be *our* joy. The deeply personal fellowship John is talking of involves *their* becoming part of *us*, and *our* becoming one with *them*. John's aim is that together we may share in the joyfully enriching fellowship which can be found if, together, we are united to God himself. John points out that our fellowship comes, not just through some shared interest as in a football supporters' club, but through fellowship 'with the Father and with his Son, Jesus Christ'.

Although John is talking of personal experience of the Lord, it is noteworthy that our message is to be preached. What is proclaimed is based on the warmth of personal testimony. Biblical truth and the experience are to go hand in hand in our preached message. Not only do we preach an objective 'word', but our message is to be evident in our lives. So John calls our proclamation 'the Word of life' (1:1).

In today's world we are faced with the overwhelming development of mass media. This opens doors for rapid communication of the gospel and enormous growth in the church of God. But communication through mass media also risks becoming remote and impersonal, losing the intimacy of personal experience and fellowship.

From paper to pixels

The technology for mass communication has been developing for more than 500 years. In 1455, Gutenberg published the great 'Forty-two Line Bible' in German. The first English book with movable type, relating legends of the siege of ancient Troy, was published by Caxton in 1476. This was facilitated by the introduction in the fourteenth century of the much earlier Chinese discovery of how to make paper.[1] Thus began more widespread production of literature in Europe which was to fuel the Reformation and, indeed, the whole course of European thought, including the history of Christianity in our countries.

But China had been using wooden printing-types since the eighth century. In 767 a million copies of a book of Buddhist charms had been printed at the command of the Empress of Japan, and the first recorded block-printed work was the Buddhist *Diamond Sutra* in 868. There can be no doubt that the ability to mass-produce literature played a significant part in spreading Buddhism from north India into China and then from China to Japan.

It is therefore nothing new that we in our day have been developing new information and communications technology. But the scale and speed of today's discoveries is unparalleled. It has become a major occupation, even for the technically proficient, to keep abreast of every computer update. Workers in administration have constantly to attend refresher courses to train in the new developments. Up-to-date companies frequently have to replace their old computers with state-of-the-art productions, lest they fall behind the times.

It is only about 140 years since Bell invented the telephone in 1876. Radio began to be used in the 1890s. How amazingly communication has changed in such a relatively short time! Of course, neither telephone nor radio entered into common use for many years, but gradually they penetrated everyday life and then began to spread around the world, bringing different parts of it into direct communication with each other. At first, only larger cities could boast a telephone; the small town where we lived in Indonesia in the 1960s did not even have a telephone in its Post Office. But by then radios had become quite common, so we suffered from their noise. Our immediate neighbours would turn their radios on full volume. Why turn them down when you pay the same amount however loud you have them on?

Of course, mobile phones, let alone satellite phones, were still undreamed of. I remember venturing with a fellow missionary deep into the Mindoro jungle in the Philippines. I was amazed when, on our way back, he got out his satellite phone, called his wife and told her approximately what time we might arrive home. In earlier days such communication had been impossible, so jungle expeditions held considerable dangers. If you slipped and broke a leg, no help was readily available. Now you would just phone for assistance. Mission has changed its character.

Soon after electric telegraphy came into use in the mid-nineteenth century, people began to experiment with the idea of transmitting pictures. The company that was to become the BBC started to work with this in 1929, and initiated an official service seven years later. But it was not until some years after the Second World War that television began to come to the attention of the ordinary public. It began to spread in the late 1940s and early 1950s. The coronation of Queen Elizabeth in 1953 stimulated many in Britain to buy their first TV sets.

How well many of us remember the huge size of early computer systems! A corporation would set aside whole rooms for its computer. Private individuals could not possibly afford the luxury of dedicating so much space to it, or of course the cost. But in just a very few years we have moved to the present state, where it is normal for ordinary people to have a computer. In many homes each person in the family has his or her own.

Email has made communication unbelievably instantaneous. As a travelling speaker, I wonder how I ever existed without email! One can make arrangements with people in remote countries in just a few minutes. The very term 'snail mail' for letters reflects the speed of electronic communication today. We used to think that some snails moved quite rapidly, for some letters in advanced countries only took a couple of days to arrive. By contrast, during our time in Indonesia it often took six weeks for our letters to travel by air to the capital city, Jakarta. Some planes are almost as slow as snails!

The invention of microchips has facilitated the development of a whole variety of other forms of communication. Spiders have been busy spinning their webs and nets. The internet and chat rooms compete for many people's time. And one wonders what will be invented next to make us all feel outdated.

The personal touch

Christian mission has always been centred on personal relationships. Jesus not only came as a prophet to preach a word from God, but he himself, in his person, was and is God's Word. Life and salvation come through our living relationship with the person of Jesus. He gives us the model for our mission. Interpersonal connections lie at the very heart of any truly Christian communication. We dare not withdraw from the risks inherent in interaction with unpredictable human beings. Of course, computer screens and other impersonal forms of communication may prove safer, but we have to venture out of our comfort zones in our mission.

While applauding modern methods of communication, we face a new danger. Rectangular screens monopolize our time and interest, so that live people can be downplayed. We have heard complaints from some mission leaders. They bemoan the way so many missionaries now work out their personal disagreements on the passive and docile screen rather than talking them through with their fellow workers and gaining reconciliation and mutual understanding. These leaders also complain that their members email them immediately if they have a problem, instead of prayerfully working through the problem themselves.

In this chapter we shall note the enormous opportunities for mission which technological advances offer us. But we need also to be aware that technology has its dangers. Instead of developing warm personal friendships with people, we can easily become very impersonal. Websites and emails can communicate efficiently and convey enormous amounts of information at great speed, but they may lack the loving relationships which open people's hearts.[2]

In my early days of college teaching, student applications came by post. These were dealt with by a secretary, whose letters were very personal and quite lengthy, and demonstrated the college's real concern for each individual applicant. Then electric typewriters came into vogue, introducing standard letters to which a directly personal paragraph could be added. Now the same college is inundated with emails from people who have seen the college's website and ask for further information. Many of these have no particular interest in becoming students, but they all require an answer. Email replies plus printed literature about the college can easily lose that personal touch. We all know how easy it is to churn out quick emails!

Good news

The heart of our mission lies in the gospel of Jesus the Messiah. In Greek, the noun *euangelion* goes together with the verb *euangelizo*, one of the foundational terms for our ministry of proclamation. Unfortunately the term 'gospel' has often become a jargon expression, to which are attached fixed aspects of the message of Jesus Christ. We immediately think of sin, repentance, Christ's atoning death, converting faith and perhaps baptism. However biblically true we may be in our understanding of the gospel, we can easily lose its inner character. The word means 'good news', and this compels us to ask in what way the message of Jesus presents its recipients with news which causes rejoicing. That forces us to consider what needs people both have and feel they have.

When Elizabeth and I returned to Britain after ten years away in Asia, we came to live in a small Hertfordshire village. At that time the local churches were moribund, and it was hard to find any Christian witness in the village. Yet God's calling to us was that we should be missionaries wherever God put us. That calling did not die when we returned to England. So we had to ask ourselves how we could preach the gospel in the context of a British village. What makes Jesus 'good news' to a villager in contemporary Britain?

Noting rows of fishermen along our local river every weekend, and the strange fact that they never seemed to catch any fish, we asked them why they came fishing. The overwhelming majority replied, 'A bit of peace from the wife and kids.' Most of these men worked all day and spent the evenings in the pub, so the weekends were the only chance they had to see their families. Why then did they need peace from the wife and children?

We realized that in today's Britain and, indeed, in many other western countries, homes often lack loving relationships. Once again, we notice the need for the church to have a witness which demonstrates and preaches true relationships of love in Jesus Christ. That is 'good news' in modern Britain and in many other societies too.

The potential of books

Straight from honeymoon, Elizabeth and I were about to take the bus three hours up into the mountains to set up home in Kabanjahe, Indonesia. Owing to the vagaries of the postal system, no money had arrived for us. Our luggage consisted of nothing but what we had brought on the plane from Singapore. There were no other foreigners in Kabanjahe and local Christians did not yet know us. So we felt very vulnerable. We would at the very least need to buy furniture, food and something to cook on. How would we survive without ready cash?

Noticing six new Indonesian Bibles on our senior missionary's desk, I asked if we could take them to sell and thus get a little money.

'Up in the mountains, people don't read, and they speak their own language, not Indonesian,' he replied discouragingly.

In desperation we took the Bibles anyway.

On arrival in Kabanjahe we quickly found how wrong our friend was. People did read Indonesian, and Christians were hungry for Christian literature and teaching. So started a major literature ministry as an extra to our training and Bible teaching role in the churches. After a while, we were selling some twenty-five Indonesian Bibles or books every day. And we reckoned that on average one person a week came to us with a significant testimony of blessing through a book he or she had read. Ever since then, we have been selling and then writing books. We believe in the important role Christian literature plays in mission.

When I travel on a train or the London Underground, I am struck by how many people are reading books. It is said that every book bought will be read on average by 2.5 people. I would assume that Christian books are lent to friends more frequently than secular books, so we may expect that secular statistic to be a minimum figure for Christian literature. Quite an ordinary Christian book will normally sell at least 10,000 copies, so it may be read by at least 25,000 people. Most Christian speakers will not have the opportunity to share their message with so many people in their whole lives.

Books also find their way into all sorts of places where their authors are unlikely to travel. We have happy memories of an occasion when we flew into the airport at Peshawar. We knew we would be met by missionaries with whom we would spend the night before travelling into Afghanistan the next day. But we had not expected to be met by a crowd of local Pakistanis. They all belonged to the same extended family, and had been reading Elizabeth's book *God Can Be Trusted* (OM 1996, 2003).[3] Having been particularly blessed as a family through her book, they were longing to meet her. What a privilege to sit with them in a large wooden house and drink cold water together! Books travel, and they speak wherever they go.

In the English language we have an enormous range of commentaries, theological books, devotional literature, biographies and other books suited for all ages and all educational levels. In many other languages this is not the case. When we worked in Indonesia, some leading Christians would come to our home to ask us if any new book had been printed in Indonesian. They had already read every single Christian book in their language.

In eastern Europe, too, when communism collapsed, there was a fearful dearth of Christian literature. Just after the Czechs' Velvet Revolution of 1989, I dared to suggest to a group of Christian youth leaders that they badly needed more Christian books – evangelistic material suitable for students and youth, foundational discipleship courses and so on.

They acknowledged that such literature did not yet exist, but questioned whether it was wise to produce it. Under communism, they said, anything printed was known to be untrue propaganda. So they were anxious about producing Christian literature, lest it too convey the message that Christianity is untrue propaganda. They also emphasized the importance of having literature that was genuinely Czech and fitted their needs and context.

They had been offered the opportunity to translate an American training course for young people. But it sounded like simplistic propaganda in their Czech context. It contained simple questions like 'Who is Jesus?' The answers consisted of over-simple affirmations like 'Jesus is God'. This would be supported by three biblical quotations without context. Such clear but over-simple teaching was quite unsuitable in the post-communist situation.

When we pastored a young Chinese church in Malaysia, we noticed that people wanted different sorts of books from Christians in Europe. They lapped up devotional literature, and the Holy Spirit used the spiritual classics of A. W. Tozer tremendously. With their Confucian background, they also benefited enormously from very pragmatic books which taught them how to pray, how to witness, how to have time with the Lord and so on. Such 'how-to' books fitted their background culture. The Taiwanese theologian Francis Wei has said that Chinese Christianity must be long on ethics and short on theology. By contrast, in our experience in Malaysia, biographies and books of personal experience fell on deaf ears, whereas in Europe such books top the lists.

A reading church and reading Christians will receive much spiritual enrichment. We need suitable, quality Christian literature in every language. Those of us with opportunities in preaching and teaching should make a point of encouraging our audiences to buy and read good books. In these days, we can no longer take it for granted that people will read books. In London's rush hour, it is interesting to see how many people are reading a book on the train or Underground, but on long-distance trains I have observed that most people read newspapers rather than books. Christians, too, must be encouraged to do regular reading of good Christian books. Preachers and church leaders need to recommend books and encourage church bookstalls.

Television and radio

People today are born with rectangular eyes. In many homes the television is left on all evening, so that it influences the lives of the whole household. Children turn it on as soon as they get home from school, and goggle until bedtime. Of course, computer games may compete for the children's attention, but in one form or another the screen will generally win over all other possible activities. When the children are small, a video, DVD or television programme keeps them occupied and quiet, so that parents can get on with other things. Often, too, the radio or a CD is left on while people are at work or studying, unconsciously permeating their minds.

An Indian Hindu, who had been stationed in West Africa for a while as an overseas aid worker, was getting on with his normal work with the radio playing in the background. Suddenly, he heard the announcer declare that the next programme would discuss the Christian attitude to the Hindu classics.

He could hardly believe his ears. For some while he had wondered about this issue and had even asked a couple of Christian missionaries in Nigeria about it. One had gaped in confused silence, without suggesting any answer. The other had told him to forget such questions, as the Hindu classics come from Satan. Neither response had been of much help. And now a Christian radio programme for West Africa was beaming a programme on the Christian attitude to the Hindu classics! It hardly seemed possible. Surely God himself lay behind the choice of such a topic for the radio – and in a programme for West Africa, where Hinduism hardly exists! Our Indian Hindu friend was converted to Christ as a result.

In TV games and quizzes, questions about television characters or advertisements elicit an immediate response. People know the answers. The medium has penetrated deep into their thinking and moulds the attitudes, morals and beliefs of our people. Even everyday vocabulary is determined by the words and expressions used. Missionaries who have lived for some years overseas will be wise to watch television extensively when they first come back to their native country. Only then will they learn to relate effectively to modern younger people, and thus have a fruitful ministry in mission and deputation in their home country.

Radio and television producers decide which music to promote among the youth of the world. And that music plays a vital role in shaping young people's beliefs. On their programmes they also glorify their fellow stars as notable celebrities, so that they become models which young people want to emulate. For example, if a media celebrity dies, it is big news, and considerable air time will be devoted to his or her death. If a leader in the business world or a top person in some charity dies, he or she is not considered worthy of notice. The thought-moulding power of the top echelon of media personnel is frightening.

In Christian mission we have to pray and work to gain a foothold in such circles. We need to encourage gifted young people to take up media studies and climb the radio or television ladder. In such circles the pressure against committed Christians may prove quite severe, so the church needs to give these strategic people considerable support in prayer and fellowship.

It is sometimes assumed that as Christians our interest lies in the production of specific Christian programmes, in which the message of Jesus Christ comes across clearly and definitely. But our purpose should not always be to aim a direct blow between the eyes. We need to be wise as serpents, and more subtle. We want the underlying philosophy of programmes to reflect Christian values. The Christian faith and the church need to be portrayed in a positive fashion.

Sadly, the opposite is often the case. In current British television, the church is constantly shown to be out of date and old-fashioned. The services are shown to be poorly attended, and the church members look dowdy. The minister may appear worthy, but irrelevant. As Christians with a mission vision for our country, we long for this inadequate presentation to be reversed. While Christians are shown in such a negative light, gay couples are shown in media dramas in a good light, rarely highlighting the dangers inherent in most homosexual relationships. The producers' agendas come across non-verbally without direct preaching.

I remember when a beautiful nature programme was made in our neighbourhood in Indonesia. The producer went to the village, from which he climbed the local smoking volcano. The programme showed traditional religious dancing and other rituals in that village, giving the impression that such practices represented the local culture in all its attractive beauty. Actually, three-quarters of the village's population had already become Christians, because tribal religion, with its fear of the spirits, had proved deeply disillusioning. Non-Christian religious rites were definitely dying out.

The producer then climbed the volcano, pausing to reflect on the deep piety of those villagers who still sacrificed food and a lighted cigarette at the little animistic shrines on the path to the top. Fearing the spirits of the volcano, silence was maintained as the party neared the summit and looked down into the crater. Again, the programme made no mention of the Christian practices concerning the volcano.

Believing in the Creator, who made the volcano with all its power, Christians would shout to each other and praise God at the summit. They would throw stones down into the crater to show their freedom from the angry spirits of the volcano. Some of these stones lodged in the sulphur-yellow crevices from which the smoke was pouring as from an old steam train. The force of the steam would throw the stones high into the air before they crashed noisily back down into the crater. All very picturesque and symbolic!

How good it would have been if the producer had been Christian! With similar beautiful nature photography he or she could have shown in the background the development of the Christian church with its life-changing power and its freedom from the fear of spirits. No direct preaching – just a beautiful nature programme with an underlying message of truth.

In some countries of southern Africa, a Christian soap has become very popular. Again, it does not directly preach the gospel, but its underlying worldview is Christian. It deals with relevant contemporary issues such as Aids from a Christian philosophical and moral base. Such pre-evangelism prepares the ground for the good news of Jesus' death and resurrection.

In many developing countries, the national radio and television companies lack adequate finance. The cost of buying attractive programmes from Europe or America may prove prohibitive. As a result, they are searching for cheap but good input. As Christians, we can offer to produce good programmes teaching about health issues or other educational material. Likewise, we can suggest that they do interviews with interesting people, including missionaries and their overseas visitors. Such opportunities abound also in local newspapers and magazines.

In some countries it is possible to buy time on national radio or television stations. Of course, it is helpful for the spread of the gospel to be able to beam the message over the air in that way. But we have to realize how professional the media are today. We dare not produce shoddy, unprofessional programmes, which will prove counter-productive. And with both radio and television, people can switch programmes with a flick of the finger.

Buying time on national television and making programmes to a professional standard would bankrupt most mission agencies. Such a ministry forces missionary societies to work together. This has been done in Japan, for example. Various missions clubbed together to pool finance and personnel with the necessary technical expertise. Together they produced a series of fifteen-minute programmes. They found that these programmes elicited more response than all their radio programmes together. Christian radio produces considerable interest, but television is enormously influential.

Sitting on the Board of the European Jews for Jesus mission, I have observed how that mission contrives to gain media interest. It is culturally very Jewish and therefore sometimes controversial and up-front in its methodology. Television and radio enjoy promoting heated debate. So they put Jews for Jesus up against representatives of the non-Christian Jewish community or decidedly liberal Christians who strongly oppose Jewish evangelism. By such means the gospel is widely debated and becomes an inescapable issue among all Jewish people. Some will come to faith in Jesus as their Messiah and Saviour. Others will at least begin to ask searching questions. Yet others, of course, will be provoked to hostile anger. So it was in the book of Acts: some believed the very up-front, confrontational preaching of the apostles, while others angrily and even violently rejected it. Even hostile and critical mention on the media draws attention to the message of Christ and stimulates curiosity and reaction.

In Europe it has been considered even more entertaining to watch a video than a live television programme. It has become culturally very acceptable to hire a video when welcoming friends for an evening or when relaxing at home. Happily, we now have a considerable reservoir of Christian videos of various kinds – Bible teaching, evangelistic, missionary reports, music and so forth. We also need to penetrate further into the currently secular video world, so that video shops will highlight our videos as well as those of the non-Christian world. But we run the danger of jumping on to a media bandwagon after it has already passed by. Videos have already been largely replaced by DVDs.

Films

A few years ago I was ministering in Almaty, the capital of Kazakhstan. The billboard outside the huge, hangar-like main cinema displayed a lurid advertisement in vivid colours. I assumed it was promoting a gangster film – until I read the wording! The following week the government was screening the Jesus Film at that huge cinema.

We have all been amazed at the way the Holy Spirit has used that film to bring many to faith in Jesus Christ. It has now been dubbed into a wide variety of languages, appealing to people all over the world and of every religious background. Before the Jesus Film, Zeffirelli's film of the life of Jesus stimulated a love for Christ in many hearts. And since then, Mel Gibson's horrendously violent film of *The Passion of the Christ* has left its audiences in awed silence. Many have gained a new interest in Jesus and in rereading the Gospels. Some have struggled through their emotional awe to actual faith in Jesus as Saviour. *The Passion of the Christ* has broken all viewing records.

Hollywood has begun to take notice of the fact that morally upright and even specifically Christian films can gain box-office success. This is true not only of America, with its huge, actively Christian population, but also of our more obviously non-Christian countries of Europe and other continents. Some years ago *Chariots of Fire*, the story of the missionary and Olympic runner Eric Liddell, gained huge viewing figures. (Elizabeth was particularly interested in this, as she suffered in the same Japanese prison camp, in China, in which Eric Liddell died just before the end of the war.) Later, despite the audiences' general ignorance of the Bible, the cartoon film of *Moses, Prince of Egypt* received general acclaim and wide circulation in the secular cinemas.

Are we now going to see a spate of films with Christian themes? Will the pendulum swing in favour of more morally upright films? How will this influence Christian mission in the coming decades?

Christian films can play a significant part in Christian mission. But they will be more effective if to the impersonal celluloid screen is added the personal witness of a living Christian. When questions fill the mind and heart after seeing a film, it is good to be able to talk with someone who knows some answers and can share from experience what it means to follow Christ. At this point Christians will need to know in a very practical way how to lead enquirers to faith in Christ, and how to help them as they take their first steps in their new life in Christ.

The internet

All over the world, the internet has become a major means of communication. Terrorists plan their attacks and co-ordinate disparate teams through it. Increasingly, consumers shop and plan their travel this way. Websites advertise everything from pornography to church meetings. Information on every subject can be found by surfing the net.

It is challenging to note the spread of internet cafes all over the world, even in poorer countries. In South American villages, rural China or poverty-stricken Central Asia and Africa, people are glued to the internet, fascinated. Through it they are gaining insights into new philosophies, cultural trends, political possibilities and other religions. Websites which advertise the good news of Jesus Christ can be influential.

The founder and former leader of Jews for Jesus spends considerable time in his retirement entering Jewish chat rooms and gradually sharing Jesus the Messiah with the people there. In this way he is able to communicate with people who otherwise might never hear the gospel at all. And he is able to do this in a way which includes quite personal interaction, thus avoiding the danger of depersonalization which threatens our use of the media in preaching the good news.

Conclusion

Technology races ahead like an unbridled horse. How can we keep up with it all in Christian mission? We run the danger of constantly jumping on bandwagons which have already passed by. By the time we catch up on working with television, videos and films, the world has moved on to chat rooms, and the restless spider is spinning new websites. What will it spin next?

Many Christians today would be surprised at the hostile reactions of previous generations to new forms of media. In its early days the cinema was suspect in Christian circles and good Christians avoided it like the plague. Then it was felt that the television screen enticed innocent Christians into the sinful embrace of Satan. Similar feelings of suspicion may surround modern music, computer games and contemporary information technology. Avoiding such old-fashioned approaches, we are reminded that Christians need to learn to be selective and discerning. All media can be used by non-Christians and even by anti-Christian forces. Immorality and sin can easily prevail. But in themselves the different forms of media remain neutral, available equally to morally upright producers and to us in Christian mission.

The challenge lies before us. Will we surrender to Satan and his servants all the most influential means of communication and thus abdicate our responsibility by all possible means to save some (1 Corinthians 9:22)? As is often asked, why should the devil have all the best tunes?

Discussion starters

1. What can we do to improve the communication skills of our church or Christian Union?
2. What dangers do you see for us as Christians in the use of modern communications technology?
3. Are we making adequate use of the range of Christian literature in our own language? What sort of Christian books are we reading? Could we do more to encourage other people to read Christian books?
4. What makes Jesus 'good news' to you and to those around you?

Notes

1. It is uncertain how or when Chinese paper-making was first introduced to the West. It may have been through the capture of

skilled Chinese at the Battle of Talas in Kyrgyzstan in 751, or through the Mongols. At least, we know that paper was being exported from Damascus by the middle of the tenth century.

2. For further thought on the significance of relationships, see M. Schluter and D. J. Lee, *The R Option* (Relationships Foundation, 2003), and *The R Factor* (Hodder & Stoughton, 1993).

3. E. Goldsmith, *God Can Be Trusted* (OM Publishing, 1996, 2003).

8 God never stands still

Jesus was asking for trouble when he healed an invalid by the pool of Bethsaida.

The man had been sick for thirty-eight years, lying on his mat unable to walk. It was the Sabbath when he encountered Jesus. But Jesus had no hesitation in healing him, despite the normal restrictions on what could or could not be done on the Sabbath. It was arguably legal for Jesus to bring healing on a Sabbath, but against the law to instruct the man to carry his mat on the Sabbath (John 5:8–11). In any case, Jesus could easily have avoided the offence he caused. He could have waited to heal the man until the Sunday, the day after the Sabbath. When you have been sick for thirty-eight years, one day more or less is not so vitally important. Alternatively, Jesus could have healed him but told him to leave his mat where it was.

John records that 'because Jesus was doing these things on the Sabbath, the Jews persecuted him'. Why did Jesus purposely provoke the angry opposition of the Jewish leaders? He was quite unafraid of their attacks against him. In fact, his response caused yet further antipathy, for his words seemed to claim that he was 'making himself equal with God' (John 5:18). Surely, therefore, he was wanting to teach his disciples a lesson of fundamental importance.

Jesus draws out one basic lesson from this Sabbath miracle. 'My Father is always at his work to this very day, and I, too, am working.' The present continuous tense of the verbs underlines the fact that neither the Father nor Jesus ever stops working.

By this statement Jesus was entering into a common debate of that time. Was God so holy that he had to obey his own law and thus rest on the Sabbath? If so, the world would surely collapse, for it depends on God's continuous caring oversight. If God sits in heaven, twiddling his thumbs with careless indifference, the world and we human beings would be in serious trouble. Nevertheless, some people said that God was so holy that he must remain inactive on the Sabbath. Others objected, and affirmed that God must be lovingly active even on the Sabbath for the sake of his creation.

Into this debate Jesus stepped with the clear statement that both the Father and he himself work all the time. They never stop working.

Today, of course, most of us find that old debate somewhat irrelevant. But actually it relates also to us in our doubts. Particularly in the ecclesiastical pessimism of Europe, we can be prone to doubt whether God is really at work in our day. Churches decline, Christians backslide, our zealous and prayerful attempts to witness bear little fruit. Is God enjoying a siesta, or a prolonged sabbatical in heaven?

No! Jesus reassures us that both the Father and the Son are always at work. So what is God doing today that is noteworthy?

One of the advantages of getting older is that church history becomes one's own personal experience. It is also the privilege of old age to reminisce, so let me indulge myself and recollect old memories of God in action. Back in 1968, the time of flower-power and hippies, John Stott attended the World Council of Churches conference in Uppsala. There he was challenged, not only by its radical and unbiblical approaches, but also by the call for justice and liberation. As the uncrowned leader of evangelical Christians, he strongly introduced us all to the need to add this dimension of mission to our emphasis on evangelism and more directly spiritual ministries. Under the one umbrella of mission he placed not only evangelism and church ministry, but also social and developmental work. The Great Commission became inseparable from love of neighbour. Later, these roots flowered into a passionate concern for justice, ecology and other outworkings of the gospel of Christ. God has been at work in this way, but we shall examine these subjects in greater detail in chapter 11.

God at work in Latin America

When I was a student in an Anglican theological college back in the late 1950s, many of my fellow students had a passionate concern for mission to Latin America. Missionary prayer meetings for that part of the world witnessed a stream of heartfelt prayer. On graduation, several of my friends went as missionaries to South America. This concern for Latin America ran through many churches, not only in Britain, but also in other countries. It was clearly a work of the Holy Spirit, stirring up his people to pray and go as Christian workers.

When the Holy Spirit raises up a spirit of prayer and also thrusts out workers into a particular area of the world, we may rest assured that he is planning to do something special there.

Back in the 1950s, Latin America represented a tough mission area. There were fewer than two million Protestant Christians in the whole continent. The Roman Catholic church wallowed in the mire of a pre-Reformation style superstition and spiritual corruption. The reforming work of the Second Vatican Council had not yet burst onto the church scene. The Roman Catholic Church was persecuting Protestants ferociously, often killing pastors, burning manses and attacking ordinary Christians. Bibles were outlawed and frequently burned. In the fury of such persecution, the gospel seemed to make little headway, and the challenge of sacrificial mission lay heavily on the hearts of my fellow students.

But God was already planning to work in very special ways in Latin America. Brazil (the continent's largest country), Chile and Argentina, especially, witnessed the sudden explosion of Pentecostal churches, whose members preached zealously on street corners and at the bus stations where new urban dwellers first arrived in the city. Pentecostals also followed the building of the new transcontinental Amazon highway as it snaked its way across the continent. As each new settlement emerged, they planted churches there. At the same time, the masses of the urban poor, disillusioned with the status quo of Catholicism, eagerly embraced this new religion of the people.

In other South American countries, more traditional Protestant churches also grew considerably, while in Central America the massive influence of right-wing fundamentalist churches flowed across the border from the United States and won the multitudes for Christ.

Twenty years after leaving theological college I had the immense privilege of touring South America. I shall never forget one Pentecostal church in Brazil, with a congregation of 36,000 adults that Sunday morning. The church met in a huge, hangar-like building with eight fountains playing beneath the great podium. Coloured lights wafted up and down as the water played beautifully in the fountains. No wonder the pastor told me how difficult he found it to get newly baptized members out of the refreshing cool of the fountains! If someone had told me twenty years earlier that I would minister in such a church in South America, I would have laughed in unbelief.

But our God is always at work. He never sleeps, leaving his world to rot without him.

But there is still much work to be done. Most of the Pentecostal churches are often weak in Bible teaching and in their theology. Because of their inadequate teaching, many younger people with education leave the churches. At first, these churches attracted the poor and uneducated, but, with education, they are climbing into the lower middle class. But the upper classes remain quite untouched with the gospel. Mission workers from overseas can often help the churches to reach out more effectively to the more educated and the upper classes.

The Anglican South American Mission Society has two schools in Chile and Paraguay, which cater for the wealthiest and most influential families. The children of leading politicians, business people and the military flock to these schools. Under these schools' Christian influence, these privileged children are introduced to link schools in the slums, visiting areas of their cities which they would never otherwise see. In this way they are taught about social responsibility. These children will grow up to occupy top positions in society and will have considerable power to change their countries' systems and structures.

The Pentecostal churches are quite unable to relate to these high-ranking people. The class divisions are too extreme.

I was flying from one city to another in South America. Sitting next to me was an elegant middle-aged lady with perfectly coiffured hair. She was smartly attired and wore expensive scent. She soon discovered that I was a missionary, and asked me which order I came from – Jesuits, White Fathers, Franciscans, or which?

I replied that I was a Protestant. Amazed, she exclaimed: 'How interesting! I've never met one of those before.'

I realized that, although she came from a city with huge Pentecostal churches, they would never be able to relate to an upper-crust woman like her. And she would feel like a fish out of water in a Pentecostal church.

God has been and is at work in Latin America, but there remains much work still to be done.

God at work in the communist world

Our God, who never stands still, moved on. In the 1970s and 1980s his Spirit earmarked the then communist world for special attention. Brother Andrew's book *God's Smuggler* became a bestseller. A high proportion of Christians read it and were moved by it. A wave of prayer for the communist world swept through the churches and student groups. And many Christians began to travel into politically closed countries in order to bring Bibles and Christian literature to beleaguered believers. In their travels they visited churches and gave extensive words of greeting to bring further biblical teaching to these persecuted Christians.

I remember being invited to speak at a conference for people concerned for communist countries. As I looked out on the audience of several hundred people, I had serious doubts. So many of them were elderly, looking distinctly out of touch with modern life. Buns and bonnets seemed to prevail. But when I talked with the people at the meal table, I had to repent of my proud and judgmental attitude. One after another told how they had travelled to even remote areas of eastern Europe, the then Soviet Union, China or Vietnam. Here they had distributed Bibles or other Christian books in the local language and encouraged the believers with their fellowship. Looking so very ordinary, they were able to slip through the nets of immigration and police checks.

How important it was for isolated and persecuted Christians to know that people in other countries had not forgotten them and were praying for them! It became a challenging joke among western Christians that we were called to be 'donkeys for Christ' – hopefully without being too asinine.

When the Holy Spirit plans to work in a special way in one area of the world, he stirs up much prayer and inspires a passion for sacrificial mission. Then, when he does actually begin the radical work he has planned, he seems sometimes to use a totally different instrument to effect the desired movement of God. In Latin America, he did use the missionaries to some extent, but his main method was through the Pentecostal and the fundamentalist movements. Likewise, in the communist countries he did use the many who travelled into these areas of extreme persecution, but mainly God worked through the existing churches there and through the sacrificial testimony of oppressed Christians.

I remember starting to deliver a sermon in a large Russian Baptist church. As I looked out on their rugged faces, which clearly reflected the poverty and suffering which Christians then endured, I commented that they had overcome all the power of the state, atheistic propaganda, persecution (which put leaders into fearful labour camps), and discrimination (which did not allow their people to gain good education or to have paid employment). Previous generations, and they themselves, had suffered all that for seventy years, but by the wonderful grace of God they had overcome all the might of the secular powers. I shall never forget the sight of the whole congregation quietly nodding their heads in agreement. It was true. Humanly speaking, they had been vulnerable and weak, but with the indwelling Christ they had won the day.

Sadly, however, the old Baptist and Pentecostal churches in the communist world were forced into rigid legalism in order to resist KGB infiltration and divisive stratagems. Now, in the relative freedom of the post-communist world, such rigidity hampers the work of evangelism and deters people from following Christ. Such churches need help in learning to discern what is truly biblical and essential to sanctified faith, while being willing to adapt on other legalistic traditions. We have, however, to confess that western Christians are sometimes so rigidly *anti*-legalistic that Christians in these countries cannot fit into churches of that background. We can easily forget, and fail to respect, their endurance and suffering for Christ in the days of fierce persecution.

On another occasion, back in the late 1980s, I attended a crowded Russian Orthodox service. Next to me stood two older ladies, who evidently knew the liturgy by heart and were prayerfully following it. They must have been born at about the time of the 1917 revolution and lived through anti-Christian propaganda at school and throughout their lives. They must have suffered anti-Christian discrimination and must never have known religious freedom. But they had endured and won through victoriously. We may wonder what biblical teaching they had received or what theological beliefs they might hold, but I could only admire their courageous endurance and praise God for his enabling grace. Of course, we now face the challenge of helping the Orthodox churches to give their people adequate biblical and theological teaching.

Under communism many Christians stuck their necks out with open evangelism whatever the cost. One old Russian lady told me how she used to board an overcrowded bus every morning and stand all day as the bus went round and round the city. Cheek by jowl in the crowd, she would preach openly. Smiling, she said the bus was so full that the KGB could not get on.

I asked her how people reacted in the worst days of persecution under Stalin and Khrushchev. She was amazed at the question, wondering why I had not studied the book of Acts. The answer was clear in Scripture! Of course, some people believed and some rejected the gospel. So it always is, she informed me. Those who rejected, kicked her and spat in her face. But she rejoiced in those who came to faith.

In eastern Europe a group of men went from village to village singing the gospel. In those days it was illegal to travel outside one's own place of residence without permission, but they knew that as Christians we are called to preach the gospel whatever the cost. Finally, the police arrested them and they were put into prison. One of them told me with tears in his eyes how his ten-year-old son visited him in prison and comforted him with the assurance that he and a group of his young friends were continuing their parents' ministry. These small boys were now singing the gospel like their dads. No wonder the gospel has prevailed and the prayers of Christians in the West have been abundantly answered.

Since 1989 and the collapse of the communist empire, the church has grown enormously. Old churches have planted new congregations as well as adding to the mother congregation. Multitudes of new churches of all sorts have mushroomed. But, as communism slips into history, materialism and disillusionment flourish. The churches have found that the post-communist context is not all sweetness and light. They need ongoing prayer and help in evangelism and Bible teaching.

Economic poverty, too, should move the rich churches of the West to wise and careful generosity. The churches of Russia and eastern Europe are littered with the casualties of unwise giving. Many have been tempted by the comparative affluence of western Christians and have pocketed for themselves money which was meant for the use of the church. Nevertheless, in our comparative wealth, we are surely called to share with our less well-off sisters and brothers. But great wisdom and discernment are needed so that our giving may be beneficial rather than corrupting. And despite their need of our help, we must not forget to be humble as we relate to those who have won through the persecution of former days.

While we stand amazed at what God has done in the former Soviet Union and Eastern Europe, perhaps greater still is his miraculous working in China.[1] When Chairman Mao gained power and the Christian church seemed almost eliminated, there were only about one million Christians in all China. Ferocious persecution was directed against the church. Church buildings were closed down and leaders were often martyred or sent for many years into horrendous labour camps. In the West, more liberal Christians and other China-watchers declared that the Chinese church had ceased to exist, except for a few remnants of pre-revolutionary old people. I remember being scorned and laughed at in a China-watching group because I referred to the church in China.

How wrong such 'experts' were! Despite all the fires of persecution and the overwhelming weight of anti-Christian state propaganda, Christians continued to share their faith. And the Holy Spirit used their brave witness, so that Christian groups multiplied in many parts of the vast land of China.

In more recent years it has been more possible for churches to show their faces above ground. We still have little accurate knowledge of how many Christians there now are in China. Estimates vary wildly from twenty or thirty million to even a hundred million. We can at least be sure that there are more than twenty million Christians,[2] of which probably about 80% belong to the house churches and 20% to the official, government-recognized churches. Whatever the actual figure may be, the growth of the Christian church in China exceeds all possible hope or expectation any of us may have had – and it has taken place in the context of fearful suffering and persecution. God's amazing working in China can only move us to further prayer, involved mission and awe-struck praise.

God at work in the Muslim world

For some years, churches and Christian Unions have often invited me to give talks on Islam and mission among Muslims. In the past I used to paint the picture of a small boy with a toy bow and arrow. He shoots his wooden arrows against the thick walls of an ancient stone castle. The arrows hit the massive wall, make no impact and drop hopelessly into the moat. That was my impression of Christian mission among Muslims.

Of course, there were always exceptions. Having worked in Indonesia in the days of mass movement into the churches, I could not be unaware of at least one exception. Despite violent persecution and many martyrdoms in more recent years, considerable numbers of Muslims continue to come to faith in Christ. This represents a relatively small stream compared with the torrent of conversions in previous years, but nevertheless it is significant.

In Algeria, among the Berber Kabyle people, we have seen the first major movement of North African Muslims turning to Christ since the time of Muhammad. They have the vision of the gospel spreading also among the majority Arabs and we see the first small signs of this beginning to happen, but the numbers still remain small.

Iranian refugees in many western countries often manifest a deep disillusionment with Islam. They have suffered at the hands of extreme elements in their own country and many feel the need to search for truth and life elsewhere. Coming to western countries, they often grasp the opportunity of religious freedom with both hands, and we are seeing a steady flow of Iranians becoming Christians.

Because of the fear of violence from other Muslims, many ex-Muslim Christians are unwilling to have their names revealed. By contrast, Muslims trumpet abroad any ex-Christian converts to Islam. This gives a misleading impression of one-way traffic towards faith in Islam. Actually, every Muslim country now has various ex-Muslim Christian believers, even Saudi Arabia and the formerly totally gospel-resistant Mauritania. These new Christians may not inform the world around them that they have become believers in Jesus as Lord and Saviour, but their newfound faith is nevertheless clear.

In these days of the internet, it is impossible to seal any society off from wider knowledge. In the past, people in countries like Saudi Arabia had no opportunity to discover anything about the Christian faith except through the negatively propagandist grid of official Muslim information. Now, many people have computers and an internet connection. They can therefore access all sorts of Christian materials. As a result, they may begin to think critically for themselves. They are able to compare the various faiths which are practised in different parts of the world. In this open market, some discover the glory of Jesus Christ and his saving work for all humanity.

In sub-Saharan Africa, relations between Christians and Muslims have changed radically. In the past in West Africa, Islam penetrated across the Sahara from the north, while Christianity came by sea along the coast. Between the Muslim and Christian tribes lay a belt of tribes which still followed their traditional religion. These acted as a buffer, so that Muslims and Christians hardly interacted. Both were busy advancing into those tribal peoples that remained neither Muslim nor Christian. Gradually, some were converted to Islam and others to the Christian faith. Today, virtually nothing stands between the two great religions, and they are forced to relate directly to each other.

A parallel movement was also taking place in East Africa. Christianity began up in the hills, where European missionaries enjoyed the cool, healthier air. They also saw the agricultural potential of the fertile hill districts, where tea and coffee flourished along with fruit and vegetables. Meanwhile, Islam came down the coast from the Arabian peninsula. Arab slave-trading also took many from those areas to the heartlands of Islam, where they were converted to Islam. Still today, one can meet many black Muslims in the countries of the Arabian peninsula. Again, there remained for many years a wedge of traditional peoples between the coastal Muslims and the hill-country Christians. But, as in West Africa, tribal religion has very largely surrendered to the more powerful Islam and Christianity. Here too the Christians and Muslims are now compelled to face each other. Will they relate together in peaceful coexistence, or will they fight each other with communal violence? In mission, will one or the other win the day and gain multitudes of converts from the other faith?

Sadly, there are signs of violence in some areas, although tolerant peace reigns elsewhere. Such communal violence has been particularly evident in the large and dynamic nation of Nigeria. The population of the northern states is largely Muslim, with particular traditional social structures. Here they have developed Muslim-dominated governments and accepted *sharia* (Muslim law) as their justice system. Even the most barbaric forms of Islamic criminal law have been enacted. The large Christian minorities have objected to the imposition of *sharia*, but to no avail. Communal violence has been initiated by Muslim crowds, with considerable numbers of people being killed and homes burned, and consequent bitterness and insecurity. Understandably, some Christians have armed themselves, seeing the need for self-defence in the light of the inactivity of the police and army, who often stand to one side when mob disturbances erupt. Regrettably, there have also been cases of Christians seeking revenge and taking the initiative in attacking Muslims and their homes.

But, as stated above, peaceful coexistence prevails in many countries, although the danger of volcanic eruptions of violence simmers not far below the surface. In some Muslim countries, like Mali or Senegal, their governments and people actively resist more aggressive forms of Islam.

How then should Christians view the biblical command to witness, preaching the good news of Jesus Christ to all people? And how should Muslims remain faithful to their equally definite call to *da'wah* (mission)? These questions challenge both Muslim and Christian. Where inter-ethnic and inter-religious relations threaten at any moment to boil over in destructive hatred, should both Christian and Muslim ignore their religious requirements? Should they just live and let live without making any attempt to share their faith with others? In practice, that is what is happening in many situations. Both feel that it is almost impossible to witness to the adherents of the other faith, and that such witness would in any case be fruitless. The only possibility of conversion in either direction, they feel, is through intermarriage.

But surely it should be possible to develop personal friendships, in which both sides can share their faith with humble integrity and love. It must always be wrong in any context to thrust one's faith down other people's throats with an arrogant and unloving disregard for their feelings. But with the sensitivity of humble love we ought to be able to witness to the reality of God's salvation purposes. Our message not only consists of an unbending truth, but also brings attractive good news for all who genuinely and humbly seek God's way of life and salvation.

In such tense and sensitive situations, the church of God needs to avoid all rabble-rousing methods of evangelism. Large and sensational meetings, with blatantly anti-Muslim preaching, can only arouse more communal disturbances, with the inevitable consequence of martyrdoms and severe suffering. One preacher even publicly boasted that God gave him a vision, in which the word *Islam* was divided into two parts, *I slam*. He then declared that God was calling him to be the divine instrument to slam Islam. No wonder reaction boils over in the context of volatile Muslim communities! In a Muslim context such preaching can only be inflammatory. *Jihad*, which is sometimes translated as 'holy war', is close to the surface.

In his letters Paul frequently refers to his need of 'boldness'(Greek, *parrēsia*) in his preaching of Christ. This word has the sense of such absolute confidence in the truth and reality of what we believe that we are emboldened to declare it courageously, whatever the cost. But confident boldness is not synonymous with unwise and provocative insensitivity. It needs to go hand in hand with wisdom – bold wisdom or wise boldness. In the context of warmly loving friendships and relationships, God calls us to share our faith in Christ and his gospel with our Muslim friends. And such sharing should be clear and unashamed, seeking to convince them of the glory and truth of Jesus' saving work through the cross and resurrection (Romans 1:16).

Where will the Spirit move next?

At present, God is still at work in his church, raising up much prayer and mission zeal for witness to Muslims. We have already begun to see a new movement of the Spirit of God in breaking down the fortress walls of Islam, but much hard mission work still lies before us.

A growing flow of Muslims is turning to Jesus Christ for salvation, but it is still just a relatively small stream. We are called today to pray and witness so that this small stream will become a mighty river. God surely purposes to bring about a spiritual breakthrough in the Muslim world, as he has done in Latin America and in the communist countries. But where will he turn his attention to next?

One possible candidate for the Holy Spirit's particular attention is southern Europe and the Mediterranean islands. In visiting the small evangelical churches of this area, one's heart is moved by the spiritual darkness which surrounds them. Surely God's heart of love must long for the message of his salvation to reach out into those countries. It is hard to imagine today that in the past the Christian church was centred on this part of the world. Christian tourists may enjoy the spiritual experience of walking in the footsteps of Paul in Turkey, Greece, Cyprus and Malta. But what a shock Paul would experience if he retraced his missionary journeys now! He would find that most of the churches he had planted have long since had their candlesticks removed. The light of the gospel has been extinguished. Spiritual darkness prevails with widespread dechristianization and churches that wallow in unreformed formality. A living faith in the glory of the resurrected Jesus, and new birth through his redeeming cross, seem far removed from the religiosity of those areas.

The Greek Orthodox and the Roman Catholic churches of that region desperately need the reviving work of the Holy Spirit. Knowledge of the Bible is minimal among the people, indeed often even among the priests and monks. Spiritual ignorance and darkness prevail among the ordinary people. This is true not only of the large countries of southern Europe – Portugal, Spain, southern France, Italy, the former Yugoslavia, Albania and Greece – but also, and perhaps especially, of the Mediterranean islands. How little living Christian witness can be found in Corsica and Sardinia, Malta and its neighbouring smaller islands, Cyprus and Crete! Many missionary societies working in the Muslim world of the Middle East have located their headquarters and offices in Cyprus because of its strategic significance; it has good communications and facility of travel. But relatively few of these can be expected to be fully involved in both the Middle East and locally in Cyprus, nor can they, realistically, learn both Arabic and Greek. Their time is fully occupied in their office work and their missionary responsibilities into the Middle East, so little energy remains for mission locally.

When the world of Islam has yielded a rich harvest for the gospel of Christ and multitudes of Muslims have come to faith in Jesus as Saviour and Lord, will the Holy Spirit raise up prayer and missionary zeal for the Mediterranean area?

But perhaps the Holy Spirit's next thrust will be into the Buddhist world. Quite a harvest has been reaped for the gospel amongst the more syncretistic Mahayana Buddhist populations. Great churches have arisen among the South Koreans and Chinese. In Mongolia, too, with its tiny population, the church grows apace and reaches out increasingly across its vast almost empty spaces – a country as large as western Europe, but with less than half the population of London. Here theological education by extension plays an important part alongside the residential Bible college in the capital city.

But Mahayana Buddhist Japan still remains resistant to the gospel. With all the advantages of high-level education, economic prosperity, technical expertise and a highly sophisticated society, its people continue firmly tied to the traditional Shinto religion and Confucian ethics with a veneer of Buddhism. The veneration of ancestral spirits holds the Japanese in spiritual bondage. Perhaps neighbouring South Korea or the vibrant city of Singapore, with their dynamic churches and passionate missionary zeal, will break through with effective mission to Japan. But we dare not leave it only to them. The church of God worldwide must face the challenge of mission to the significant and influential country of Japan. Its little churches need all the assistance we can give them in their call to evangelize their own people.

The stricter Theravada and Hinayana forms of Buddhism present the church with unyielding lack of interest in the Christian faith. Those witnessing among the Thai, Sri Lankans, Burmese and other Theravada Buddhists sometimes feel that they are engaged in a boxing match against a jelly mould. However far their message penetrates into the jelly, the mould will afterwards return to its original shape. The preaching of the gospel seems to make little impact in societies which glory in passive non-feeling.

Western forms of Buddhism draw over-busy westerners, with their offer of peace and calm in the midst of a frenetic society. Such escape from the harsh realities of a fraught world acts like a magnet among people who work to live, live to work, and work to live. So Buddhism is winning large numbers of converts among us here in Europe. Once people get caught up into the subtle spider's web of Buddhism, their minds become immune to the life-giving truth of Jesus Christ. Few such people are becoming Christians.

We cannot doubt the enormous needs of Buddhist societies, in which the spirit world is an ever-present threat. A Thai tourist guide announced in my hearing that 'all of us in Thailand believe in the spirits'. She pointed out the ubiquitous spirit houses outside almost every home and business. The doctrine of reincarnation, so widespread now in western thought, leaves its followers with little hope for the future and no assurance of eternal salvation. It also removes all compassion for the handicapped and needy, for it teaches that present disadvantages are the natural consequence of bad karma in a previous existence.

As God observes the spiritual needs of the Mediterranean and the Buddhist lands, which will he choose for the next mission thrust? Latin America – the Communist countries – the Muslim world – and what next? As Christians we are called to pray and serve as Christ's fellow workers. Let us keep in step with the Holy Spirit and the mind of Christ.

Discussion starters

1. With your gifts, training and personality, what could you contribute to mission today? And as you see the needs of different areas of the world, where could you see yourself fitting into God's purposes?
2. If you could choose, where would you arrange for the Holy Spirit to concentrate his working in the coming years? Give your reasons.

Notes

1. T. Lambert, *China's Millions* (OMF and Monarch, 1999).
2. 'The state-sanctioned churches (Catholic and Protestant) claim up to 35 million followers. More significant are the underground or "house" churches, which are said to have 80 or even 100 million members.' Overseas Missionary Fellowship, *International China Prayer News*, October 2005.

9 United for mission

In John 17, Jesus asks in his prayer to his Father that Christians may come to 'complete unity' in order that the world may 'know that you sent me and have loved them even as you have loved me' (verse 23). This unity will be evidenced among those who believe in Jesus (verse 20), those to whom the Father has been made known by Jesus (verse 26). He prays that 'all of them may be one ... just as you are in me and I in you' (verse 21). Christian unity is based on the model of Jesus' relational oneness with the Father.

Paul also longs for Christians to 'keep the unity of the Spirit through the bond of peace' (Ephesians 4:3). He affirms that we are one in the body of Christ because we have the same Holy Spirit in us and share 'one hope, one Lord, one faith, one baptism, one God and Father of all' (verses 4–6). Just as Jesus, in John 17, declares that such unity is to be experienced by those who believe in him, so also, in Ephesians 4, Christian unity is found among people to whom 'grace has been given as Christ apportioned it' (verse 7). Paul's teaching on unity has a specific aim: that the Ephesians may 'live a life worthy of the calling [they] have received' (verse 1). It has a specific mission purpose: that our lives within God's church may match God's call to be his apostles, prophets, evangelists, pastors and teachers (verse 11).

He notes that this will require humility, gentleness and patience as we bear with one another in love (verse 2).

So our desire for unity is tempered by God's call to hold fast to the central truths of the Christian faith. While we can patiently disagree on secondary matters, we cannot compromise on the basic essentials of our faith in Christ. It is not easy, however, to draw the line as to which truths are central and which are secondary.

The issue is complicated by another problem. Sometimes individual Christians may hold to basic Christian truth despite the official teaching of their church, but still they do not always feel called to leave that denomination.

When unity gets tough

Battles raged in the latter decades of the twentieth century on the questions: With whom could we walk in genuine spiritual fellowship? With whom could we co-operate in the great task of world mission, whether in our own country or abroad?

Billy Graham, in his influential evangelistic meetings in Britain, encountered a storm of critical protest because he invited Roman Catholics onto his platforms. Likewise, pastors of theologically liberal churches sat alongside more conservative ministers. They had often never met each other before and had certainly not enjoyed fellowship together, although they perhaps worked in neighbouring areas. Was Dr Graham going beyond the teaching of Jesus and Paul in John 17 and Ephesians 4? Did these Roman Catholics and liberal pastors share the one faith and hope through the grace of Jesus Christ? Were they believers who, in the one Spirit, had received the grace of Jesus Christ through his death and resurrection?

Where do we draw the line in opening doors to mutual acceptance and co-operation? Somewhere a dividing line does have to be fixed, for otherwise we betray the biblical gospel and will end up in an adulterating compromise. To give an extreme example, Billy Graham would not have invited representatives of the Jehovah's Witnesses to share the platform with him. Their denial of the deity of Jesus Christ would have made this unthinkable.

Evangelical Christians have wrestled with the issue of an inter-denominational fellowship which straddles divergent views on many topics. This has led the way for the development of the ecumenical movement, with its goal of church unity. This started among Protestant denominations, but, later, Orthodox churches became involved. And now the question arises of Roman Catholic participation. The danger has been that unity has sometimes become more important than true faith and teaching.

We always have to ask: On what foundations is our unity built? The movement towards such breaking down of barriers between Christians started in the context of the international mission of the church. In pioneer mission, Christian workers realized that they were facing bigger issues than those which might divide them in their home countries. In the context of evangelism and church-planting in Buddhist or Muslim societies, it no longer seemed so important whether one had a 'right' or 'true' theology of the millennium or whether one baptized both adult believers and their children. But the central tenets of the Christian faith remained essential for any fellowship or co-operation. Christians with differences in peripheral and non-essential views were increasingly finding that they could still work together, but fellowship died if it was not built on faith in Jesus Christ and his atoning work on the cross and resurrection.

Likewise in China, as formerly in Russia, Christians in prison camps found vital fellowship with believers across denominational and even doctrinal borders which in other contexts could not be crossed.

Before he went to China as a missionary in 1913, my father-in-law attended the great Edinburgh Conference of 1910. At breakfast one day, as they cracked their boiled eggs, tears ran down the cheeks of those who shared the breakfast table with him as they realized that they all came from different denominational backgrounds. A Baptist was sitting next to an Anglican; a Methodist passed the salt to a Reformed Presbyterian; a member of the Brethren shared fellowship with someone from an independent evangelical church. But at that time they did not have to face the more difficult questions of whether they could share fellowship with people who belonged to churches whose teaching differed significantly.

For us today, such an experience no longer seems worthy of mention. But in those days it was rare for Christians to meet together with sisters and brothers of different denominational backgrounds. Even the smaller issues which divide Christians still seemed tremendously important. Most Christians had not yet experienced the liberating interdenominational fellowship of movements such as the Universities and Colleges Christian Fellowship. What a joy it was for those conference delegates, over their boiled eggs, to find that they shared together the heart beliefs of the Christian faith and that they loved the Lord Jesus with equal devotion! Together they were called to proclaim the glorious message of Jesus Christ with all the world.

And so the boundaries of fellowship began to widen. But the question remained and remains still today: how widely can we enjoy true biblical fellowship in the unity of the Holy Spirit?

Openness to the Holy Spirit

Superb gateau and excellent coffee graced the conversation in the elegantly furnished study. The Principal of the German Bible school strongly desired an official link and co-operation with an English Christian College. His Bible school was known for its clear biblical theology and its rather right-wing conservative approach. The guest lecturer from the English college had lived for a while in his childhood with his German-background grandparents, and so felt comfortable, personally, with the somewhat old-fashioned German culture, although his missionary heart also reacted against such an out-of-date cultural worldview.

At first, it seemed mutually advantageous to join forces, at least in some form of unofficial co-operation in which students from the one college could easily complete their studies in the other. Then came the bombshell.

'Of course, if we relate together, even unofficially, your school will not allow anyone on to the teaching staff who has had anything in the way of a charismatic experience. And you would obviously not accept any student with such a background.'

The English lecturer explained that such a condition would spell suicide for an English Bible school. The charismatic renewal has long ago become an integral part of everyday Christian life in the British church and Bible schools. This is now so taken for granted that no-one even distinguishes between 'charismatic' and 'non-charismatic' staff or students. We may assume that in most theological and Bible schools at least half the students will have enjoyed some form of charismatic experience of the Holy Spirit and his gifts.

This explanation fell on deaf ears, and the suggested relationship between the two schools collapsed. But the English lecturer silently reflected on how the Holy Spirit had worked over the years in Britain. When he had studied thirty years before in an evangelical Anglican theological college, a fellow student had 'gone charismatic' and become wildly extreme. He began to pray emotionally for all sorts of unnecessary miracles. Some of the other students began to fear even having a cold, lest he fall upon them with fervent prayer and laying on of hands.

In those days, most evangelical Christians had been understandably suspicious of this new movement, accompanied as it was by such excesses. Fairly quickly, however, Hegel's traditional theory came into play, the thesis and antithesis gradually forming a new synthesis. Many anti-charismatic evangelicals began to see the renewing and life-giving work of the Holy Spirit. They also did their biblical homework more carefully and discovered the reality of signs and wonders in the New Testament church, with the gifts of the Spirit. They then found to their surprise that such spiritual gifts had continued on in the early centuries of the church's history, and had not ceased with the closing of the canon of Scripture. They also experienced the worship and music of the charismatic movement, enlivening their meetings and services. In outreach to an increasingly unchurched society, the new worship music attracted people into the church and thus also to faith in Jesus Christ.

Meanwhile, the 'charismatics' gradually settled down and lost their wild extremes, while generally maintaining dynamic enthusiasm and life. They also began to examine the Scriptures afresh, learning to distinguish between what was essential in the infilling of the Spirit and what had been peripheral. They began to appreciate that other Christians, too, had something to offer. Despite their emphasis on the Holy Spirit speaking directly to people apart from Scripture, many began to hunger for more Bible-based preaching and teaching.

In the wider international church, history intermeshed with biblical understanding – or sometimes with biblical misunderstanding. The Protestant churches of South America and southern Europe had been dominated by an aggressively antagonistic Roman Catholic Church.

While the great council of Vatican II in the early 1960s had opened the door to a more tolerant theology and practice, their past experience of ferocious persecution had forced the evangelicals into a ghetto-like narrowness. In their conservatism, they therefore found the new movement of the Spirit in Pentecostalism unacceptably threatening. Having suffered so severely at the hands of the Roman Catholic Church, they found it impossible to believe that anything positive could happen among people who were different from themselves.

They then noted the biblical inadequacy of most Pentecostal churches in the Latin American continent. Seeing the mushrooming growth of the Pentecostal movement in South America, they closed ranks in defensive opposition. God does not judge by numerical growth, they asserted, but by biblical faithfulness. How true! But this affirmation easily became an excuse for a closed mindset which would not re-examine the Bible's teaching concerning the life and work of the Holy Spirit. They thought their rejection of the Pentecostals was biblical and theological, but actually it was mixed with history-based experience, their suffering under Catholic persecution, which had pushed them into isolation. As a result, they failed to question their traditional approaches and did not face the mission challenge of the church: how can we remain fully faithful to the revealed Word of God in Christ and in the Bible and at the same time relate to the changing world in culturally relevant ways?

Because of the determined opposition of the evangelical churches of Latin America and southern Europe, the earlier mission congresses did not invite delegates from Pentecostal or specifically charismatic churches. Although many of the delegates might have been open to fellowship with such Christians, official acceptance could have split the world evangelical movement. Both the World Evangelical Fellowship and the Lausanne movement, umbrella groups representing evangelical churches and missions worldwide, felt they were walking on eggs as they tiptoed through this particular minefield.

Yet it was becoming increasingly clear that in world mission God was richly blessing Pentecostal and charismatic churches. At the grassroots level, evangelical Christians were experiencing true fellowship with their charismatic and Pentecostal sisters and brothers, although they might still have reservations about the more extreme wings of this movement of the Holy Spirit. It was evident that they shared the basic fundamentals of biblical faith. Differences concerning their experience of the working of the Holy Spirit and his gifts did not necessarily affect their shared dependence on the ultimate authority of Scripture and the saving work of Jesus Christ, his atoning death, physical resurrection and second coming.

Breakthrough

The breakthrough in relations came at the 1989 Lausanne Conference in Manila, at which Pentecostalism and the charismatic renewal were fully represented. In presentations on the big screen as well as on the platform, the conference rejoiced in all that God was doing through such movements of the Holy Spirit. The danger was that the conference seemed to accept uncritically the prosperity movement (which teaches that God always gives wealth and health to his people in answer to believing prayer), and churches which practised wild excesses, as all being equally a work of the Holy Spirit. In the desire to assert that evangelical fellowship overcomes the barriers of differing understandings of the gifts of the Spirit, sometimes questions were not asked concerning doctrinal teaching. In particular, some of the newer African Zionist churches are closer in their teaching to African traditional religion than to true biblical Christianity. And some more extreme churches put their faith in a God of prosperity rather than in the suffering Saviour. Such churches reject the biblical emphasis on taking up our cross to follow Jesus (Matthew 10:38; 16:24). They cannot accept that it is by God's grace that we are allowed the privilege of suffering for him (Philippians 1:29). In Philippians 3:10, Paul declares that by sharing in his sufferings, becoming like him in his death, we share fellowship with Christ. Worldly prosperity cannot be compared with the glory of such deep fellowship with the suffering Servant (cf. Isaiah 53).

In many countries today, the issue is not fundamentally division between charismatic and non-charismatic. More moderate and balanced charismatic Christians are now accepted by most Christians as part of the mainstream of the Christian church and mission. But there are still some more extreme charismatic churches which teach that every Christian must exercise particular gifts of the Spirit, for these are seen as essential marks of the reception of the Spirit. It is often, therefore, more a question of discerning between a genuine charismatic work of the Spirit and forms of belief which ignore biblical teaching that God's Spirit gives different gifts to the members of his church in accordance with his will (1 Corinthians 12:7ff.).

Christians also need to be aware of the danger of experiential extremes which are more psychological, artificially induced or even demonic. Tongues and other charismatic phenomena are experienced in other religions and are not always necessarily the working of the Holy Spirit. Such experiences can be the result of psychological pressures. So in 1 John 4:1 we are exhorted not to 'believe every spirit', but to 'test the spirits to see whether they are from God'. Likewise, in the context of the gift of prophecy, we are commanded to 'test everything' (1 Thessalonians 5:21). True gifts of the Holy Spirit will lead to increased holiness, with a growing experience of the fruit of the Spirit in our lives (Galatians 5:22–23). Such a work of the Holy Spirit will include crucifying 'the sinful nature with its passions and desires' (Galatians 5:24). And the true working of the Holy Spirit not only will result in blessing for the individual concerned, but will also spill over to build up the whole church. So, before listing some of the Spirit's gifts in 1 Corinthians 12:8–11, Paul notes that 'the manifestation of the Spirit is given for the common good' (cf. 1 Corinthians 14:5).

Issues with the Roman Catholic Church

Some years ago a visiting lecturer to São Paulo in Brazil described current movements within the Roman Catholic Church. He noted the old-fashioned, pre-Vatican II stream, which looked very much like the old pre-Reformation Catholic Church. He rightly observed that this type of Catholicism predominated in the whole of Latin America. But he also talked of the liberation theology movement, which originated in South America and became so evident in the Catholic congress at Medellín. Alongside the liberationist movement, a more liberal theological approach has flourished. The influence of German liberal theology makes its mark on this part of the Catholic church.

But then the speaker commented on the reality of a biblical renewal within the Catholic Church, which is often associated with a charismatic experience. This stream within the Catholic Church may be small, but it does exist. Even if it remains a minority movement, we have to face the fact of what is beginning to happen in the Catholic Church around us.

Since Vatican II, the Catholic Church has promised particular blessings on people who read the Bible, and this has played a significant part in spreading copies of the Bible among its members. But the charismatic experience in the Catholic Church calls for discernment. It appears to be a genuine work of the Holy Spirit with some people, but in other cases it represents merely an existential experience which does not exalt Christ or the Scriptures' authority.

Let us see two opposite examples.

A Chinese Catholic lady in East Malaysia excitedly described her experience of the baptism of the Holy Spirit. He had given her a new love and joy with a warm spirit of worship. But when she was asked whom she now loved with such joyful warmth, she talked only of Mary. She had even built a new grotto to Mary in her lounge. To her, Jesus was merely the son of Mary. Questions about Jesus only led to enthusiastic eulogies of Mary, the mother of Jesus. Her charismatic experience had reinforced her very traditional pre-Reformation Catholic faith with its emphasis on Mary as co-redemptrix.

By contrast, the head of the Roman Catholic Church in Denmark some years ago also enjoyed a charismatic experience. He then asked an evangelical speaker what he could do to bring the Catholic Church of Denmark back to a right biblical faith. He longed for Danish Catholics to centre their faith on Jesus Christ and his saving work on the cross. He had brought with him an elegantly attired nun who was responsible for all Catholic use of the media in that area. She commuted twice a week to Paris to lecture at the Sorbonne – not perhaps the usual routine for a nun! She, too, had entered a new experience of the Holy Spirit. These two church leaders had come to a vital new biblical faith in Jesus Christ as their Redeemer and Lord.

Sometimes it is not immediately obvious whether Roman Catholics' charismatic experience is merely existential or genuinely from the Lord. In a Catholic charismatic meeting in Lima, Peru, I observed that the church ornaments were very traditionally Catholic, with a large golden box for the reserved sacrament on the altar. The notices in the meeting also glorified Mary and majored on celebrations of her 'immaculate conception'. But the prayers and worship concentrated exclusively on the Lord himself, with no mention of Mary or the saints.

When I asked the leaders about this apparent contradiction, they replied, 'In charismatic prayer, one prays to the Father through the Son by the Holy Spirit. Mary and the saints play no part in charismatic prayer.'

Someone then added, 'And our salvation comes from Jesus Christ, not from Mary.'

Surely the Holy Spirit was leading them into new theological ways, but they had not yet realized that their new biblical faith was incompatible with some elements of their old traditional beliefs.

As with the adherents of other denominations, Roman Catholics vary enormously. With many we shall come up against the traditional teachings of the Vatican Curia concerning the mass, prayer to the saints, unacceptable beliefs concerning Mary, and the infallibility of the Pope when he speaks *ex cathedra*. The official teaching of the Roman Catholic Church remains firmly entrenched, and the Vatican shows no sign of changing its position on central issues. With a few Catholics, however, evangelicals quickly sense a deep unity of the Spirit. We may discover differences in emphasis and in some doctrinal matters, but we find a oneness of heart in a shared faith in the Bible as God's Word, and in Jesus Christ and his work on our behalf on the cross and in the resurrection.

Evangelical interdenominational missions and Bible schools will have to be discerning as they decide whether to include or exclude particular Roman Catholics. The lines of division are no longer always clearly marked, as they used to be fifty years ago.

In the whole question of mission co-operation, we have to make a clear distinction between the official structures of the Catholic Church and individual members of it. While we may well find a biblical oneness with some individual Catholics, biblical Christians will disagree strongly with some of the unchanging teaching of the Roman Catholic Church in its authority structures in Rome.

The Orthodox churches

In earlier centuries, it was not only theology and church order which divided the Eastern Orthodox churches from the Rome-based western church. Language, too, formed an almost insuperable barrier. While the western church used Latin and therefore the Vulgate translation of the New Testament, the Orthodox churches used Greek, the language of the New Testament.

One element in the Reformation struggles was the Reformers' emphasis on the use of New Testament Greek rather than the continued use of Latin. The Orthodox churches have always emphasized that their history goes right back without a break to the New Testament church. The ancient patriarchates of Jerusalem, Antioch and Constantinople demonstrated this direct continuity.

There were other fundamental differences. In the western churches, theological study resided particularly in the hands of the ordained ministry. In the Orthodox churches, another tradition ruled (although in more recent years this has yielded to the western pattern). Historically, theological study and expertise, and the ministry of teaching the Scriptures, lay in the hands of educated laity. Orthodox clergy were usually somewhat uneducated, merely having the task of reciting the various church liturgies and leading the sacraments. Little education is required for such a ministry.

With the increasing shortage of ordained ministers in western churches, perhaps we need to change our patterns of ministry. It might be helpful if laity became responsible for leading worship and celebrating the Lord's supper, while the clergy could use their biblical and theological expertise in teaching and training. While the tradition of the church has developed the pattern that the sacraments should be led only by ordained ministers, there is no biblical necessity for this tradition to be unchangeably set in stone. In Britain, and some other countries too, many ministers have responsibility in a variety of congregations, so there is a danger of their rushing from one church to another in order to administer the sacraments. In this way they can become too busy for the vital ministry of teaching and training. Thus the ministers' theological training may not be utilized, while the laity often remain inactive and untrained, with a strong sense of inadequacy.

During the 1,000 years after the great 1054 split, the western and eastern churches drifted further and further apart. Indeed, the Orthodox churches stressed the ancient credal affirmation that because we believe in *one* holy, catholic and apostolic church, schism can arise only *outside* the church, not *within* it. They therefore did not recognize the western churches, because they had split off from the one true Orthodox Church. Only in more recent times have the two edged gradually towards each other in ecumenical relationships.

Theological books and biblical commentaries reflect the gulf between the western and eastern churches. Books from the western churches outline the varying views among different streams of Catholic and Protestant thought, but normally they contain nothing about Eastern Orthodox beliefs on the subject. Likewise, most books on church history or mission hardly refer to developments in the Orthodox Church. Most Protestant or Catholic Christians are fundamentally ignorant of the Orthodox churches. It must also be said that Orthodox Christians reflect the same ignorance of western Christianity.

When, in the early 1970s, the college where I taught introduced a course on Eastern Orthodoxy into its syllabus, this was rare indeed (perhaps even unique) in western Europe. Still today, very few training colleges include Orthodoxy in their teaching.

But in twenty-first century mission, western Christians are encountering Orthodoxy in a new way. In America, several well-known evangelicals have shocked their churches by converting to Orthodoxy. And the Orthodox Church, while remaining a relatively small minority church, is growing apace in the United States. This movement reflects a discontent with the lack of awe-inspiring worship and a desire for a deeper experience of the absolute holiness of God in a more mystical way. It stems from a search for spirituality with forms of worship and experience of God which reflect the reality of God's presence with his people. In the postmodern world, people are not content just with biblical and theological truth or with good music and traditional worship. We need a combination of true biblical teaching and a deeply spiritual sense of God's presence.

With the opening of the former communist countries to the western world, the Orthodox Church has also come out of the cold. Christians working in the former Soviet Union, Yugoslavia, Romania or Bulgaria find themselves in a context where the Orthodox Church predominates. Many overseas workers in those countries fail to do their homework and assume that the Orthodox Church must be similar to the Roman Catholic Church; both have ornate liturgies, use incense and so on. They may fail to realize that the local Orthodox Christians equally assume that Protestants and Catholics are fundamentally the same; both have a Latin-background theology, leadership which assumes hierarchical authority and so forth.

With the current emphasis on mission among Muslims, many evangelical Christian workers find themselves drawn as by a magnet to the Middle East and Egypt, Sudan and Ethiopia. Here they encounter the ancient Orthodox churches, which have survived fourteen centuries of Muslim domination and discrimination. Some evangelicals write these churches off as obviously spiritually 'dead', failing to honour their endurance and perseverance in faith over long centuries.

I remember a dynamic charismatic Brazilian student wagging his finger in the face of an Egyptian Coptic pastor. He asserted that, if the Egyptian pastor would only receive the baptism of the Spirit in a charismatic-style experience, he would surely find his church coming to new life and growth. 'As it is,' he argued accusingly, 'your church and you yourself know nothing of the power of the Spirit.'

When the Brazilian eventually drew breath, the Egyptian quietly responded, 'When you and your church have endured and survived 1,400 years of discrimination and oppression, come and talk with me again.'

Moves towards unity

Over forty years ago the Orthodox churches began to associate with the ecumenical World Council of Churches. But in evangelical international mission conferences, it never entered the leaders' minds to invite Orthodox representatives. A very small beginning was made at the Lausanne Manila Conference in 1989, when an Orthodox priest not only attended as a delegate but was also invited to share a small testimony from the podium in a plenary session. Father Alexander Men reflected in his manner something of the beauty of Christ, and people responded warmly to him. Knowing little or nothing of Orthodox beliefs or practices, the hall broke into spontaneous applause. Was this a sign that Orthodox Christians could now begin to find a welcome in evangelical mission circles? Or will the doctrinal differences prove too fundamental for any possibility of true fellowship and co-operation?

Of course, like all barriers, the problem of division does not stem from one side only. The Orthodox churches still will not normally accept non-Orthodox churches as being genuinely part of the body of Christ. Believing that they alone represent the true body of Christ, they assert that they alone represent the continuation of the divine incarnation. As the one true church, they alone enjoy the Pentecostal presence of the Holy Spirit. Non-Orthodox forms of baptism are not accepted as valid.

It takes time for long centuries of divorce to find a new life of acceptance and reconciliation. It cannot be rushed. But gradually we look for a new theology of the church and new attitudes of acceptance of other Christians of like faith. Meanwhile, we rejoice in the small beginnings of interaction and working together in the missionary calling of the Christian church.

Jewish Christians

The appearance of Father Alexander Men on the Manila platform was more radical than many realized. He was not only an Orthodox priest, but also a Jewish Christian.[1] The Manila Lausanne Conference was the first occasion in recent history when a Jewish Christian was welcomed onto the podium of an international missions congress. At that conference, too, Susan Perlman of the Jewish mission Jews for Jesus was even invited to share her testimony publicly.

What a difference from a previous Lausanne Conference, when one of the main speakers read publicly a passage from the book of Acts in which Paul had to endure fierce persecution from the Jewish leaders. He interrupted his reading to say, 'Happily, we don't have any Jews among us here!' Actually, there were some thirty Jewish believers present.

At the second Pattaya Conference in 2004, as in the first one in 1980, a successful study group on Jewish evangelism made something of a mark. In these days of heady pluralism, Jewish evangelism has become a very controversial issue. Supersessionist or replacement theology asserts that the Jews and the Mosaic covenant have been 'replaced' by the Gentiles and the new covenant, so Jewish evangelism and Jewish Christians are no longer allowable. This may be linked to a dispensationalist theology in which God's grace in the present era is for Gentiles, while the time of the Jews will come in the last days.

Others preach a two-covenant theology, in which the old Mosaic covenant is for Jews while the new covenant in the blood of Christ is only for Gentiles. So Jesus Christ is the Saviour only for Gentiles, not for Jews, they maintain. What Peter, Paul, John and the other apostles would have thought of such theology defies imagination.

Other Christians have felt the weight of guilt lying heavily on their Christian shoulders from the Holocaust. They therefore maintain that Christians have lost the right to preach to Jews. But the Christian gospel is built on the reality that repentance leads to the cleansing of all sin (1 John 1:9). We dare not, therefore, continue under the burden of guilt. In our new life in Christ and through his atoning work on the cross, we can regain the right, and indeed the compelling duty, to share Jesus Christ with Jew and Gentile alike.

At both Pattaya conferences, Jewish delegates not only enjoyed rich fellowship together, but also struggled with particular issues concerning the role of Jewish Christianity in a church which has been almost exclusively Gentile for many centuries. What does the word 'Israel' mean today? How can we relate the gospel to Jewish people? What forms should Jewish Christianity take in the light of contemporary Jewish cultures and the history of Gentile Christianity, with its particular forms of theology, biblical under-standing, worship and so on? We shall look at these questions in a later chapter.

Sadly, it remains a struggle for some Gentile churches to accept that Jewish Christianity has a place in the contemporary life of the church and in Christian mission. And still today, no Jewish Christian has been invited to be a main speaker at a major international missions congress. One wonders why Jewish Christians are not asked to expound the Scriptures in such circles? Although Jewish cultures and worldviews today vary considerably from those of New Testament times, there also remain considerable parallels. Jewish Christians might therefore be in a position to make some contribution in the understanding and missionary application of the Bible.

But we rejoice at the first beginnings of official acceptance. The appearance of Susan Perlman and Alexander Men on the platform encourages us that these small beginnings may grow into greater things in the days ahead. As the Chinese proverb declares, small tigers become big tigers.

Conclusion

When the church is large and strong, the need for fellowship and co-operation with others hardly arises. But when the church is in a minority, facing a tough mission challenge, then it senses a deep unity in Christ with all fellow believers. In western Europe today we are seeking to keep our heads above water in the midst of a swirling tide of pluralism and rejection of the Christian faith.

This struggle takes place not only in western Europe, but equally in many other parts of the world. Strongly Buddhist or Muslim societies also confront us with their vehement opposition to the preaching of the gospel. In such situations, ancient divisions within the church begin to melt before the heat of persecution and rejection. But the desire for such mutual support must not lead to the watering down of the biblical gospel. Our unity is centred in Jesus Christ and our faith in him, his atoning work on the cross and his resurrection. In this context, we look for the one Holy Spirit who indwells all believers in Christ.

All Christians and Christian organizations have to determine for themselves individually where they draw the line. Which churches can we openly work with? Which doctrinal truths are essential to the faith, and where can we be flexible? We are being compelled again to clarify the line which divides essentials of the biblical faith from debatable peripherals. In the mission calling of the twenty-first century, we cannot just continue to live with the traditional barriers and divisions of past centuries. Both the world and the church move on. The Holy Spirit calls us to re-examine our relationships with non-evangelicals, Roman Catholics and Orthodox believers. No longer can we allow our experience and understanding of the work of the Holy Spirit to break our fellowship and prevent us from honouring one another in love. But we must not allow such questions to push us into compromise of biblical truth. In every generation new questions arise and new situations emerge, but 'the living and enduring word of God' stands for ever (1 Peter 1:23–25). The contemporary pluralist pressure for tolerance must not move us to adulterate 'the word that was preached' to us; we have a duty to pass it on faithfully to other peoples and to future generations.

In Acts 1:6–7, Jesus' apostles asked him about the coming of the kingdom to Israel. Christians are easily sidetracked by questions about prophecy and the place of Israel and the Jews in God's purposes. But Jesus rejects any such sidetracks. He commands us to know the power of the Holy Spirit and to work as his witnesses to all people, both to Jews and to Gentiles all over the world. In this international and inter-ethnic calling, those first Jewish disciples of Christ soon found themselves standing shoulder to shoulder in unity with Gentile believers.

Today, too, God calls us to work together with Christians of other ethnic and denominational backgrounds to bring the saving message of Jesus Christ to all people everywhere. Nothing else must get in the way of this priority calling.

Discussion starters

1. What are the basics, biblical and practical, when considering unity with other believers?
2. Where do you stand *vis-à-vis* the charismatic movement? Can you support your position biblically and theologically?
3. Does God still have particular purposes for the Jewish people? Should evangelism among Jews hold a special place in the hearts of Christians?

Note

1. To many Jews, words such as 'Christ', 'Christian', 'church' and 'conversion' are reminiscent of the sad history of Jewish persecution by Christians through the centuries of history. Nevertheless, I have used the more usual term 'Jewish Christians' in this book, rather than 'believers in Yeshua' or 'messianic believers'. The term 'Jewish' is, of course, ethnic rather than religious. We are reminded of the New Testament emphasis that Jesus, the Jewish Messiah, has come not only for Jews, but also for Gentiles of all ethnic backgrounds.

10 No ruts in mission

All of us are vividly aware of the truism that we live today in a world very different from that of just a few decades ago. This inevitably affects the whole pattern of mission practice. Enormous material wealth has overtaken the western world and many of the countries of east and southeast Asia. Even within the poorer countries of the world, the upper classes' accumulated monies underpin the large Swiss banks, and they revel in every splendour money can buy. On his death, it was discovered that Yasser Arafat had several hundred million dollars in his personal bank accounts. Where did this money come from? Was it from aid given for Palestinian refugee camps? Sadly, this can be paralleled in the leaders of many poor and developing nations. However much we may criticize such disparities between the haves and the have-nots of such countries, the fact remains that in Britain, too, a small minority of people dwell in splendid homes and travel the world in luxury.

As we have already noted in a previous chapter, increased wealth has gone hand in hand with the amazing evolution of speedy and relatively inexpensive travel. In my youth it was a source of wonderment that my father had travelled on business to China, Japan and other 'exotic', far-away countries. And we felt that my mother was very adventurous in the early post-war years to take us three boys by car on holidays to France. Later, Elizabeth and I travelled by sea as new missionaries through the Mediterranean and the Red Sea to Aden, and then on to India, Sri Lanka, Malaysia and finally to Singapore. We had never seen pictures of these countries, for television was not yet common. What an exciting adventure to visit such remote places and see for ourselves so many different peoples and societies!

Now in the twenty-first century it is quick and cheap to fly to any part of the world. Gap-year travel between school and university has become common. Tourism ventures into ever more unusual places as people seek novelty and adventure. Business travel brings big money to the travel industry. The availability of modern travel enables Christians from richer backgrounds to visit overseas with unprecedented ease.

Tourists can be missionaries

Back in the 1960s we were involved with a local church-planting team. Each week we visited a large village called Lingga, which at that time had never previously heard the gospel of Jesus Christ. The beautiful, traditional eight-family houses, with their wonderfully shaped sago-palm roofs, stretched up into the sky, outlined against the huge full moon. Inside, the wood-fire smoke so filled the air that the eyes smarted and the throat tingled. But large numbers came to Christ and the new church multiplied.

Years later I took my young daughter to see this village which had been so important in my life. As we approached the village, a huge tourist bus drove past with white faces straining at the windows to see the sights. At the entrance of the village stood a gate with a large sign, announcing the price for tourists to enter. When we had been missionaries there, no Europeans ever came near our region. I was shocked to see that Lingga had become a tourist site.

'How many of us here have visited a Muslim country in the last five years?'

The question did not surprise the congregation, and about half those present raised their hands. Tourism to countries of other faiths is a normal part of everyday life today. Mission theory and practice have to take this into consideration. No longer is it only full-time 'missionaries' who are interacting with people overseas. Mission lies also in the hands of ordinary Christians who travel for business or on holiday. They, too, need encouragement and training in the task of cross-cultural mission.

But the growth of tourism is not restricted to western lands. Japanese and South Korean groups flock to the great cities of the world every summer like migratory birds. Unlike western holiday-makers, they do not usually come as individuals or as nuclear families, but in whole travel groups. There are so many of them that sightseeing notices are posted not only in European languages, but also in Japanese.

In Cyprus and other countries surrounding the Middle East, the newly rich Russian elite frequent the smart restaurants and bars. Likewise, in London, Paris and other western city centres, rich Arabs from Saudi Arabia and the Gulf are often seen in our city-centre shops. The tourist industry has become a major part of national economies.

Particularly among the western and South Korean tourists, a certain percentage will be Christians. The question inevitably arises: Will they go overseas merely to soak up the sun, shop and visit ancient sites? Or will they also be conscious that they visit these other countries as ambassadors for Christ, with his message of reconciliation?

How can a tourist witness for Christ?

Encourage national Christians

What an encouragement it can be to local believers when they receive a visit from foreigners who are visiting in their area! This is particularly true when the church is just a small beleaguered minority and feels its weakness and isolation. The glory of relating to the church worldwide can give them renewed strength to stand fast against all opposition.

In China, the leader of a small church we visited was a man who had formerly worked as an untrained 'dentist', with virtually no equipment but with much experience in pulling teeth. He oversaw a little church of about fifty baptized Christians. Every Sunday their dreary little meeting place was packed to the walls, with further crowds outside in the courtyard, but the authorities would not permit any expansion of the church building and constantly pressurized the church and its leaders.

'We thought we had been completely forgotten by other Christians around the world,' he exclaimed, tears running down his cheeks.

The presence of overseas visitors, plus our assurance that Christians elsewhere were praying for his church, warmed his heart. This church had not seen foreign Christians since the revolution in 1949.

Encourage expatriate workers

Particularly in those Muslim countries which do not have large minority Christian populations, it may not be wise for expatriate Christians to try to visit the small, local Christian fellowships. Such visits can endanger the believers. But expatriate Christian workers in the area may appreciate a visit. Many such Christian workers face very real loneliness, so they will enjoy living fellowship with visiting Christians.

A Christian couple went to a North African tourist city, enjoying the warm weather and the good swimming. In that city there were no local believers yet, and just one expatriate Christian husband and wife, seeking to share the good news of Jesus Christ in the strongly Muslim society around them. What a joy for them to be invited to the visitors' hotel for worship and fellowship together! They could also enjoy the luxury of the hotel swimming pool and a leisurely time in peace on loungers by the pool. Relating to the missionary couple also made the tourists' visit much more interesting.

Seize opportunities while touring

Local governments covet the dollars, euros and pounds which flow from the tourist trade. They are therefore very loath to cause any trouble to foreign tourists. On the other hand, local believers may be carefully watched and, if they step out of line, the police may fall upon them.

In a North African country, for example, a local Christian leader once bewailed the fact that Christian tourists failed to take the opportunity to give Christian literature to the people they met. If he, as a local, distributed literature, he suffered persecution from the authorities. But tourists can so easily give a gospel or even a New Testament in the local language to someone in the hotel or to the person they buy postcards from. They may of course be wise to wait until their final day in the country before they give out literature!

While staying in their hotel, they can keep a local language New Testament by their bed, so that the cleaner has the opportunity to read it each morning. Then, when their holiday comes to an end, they can leave the New Testament with their tip. If every Christian tourist took such opportunities, a lot of New Testaments, Gospels and Christian literature would circulate locally.

Seize opportunities on business trips

Travelling Christian business people have parallel opportunities for discreet witness. They too can visit a local fellowship or church. They can also contact a mission working in the area where they are visiting. From the mission they can obtain the name and address of a Christian worker to visit. They will need to be wise about giving out Christian literature, but, with prayer and care, opportunities may well present themselves. Thus, as we have seen, many business people will be invited to a meal in the home of some local business leader. It will be customary in most cultures to bring a gift. A nicely wrapped copy of the New Testament can make a very acceptable present. The gift may be accompanied with the words, 'Would you be so gracious as to accept a copy of my Holy Book?' Even in staunch Muslim situations, such a gift will normally be warmly welcomed. The hosts may well be curious to read the Christians' book and will be glad of the opportunity to do so within the privacy of their own home.

Short-term mission

What a challenge it is to our comfortable generation to read the stories of former missionaries' epic journeys in Africa or Asia! They remind us how our current practice of short-term mission stems from our twenty-first century situation of wealth and easy travel. Even as late as the 1930s it could sometimes take a year to travel from the coast of China up to the far northwest, walking on foot the last stretch of at least 500 miles. In such circumstances one can only intone, 'Here endeth short-term mission!' But for Christians in wealthy countries, times have changed. And short-term mission is now not only a real possibility, but has indeed become the norm. Relatively few western mission workers commit themselves to life-long service overseas.

Even five years' service may be considered 'long-term'. However, Asian mission workers seem more willing to commit themselves for long-term service.

Short-term mission has both advantages and disadvantages. We need to consider honestly both the pros and the cons.

Talking of a mission society other than his own, a Christian worker exclaimed, 'Their missionaries are so gifted, they easily dominate the local church leaders. Our members are so ordinary that we couldn't outshine local leaders even if we tried!'

Well-trained and gifted ministers easily gather into their own hands all the work and decision-making of the church. Likewise, professionally trained and theologically well-educated overseas missionaries can steal the limelight from the leadership of the church overseas. The history of the Christian church is littered with sad examples of such domination, both in Europe and elsewhere. But short-term workers do not have the time to get their roots established and threaten local leaders.

Short-term workers know they will stay only for a few months, or perhaps a year or two, so they must inevitably promote local leadership. And the local Christians also know that the short-termers will soon leave, so they are less tempted to hand over to them the reins of responsibility. This applies to temporary leaders during an interregnum before a new minister arrives, as also to foreign mission workers. Long-term workers or pastors may find it harder not to dominate in the life of the church.

Short-term workers can also prove very useful in filling a particular need. A church can benefit enormously from a team or an individual coming to share their particular skills or expertise. Many British churches are lacking in children's or youth work. It may prove helpful to have a short-term worker in the church to train local believers in such work and to get an effective ministry of this sort established. Local Christians can then take it over. But if the children's or youth worker stays long-term, there is a danger that the church may just leave that area of ministry to them. That means that the church becomes dependent on outside help rather than developing ministry skills itself.

In overseas mission work, short-termers may fill a particular need in supplying medical, building, computer, or business and administrative skills. They may also play a vital role in caring for and teaching missionaries' children.

In these days of ever-increasing life expectancy, many people still have before them several years of health and strength after retirement. During their working life they have gained much experience and expertise which can be used in active Christian mission in their own country or overseas. In many cultures outside the West, older people are specially respected and so can have a particularly effective ministry.

We have to recognize that often it is the short-termers themselves who gain most from their time of service. They learn a great deal from their experience. We all know of gap-year students who have gone overseas for some months or worked in a local church in their own country. Through their experience, such young people mature amazingly, both personally and spiritually. And when they return to their own circle of friends and their own church, they can share what they have learned. Their experience of a totally different church and perhaps also a different culture will enable them to widen the perspectives of their home circle. The British church has so much to learn from God's work in Africa, Asia or Latin America. Christians returning from such experience can mediate blessing from the church overseas. So God's ultimate purpose in sending short-termers overseas may turn out to be for the blessing of their home church or Christian Union. We think we go to serve, but actually we may receive more than we give.

The limitations of short-term mission

Short-term workers do have some definite advantages. But there are also some negatives, particularly in service overseas. Outside the western world, most cultures are built on personal relationships. Such relationships have begun to be sadly corrupted by the depersonalized computer world, the impersonal supermarket, and forms of city life which destroy wider relationships. Nevertheless, traditional culture, with its reliance on family and societal relationships, still underlies everything. Short-term workers can form only relatively superficial friendships, in which more intimate sharing cannot generally surface. The very fact that short-term workers have clearly come with the firm intention of leaving quite quickly can be misinterpreted as a lack of love. The thought may lurk unspoken in people's inner feelings: 'If you loved us, you would not rush away.' Has the short-termer come only for their own sake, in order to gain experience or to enjoy the travel experience?

Perhaps the greatest difficulty in short-term work lies in the area of language and culture. In today's world, European languages like English, French and Spanish are commonly spoken in many countries, so it may prove wise to choose such a situation when wanting to go for brief periods of service overseas. That allows the possibility of communication and relationships at an everyday level, but more intimate questions of faith and personal concerns still require knowledge of a person's mother tongue. In six months or a year, language study is bound to be only elementary.

In just a short stay in another country, it will also be impossible to gain a deep understanding of another culture. Short-termers inevitably bring their own cultural background with them. Cultural imperialism is a real danger. As we have seen, in cities, globalization may have a superficial impact on cultural expressions, but beneath the surface the old cultures reign supreme. A good knowledge of both culture and language is required for an effective communication of the gospel and for the teaching and training of the church. Even within one's own country it takes time to understand the local background when one moves to a new town or village.

It has become common today for ministers and other church leaders to visit another country, even for just a couple of weeks. This can be very helpful in giving support and fellowship to their church members working there. Such visits can also encourage local believers, particularly in places where the church is small and weak. But we need to go with such humility that we desire to learn rather than to teach. Some church leaders fall into the temptation of trying to teach overseas Christians about Christian leadership. How dare we attempt such teaching with little or no understanding of the local leadership structures! Christian leadership must relate to local cultural and religious patterns. We don't want to export our forms of leadership; that is cultural imperialism.

I remember leading seminars in an Overseas Missionary Fellowship workers' conference in South Thailand, where they were seeking to plant churches both among Muslims and Buddhists. For the work among Buddhists we looked together at the patterns of leadership in a Buddhist temple with the order of monks. For mission among Muslims we studied the role of the mosque committee and the imam. Then we asked each other what forms of Christian leadership should be developed for the church in South Thailand, still bearing in mind fundamental biblical principles.

The opportunity to learn

As we have stated, perhaps one of God's purposes in allowing ease of travel in our times is that all of us may learn from working elsewhere. Most short-term ministry stems from the wealthy countries of the West and from East Asia. All of us have much to learn from God's patterns of work in other countries.

For example, South Korea tends to be rather monocultural, with little inter-ethnic or intercultural understanding. While this is just beginning to change a little, it still remains true that most Koreans have never had any personal relationship with someone from a non-Korean background. While this monocultural background gives Koreans a strong sense of identity and cultural confidence, they are not accustomed to adapt culturally, and this can cause real problems in overseas mission outreach. Their dynamic evangelistic zeal, personal warmth and vibrant spirituality and prayer can be spoiled by cultural and ecclesiastical rigidity. Within South Korea today, many churches are finding it hard to adapt to the changing patterns of life among the younger generation and in the major cities. Sadly, they often make their overseas trips in whole groups together and never really escape from their own culture. How helpful it could be, therefore, for Korean Christians to see God at work in different ways in other countries! They could then bring back what they have learned overseas to their churches in South Korea.

Many European churches are in a state of decline, in which they find it very hard to develop an effective, outgoing mission character. In Europe, we have so much to learn from the growing churches overseas and from churches which have had evangelistic witness at the heart of their structures throughout their history. Large numbers of young church members are now going to serve overseas for short periods, and many of our church leaders have the opportunity of visiting more dynamic and biblically confident churches. And Christians are going abroad for their holidays or on business, and so have the chance to see God's working elsewhere. We should pray that western Christians will learn from what they see and bring it back to our churches here. We could wish that the work of the Holy Spirit in other countries might be so contagious that their fire might spread also to us.

Prayer walks

Some Christians sense God at work when engaging in prayer in a particular place. Thus, in praying for Egypt, they may walk around the pyramids, asking God to deliver that country from Pharaonic spirits. Or some may go to a central mosque to pray for deliverance from the power of Islam.

None of us would wish to discourage vibrant and informed prayer. We believe that prayer is the vital ingredient which puts the match of the Holy Spirit to the witness of the church. Even well-laid fires still need that match to set them alight. Without the fire of the Holy Spirit, wonderful biblical teaching and preaching, beautiful and relevant worship or solidly orthodox theology will lack powerful fruitfulness. If our people are moved to more fervent and faithful prayer through travelling to other countries or places in order to pray, we can only rejoice. And it is true that our hearts may be stirred to pray when we witness for ourselves the places and situations which desperately need prayer. We may feel the strength of Satan's fortresses and be moved to pray in the power of the Spirit that God would pull down such barriers to his gospel. The sight of Satan's strongholds, where Christian witness seems so ineffective, can arouse a longing within us that the glorious name of Jesus Christ be loved, worshipped and served as it ought to be.

But travel costs money, time and energy. The very fact that prayer walks abroad depend entirely on financial wealth and ease of travel is an indication that they are not an essential part of God's purposes. That does not mean that they are outside God's plans for us today. He can use such prayer walks for his glory. But we need to think carefully about the costs involved. How much money will be expended on a visit to Egypt, for example, with a prayer walk around the pyramids and the ancient temples down the Nile? Might it be better to give that money to Christian mission in that part of the world? We can bind the forces of Satan by Spirit-led prayer just as effectively from our bedroom at home as during a march around the pyramids. God's answers to prayer are not limited by geography.

Prayer walks have sometimes been linked to trying to discover which demonic spirits have power in a particular location. The idea is then to design a map with the names of the spirits attached to the areas where they rule. The biblical evidence for demonic spirits being so narrowly tied to one place is very weak indeed. And the Bible never suggests that we should engage in such mapping activities. It is surely also spiritually dangerous to communicate with the evil spirits in order to discover from them what they are called. Even if one could persuade an evil spirit to divulge his name, could one really be confident that he will not deceive us? Satan is known as the father of lies, so presumably his minions are not always totally truthful.

Some Christians today are easily attracted by novel ideas and strategies which sound exciting. But we are called to discern such movements and ideas biblically. We need to encourage Christians today so to study the Scriptures that they are able to apply God's Word to every situation and know God's mind (1 Corinthians 2:16).

'Tentmaking'

While tentmaking is no new form of Christian mission, it has recently gained a new central place in mission thinking. Already in the first century Paul gave us a model for our mission practice.

Sometimes it seems that he received support gifts from a church which he had previously planted (Philippians 4:10ff.), but at other times he made use of his professional skills as a tentmaker (Acts 18:3). We observe in Acts 18:3 that this work gave him a oneness with Aquila, who was also a tentmaker. Paul may not just have had his own financial needs in mind as he worked with his hands, but may also have used his profession with the direct purpose of sharing together with the man he was staying with. Paul was new to Corinth and had only just met Aquila for the first time, so it was doubtless helpful to have some means of forming closer relationships. As it turned out, this was to prove a vital contact for Paul. Aquila and his wife Priscilla became his long-time fellow workers, who even 'risked their lives' for Paul (Romans 16:3–4). And as the witness developed, a church actually met in their home. By the time Paul writes his letter to the Roman church, it is evidently Priscilla who is the leader in that church, for her name is placed before that of her husband.

But with his background of rabbinic teaching, Paul must have also been aware that in those days a Jewish rabbi had, by law, to earn his own living. A rabbi should not be dependent on other people. So it is possible that Paul sometimes worked as a tentmaker even when he was also receiving gifts from the Philippian church and his needs were being met in that way. The New Testament does not give us adequate information on this point, so we can only speculate.

But it does seem clear that Paul gave priority to his preaching and teaching ministry. Judging by his association with Priscilla and Aquila, Paul used his daily occupation in making tents to evangelize those he worked with. And even when he was busy making tents, he went every Sabbath to the local synagogue with the aim of persuading both Jews and Gentile God-fearers concerning Jesus the Messiah (Acts 18:4). Did this synagogue preaching require Paul to spend time in midweek preparation too? Or was he so biblically well versed that he could debate and preach in the synagogue without preparation? Again, the New Testament does not tell us the answers to such questions and we are once more left to speculate.

But such questions make many of us today feel that we would require time to prepare for our active witness at weekends. So perhaps our 'tentmaking' should not be so heavily time- and energy-consuming that we cannot engage adequately in witness and church ministry. The tension between our professional work and our mission witness will always require careful prayer and planning. It is very easy to allow our preaching and teaching ministry to be crowded out by our everyday employment. Of course, our regular work often also provides natural opportunities for sharing the good news of Jesus Christ. We need to pray specifically for such openings and keep alert for them.

In Acts 18:5 we discover that Paul's tentmaking in Corinth did not last. When his fellow workers Silas and Timothy arrived, he gave his energies exclusively to his preaching. So he evidently did not follow too strictly the rabbinic injunctions that God's workers should earn their own living. While he was willing to use his hands professionally when financially necessary, or when it was helpful in forming closer relationships, he still gave clear priority to his preaching and teaching ministry.

Tentmaking today

Is full-time ministry a higher calling than remaining within a 'secular' profession? Should every Christian have the aim of moving on into the ordained ministry or some other full-time church and mission work? The very questions are likely to raise hackles and suggest an un-biblically clerical view of the Christian life. Sadly, the perverted view that ordained ministry is somehow a specially high and privileged calling is still often taught in our denominational theological colleges. This can easily lead to pride, clericalism and a separation of the clergy from the laity. This in turn can result in burnout among full-time Christian workers and a failure to mobilize all our church members for local mission.

Yet we have seen from Acts 18 that Paul did give priority to his preaching and teaching ministry. It is striking that, immediately after Luke mentions Paul's tentmaking, he goes on to tell of Paul's witness in the synagogue and then says that he later 'devoted himself exclusively to preaching'. Paul's model challenges Christians who remain in their professions. How eagerly do they desire their daily work and relationships to convey the gloriously relevant message of Jesus Christ? Are they praying for and constantly seeking suitable opportunities to share their faith verbally? Of course, they will not want to ram the gospel down people's throats or be in any way insensitive in their witness, but at right times and in appropriate ways we long to introduce Jesus to our neighbours.

Witness at work

Our witness, however, is not only verbal. The way we work should speak volumes. Our attitudes and motives should stand out as radically distinct from those of our non-Christian friends. And our relationships should demonstrate the reality of Paul's command to 'serve one another with love' (Galatians 5:13). The non-Christian world around us is not usually characterized by such a love that people are as concerned about others as they are about themselves. In our workplaces, such an attitude of deep concern for the welfare of our neighbours will make the gospel of Jesus Christ shine as 'good news' indeed in a selfish, cut-throat world. Paul encourages us also to serve one another with evident humility, doing everything we can to promote other people's welfare at whatever cost to ourselves. The workaday world desperately needs that sort of Christian witness. So our work and our words hold hands together in our mission.

As Christians, we have to confess that some of us are merely using our 'tentmaking' jobs as a means to get a visa and so to have the opportunity of doing evangelism locally. Such people may be tempted to short-cut their work in order to have more time and energy for specific evangelistic activities. As Christians, we need constantly to be reminded that our 'secular' work has divine value in and of itself. Whatever God calls us to do, we should do it with all our heart (Colossians 3:23). And if our work is substandard, that will in itself be a negative witness. If we undervalue our daytime jobs, we can also become very frustrated. We shall be spending long hours going through the motions of doing our work, while our hearts are not in it. Lack of God-given job-satisfaction can only lead to bored frustration. We then have to ask ourselves: What does this say to the people we are with? They will almost certainly have to spend their lives doing ordinary everyday jobs. If they become Christians through our testimony, how will they relate their faith to their work? What sort of model are we giving?

In many countries corruption and dishonesty prevail, complicating our witness at work. Perhaps patients cannot get medication without bribing the medical staff. Business people have to grease palms before they can clinch a contract. To obtain a visa, to pay one's tax or to avoid a speeding fine, one may have to pay bribes. Incorrupt honesty can shine like a bright beacon in such dark situations; but multitudes will feel impotent as they suffer under unjust social systems. The world needs godly Christians with the sanctifying power of the Holy Spirit to leaven the workplace lump.

Workplace opportunities
Whether we are in our home country or overseas, the workplace presents us with natural opportunities to relate to other people. Paul

evidently got alongside Aquila through their shared tentmaking, won him for the Lord and discipled him. Sitting side by side stitching tents arouses a natural personal affinity which is the ideal context for witness. Most of us today will not be making tents, but the principle applies equally to other professional activities. Sitting for long hours at neighbouring computer screens, working together as nurses on a hospital ward or drinking coffee in a staff common room between classes can also engender a sense of shared camaraderie. This proves true also for the missionary 'tentmaker', building natural relationships with local people as they work together. Ordinary working people may identify more easily with someone who has a job than with an ordained or full-time Christian worker.

In the overseas context, western 'tentmakers' are normally drawn from the higher echelons of education and skills. Most are well-trained engineers, doctors or nurses, top business executives or graduate teachers and lecturers. Such well-educated and highly trained people have status overseas which allows them to relate naturally to local people of similar educational background. It also gives their Christian faith some credibility and authority. But at the same time it has a disadvantage. Our high level of training and education puts us in a position of authority. This can prevent us from relating with ordinary local people on an equal footing. And our wealth and high standard of living may also prove a barrier to easy relationships with no ulterior motives. Most cultures overseas are far more status-conscious than in western societies, in which people are reacting against all class or status distinctions.

But 'tentmakers' from other parts of the world may sometimes be in more menial work. Most wealthy Middle Eastern homes employ Filipino servants who may also look after the children. Bangladesh and Sri Lanka may supply unskilled labour for the building industry. North Africans do many of the more menial jobs in France, while in Germany and Holland, Turkey provides people for the lowest-paid work. Many Filipino and some of the Sri Lankan workers, as also perhaps a few from other countries, will be Christian. Let us not underestimate the witness of Christians with unskilled work. As we have already noted, such anonymous Christian mission workers may be encouraged by the story of Naaman, the commander-in-chief of the powerful Syrian army. We are again reminded that it was through the witness of Naaman's wife's servant girl that Elisha was finally able to bring healing to Naaman.

Being a 'tentmaker' overseas gives us an obvious *raison d'être* for being in the other country. Full-time missionaries constantly face the questions: 'Why have you come to our country? What is your work? What do you do all day?' The last two of these questions also irk pastors in their home countries, as people wonder whether they work only on Sundays plus the occasional midweek funeral or Saturday wedding! With professionals, however, it is obvious what they do each day and why they are there.

Local governments and people in general are more likely to feel positive about the Christian witness of God's people if they contribute to the welfare and development of the nation. The Christian faith has often gained a good name in society because of our input medically, educationally or in job creation. Our care for the rejects of society can also demonstrate the loving kindness of the Lord as we obey the Bible in caring for the mentally or physically handicapped, orphans, old people, the homeless and the destitute.

Mission workers and tentmakers in partnership

Tentmakers and regular mission workers have much to give to each other. They often relate to different sorts of people and can therefore give each other wider contacts and friendships than might otherwise be possible. For example, a Christian neighbour of ours in Singapore headed up the whole Asian chain of Bata shoes. He would invite top business people from the various multinationals to his home, introduce me to them and ask me to give a short evangelistic after-dinner talk. Without him I could never have related to such people.

In Indonesia we were able to give the head of Goodyear Rubber a totally different experience. In his life and work he could never normally enjoy equal relationships with ordinary people. From time to time he would drive some three hours to visit us in our very basic little home in North Sumatra. Then together we would go out into local villages, sit in a coffee shop and share the gospel with people in conversation. Once or twice, too, he came out with me in church-planting in a traditional village. He loved these sorties into grassroots life.

But what a pleasure it was for us to visit him in his luxurious home! Our house had no running water, no gas or electricity, no kitchen, and only two rooms, with an outside staircase. As the only white people in the whole area, we were like three-humped camels in a public zoo. Eyes peered through the cracks in the walls to observe our every move from dawn to dusk. But in his home we could relax and enjoy every convenience and comfort, with servants to do our every bidding and bring us delicious cool drinks at regular intervals.

Christian professionals often have a nice home in which to entertain tired missionaries and give them a bit of a break. They may also have money which they can use for the advance of the gospel, but sometimes the full-time missionary is better placed to know how that money can be effectively used without causing problems. Money can ruin a local Christian and can distort the life and work of the church, if it is given unwisely. Co-operation between the 'tentmaker' and the missionary may prove helpful.

Missionary societies have usually developed good-quality language courses and have much experience in local cultures. New workers will be required to spend a year or sometimes even two in language study. During that time they will be helped to understand and adjust to the local culture. But secular employers expect their employees to get stuck into a demanding job as soon as they arrive in a country; their bottom line is the bank balance, not close personal relationships. Paying a high salary, they demand their pound of flesh.

While the 'tentmaker' may have professional skills which the missionary often lacks, the missionary may be able to help in language and culture. Often the professional's job involves only the husband, leaving the wife with little to do. Christians may expect more from life than the expatriate round of cocktail parties and coffee mornings! The wife may even be robbed of responsibility for the home, if she is expected to have servants. With time on her hands, she can be such a help to the full-time Christian worker. Equally, she may be glad of assistance in making local friends, learning the language and understanding the culture. Her time overseas can be much enriched by more grassroots involvement.

In the western world we assume that God's work benefits from the combination of so-called 'full-time' and ordained Christian workers together with lay Christians who remain in their secular jobs and represent Christ in their professions. This applies equally to the mission of God's church overseas. False ideas have gained currency in our times. People sometimes say that the day of full-time missionaries is over. No! We still need them and most countries still welcome them, the main exceptions being some of the strongly Muslim nations. Other Christians think that 'tentmaking' is just a necessary second best in countries which will not grant entry to those who have 'Missionary' on their passports or visa applications. It is of course true that, in countries without religious freedom, only foreign Christians in secular professional work will be able to gain entry. And we need Christian workers in all situations, both in the more skilled professional positions and also in less skilled work, in secular employment and in full-time ministry.

Discussion starters

1. What positives and negatives do you see in (a) short-term mission, and (b) tentmaking mission?
2. How can full-time Christian missionaries and tentmakers help each other?
3. How can we weave Christian tourists more effectively into the fabric of Christian mission worldwide?
4. How can we better assist Christians to become missionaries in their workplace?

11 Everybody and everything

The Old Testament presents us with a threesome: God, land, and people, each of which influences the development of the other two. God relates intimately to his people and they in turn are inseparably linked to the land. Then there is another threesome which the rabbis of Israel noted in their teaching: Israel, the *torah* (law) of God, and the land. Perhaps we should introduce a theological innovation, namely a foursome: God, his people, his law, and his creation, all intimately linked together.

In the first eleven chapters of Genesis, God relates directly to all humanity and to all the created world. But after the tragic event with the tower of Babel (Genesis 11), God narrows his direct dealings to Abraham and his children, the people of Israel (Genesis 12:1–3). And with the particular election of Abraham and his children comes God's promise to them of the land of Israel, which with Moses becomes inseparable from life under the law. But God's desire for all humanity and all the world never languishes. He still aims to bring his blessing to all people through the elect people of Israel. And the land of Israel is merely a stepping-stone towards the totality of all creation. Israel, both as a people and as a land, has a universal purpose in God's worldwide plan.

God revealed his *torah* to show Israel how to live in order to bring blessing to its own people and thus also to all nations. Redeemed in the shed blood of the Passover and in the exodus from Egypt, Israel, as God's chosen people, is commanded to follow God's will in obedience to his law. When holiness characterizes their national life, God pours out his blessings, not only on them as a people, but also on their land. The earth flourishes as a land of milk and honey. The desert blossoms, and even the trees clap their hands in delighted praise (Isaiah 55:12). But when Israel rebels against God and falls into idolatry and sin, then the land is blighted and hisses at Israel. When Israel 'defiles' herself like the idolatrous nations around her, then the land, too, is defiled and vomits out its inhabitants (Leviticus 18:24–28).

The New Testament reiterates the initial purposes of God which stretch right back to the first creation (e.g. John 1:1–3, 10). He longs for Godlike holiness in his people (1 Thessalonians 4:3) and so for perfect *shalom* (harmony) between himself and his people, as also between his people and the land. His people await and work for the great climax of history, when there will be a new redeemed humanity and a new heaven and earth. God's final purposes touch all nations and peoples, not just Israel. Likewise, the whole earth, not just the little Middle Eastern land of Israel, will return to its perfect Garden of Eden state.

The prophets Isaiah and Habakkuk had already foreseen this final consummation of God's plan in history. They looked forward to the day when the whole earth would be 'filled with the knowledge of the glory of the LORD, as the waters cover the sea' (Habakkuk 2:14; cf. Isaiah 11:9). This filling is both ethnic and geographical – all nations and all lands.

Mission to all creation

So the task of mission must be holistic, aiming to bring all humanity into a holy relationship with God through Jesus Christ. This must lead to God's redeemed people living lives of holiness in accordance with God's law in his revealed Word, including a practical and active concern for the poor and oppressed. This in turn must impact on the created order. Ecology is not just a by-product of the Christian faith; it is an integral part of God's, and therefore our, purposes for his world.

Thus, in Romans, Paul's fundamental concern for the salvation of both Jew and Gentile is inseparably linked to their holy living and to the redemption of all nature. In chapters 1 – 3 he shows that both Jew and Gentile are equally under sin (3:9–18) and in need of salvation. He then declares that God's righteousness comes 'through faith in Jesus Christ' to 'all who believe' (3:22), both Jew and Gentile (3:28–30). As in his other letters, Paul continually underlines that justification and salvation must be worked out in holy living (e.g. Romans 6:5ff.), and the letter climaxes in a call to righteousness in chapters 12 – 16. But human salvation is linked also to God's purpose: that 'the creation itself will be liberated from its bondage to decay and brought into the glorious freedom of the children of God' (Romans 8:21). Finally, God will 'reconcile to himself all things' (Colossians 1:20), and there will be 'a new heaven and a new earth' (Revelation 21:1). So God's purposes embrace the salvation of people from all nations, their growth in holy living, both as individuals and in human societies, and the redemption of all creation.

We may notice, however, that holistic approaches in mission need to be radically distinguished from an all-embracing pluralism. God's universal purposes still include a particularistic narrowing of his purposes to the elect people of Israel. In the New Testament the congregation of Israel widens out to include not only believing Jews, but also the redeemed people of Jesus Christ from all nations. The open arms of God's love are stretched out to embrace all who will come to him in repentant faith, desiring that through his people he might bring healing to broken and hopeless societies. He longs, too, to reverse the tragic consequences of the fall compounded by humanity's corrupting influence on God's creation.

This is no bland pluralism, which assumes that God is not concerned whether people believe in Christ or reject him. A true holistic approach to mission will refuse any easy-going rejection of the notion of sin and its fearful consequences both for humanity and for the created order. Pluralism conveniently sidesteps God's desire to redeem and sanctify a special people as his means to bring the world into his salvation. But twenty-first-century mission practice must conform to the purposes of God as revealed in Christ and in his biblical Word. We dare not surrender to a politically correct pluralism. Rather, we adhere to the revealed universality of God's saving purposes with his glorious grace channelled through his elect people. We can express this as a formula:

Holistic = spiritual + social + environmental

Everything under the lordship of Christ

'He's an atheist,' declared the Malaysian church leaders. 'We don't want him ministering in our church at all.'

I insisted that my young American Peace Corps friend was a definite believer who really loved the Lord. He had come to Malaysia with the desire to serve the church there and witness for Christ. Why were the church leaders so convinced he was an atheist? He prayed aloud regularly in their prayer meetings, faithfully attending everything possible in the church. In the school where he taught, he went regularly to the Christian Union.

'He's a good young man,' the local Christians testified, 'He has adjusted well to our more Christian context here, and so does all the right things in relating to the church and Christian Union. But he's an atheist. He has taught physics in our local high school for a whole year and has never once mentioned God in class. How can he be anything but an atheist?'

I tried in vain to explain that in western countries Christians have lost the educational battle, so it is considered unacceptable to talk about God in the context of so-called 'secular' subjects. It is assumed that 'objective' teaching will come with a secular humanist viewpoint. The Malaysian Chinese Christians were baffled by such spiritual compromise.

'But science depends on the reality of a God of order who created all things to be subject to his ordered laws. If you are nihilistic in philosophy, scientific experiments and laws become impossible. Why should Christians teach in a godless humanistic way?'

It was not easy to defend our western predicament.

We actually believe in a God who is Lord over all. We don't accept that the world is departmentalized into spiritual areas and secular areas. God created the whole world and everything in it. His kingdom reaches out to every aspect of life.

God therefore sends us out into the world in order to bring everything under the lordship of Christ. In every matter and on every subject we want to 'take captive every thought to make it obedient to Christ' (2 Corinthians 10:5).

When we look back to the forms of mission practised in previous generations, it is customary to criticize our forerunners for not being holistic in their mission. They are often accused of having so concentrated on evangelism, church-planting and pastoring churches that they forgot the biblical emphasis on practical love for our neighbour. Actually, when we examine mission history more carefully, we find that they were heavily involved in social and developmental issues. But they still stressed the priority of their more directly spiritual ministries.

Then, in the twentieth century, it was increasingly realized that we are called in mission to help in development ministries, serving particularly in education, medicine and agriculture. Disaster relief also came into play more and more. In more recent decades, Christians have realized gradually that developmental ministry can sometimes be like placing sticking plaster on a sore without healing the underlying disease. Political injustice and corruption often form the background to such social ills, so we may be forced into political involvement. In more democratic countries this can be relatively easy, but in autocratic dictatorships it may result in prison, torture or even death. It may also be debated whether expatriates have the right to meddle in the politics of the host country where they serve as mere guests.

In mission therefore we fight on two fronts. We seek to change the world through evangelism, thus changing more and more people in society. This approach seems very slow, but we see how the early church grew amazingly and gradually infiltrated the whole Roman Empire. At the same time we struggle politically with the leaders of society and the governing structures, for unless they are changed, social development is inhibited. So much depends on world leaders and their policies.

No-one an island

Western individualism tends to underplay the importance of societal relationships. But all of us exist within our relationship to our immediate family, our wider family, and our local and national societies. At our birth we automatically became the child of our parents, brother or sister to any siblings, a member of our local society and a citizen of our nation and of the world. None of us live as isolated islands, apart from relationships. We also relate to those who have gone before us through the long centuries of history. Equally, we are inseparably connected to those who will come after us and walk in our footsteps.

In mission, therefore, we are concerned not only for the welfare of each individual, but also for that of whole societies at every level. We need to be constantly asking ourselves what we can do to help and serve within the structures of society. We see all around us the tragedy of fractured relationships, in which people treat one another with violence and injustice. The consequences are clearly evident: sadly insecure and disturbed people; broken marriages and dysfunctional families; child abuse and the sex trade; white slavery and human trafficking; poverty and unemployment; violence and injustice; warfare and desolation.

The Christian church responds in three basic ways.

Love

First, we want the life of the church to model more ideal relationships of love. Mutual service and concern should characterize true Christian fellowship. The relationship of loving service between the three persons of the Trinity and the love of Christ for his people form an example for the church. God calls us to integrate the lonely, the single parents and the elderly into our fellowship. Practical service among the unemployed, the bored and socially alienated youth and dysfunctional families forms a vital part of the church's mission. Ministry in prisons and hospitals, among Aids sufferers and the outcasts of society, will benefit the world and add salt to the church's witness. The fruit of the Spirit (Galatians 5:22–23) should form an example to the world outside the church. And we pray that this model might prove contagious, spreading its benign influence outwards into our society and nation.

Immediately, on saying this, we sense God's urgent call to repentance, and we must humble ourselves before the Lord. We cannot help being deeply aware of our desperate need of the renewing work of the Holy Spirit. So the call to true mission demands contrite repentance and the Holy Spirit's transforming power within the life of his people. Only then can we adequately fulfil God's call to mission, both in our own neighbourhood and in the wider world.

Service

Secondly, in Christian mission we are not only called to present the world with a model of God's ideals for society and for all human relationships at every level. We are also called to go out into the world to get our hands dirty in practical service. With careful research and observation, we are to see which needs in society we can help to meet. For example, mission calls us to very down-to-earth service for the sake of sex slaves, asylum seekers, ethnic minorities, the unemployed or the victims of natural disasters. Some of us may have the necessary skills to mediate reconciliation in war-torn areas or to broker peace where conflict rages. In the name of Jesus Christ we want to serve our world and introduce the characteristics of God's kingdom – love, peace, righteousness and justice.

Proclamation

The third response of the Christian church to the sad needs of human society is the proclamation of the gospel of Christ. In the Old Testament, Israel was called to *live* lives of holiness, so that the nations would *see* God's glory and come to worship him (e.g. Isaiah 60:1–3; Zechariah 8:16–23). To this Old Testament exhortation to witness by *life*, the New Testament adds the call to be sent out to *preach* (Mark 3:14). Discipleship of Christ not only involves Godlike living and loving. It also requires that we follow Jesus as fishers of men and women (Matthew 4:19). The good news of the kingdom must be preached verbally 'in the whole world as a testimony to all nations' (Matthew 24:14). No-one can enter God's kingdom without being born again through faith in Jesus Christ (John 3:3–5), becoming like little children with trusting faith in Jesus (Matthew 18:3). To experience the kingdom of God, people need to be in such a relationship with Christ that they begin to develop a righteousness which outshines even that of the Pharisees and the teachers of the law (Matthew 5:20).

As a Jewish Christian, I am often asked about the possibilities for lasting peace and reconciliation in the Middle East. With a long history of broken promises, violence and injustice, glib answers seem out of place. Islamic law can never allow a significant area formerly under Muslim rule to come under non-Muslim power. Dar-ul-Islam (the world of Islam) should never revert to become Dar-ul-Harb, the world of fighting and enmity which is not yet under Islamic rule. But likewise, strongly Orthodox Jewish views of the Bible forbid an exchange of parts of the 'promised land' for peace. There seems little prospect of any happy solution. But peace and reconciliation are biblically linked to the kingdom of God, so true Christians will find the vital characteristics of love, peace, justice, forgiveness and reconciliation within the life of God's kingdom. For this to become reality, we need effective evangelism among both Muslims and Judaists.

In the 1970s and 1980s it became fashionable to ridicule the assertion that by changing people we could change society. A Marxist-influenced ideology stressed the reverse. Changing society can lead to people being transformed, it was asserted. To some extent, both are true. If the structures and values of a society change for the better, this will influence the character of people within that society and their relationships. A piece of coal becomes red hot if placed in a fiercely burning fire, but grows cool in a situation with no fire. If people are placed in a position of unbridled and amoral power, they can develop a fearful licence for cruelty and abuse. The mores of a society can form the character of its people.

But it is also true that society is made up of people. As the gospel gains wide influence in a culture, it increasingly produces the fruit of the Spirit. We observed this in North Sumatra, in a context of massively growing churches. Under the influence of the gospel, many things gradually changed. Men began to join their wives in physical work, and this benefited relationships as well as the economic situation of the area. People no longer wasted their money on habitual gambling, so they had more for the welfare of their homes and the education of their children. Such changes to a whole people do not happen overnight. It takes time, but it does occur.

We observed the same in East Malaysia, when revival spread throughout one whole area. Schoolteachers began to enjoy their teaching in a new way, for discipline problems virtually disappeared. Domestic violence stopped and people no longer needed to lock their homes or shops.

Cynical Europeans may find it hard to believe that the Spirit of God can have transforming power in a whole society. We have witnessed how the decline of the church has gradually led to moral degeneracy with a lack of ethical standards in the public sphere. European society has been gradually transformed, but in a negative direction. But actually we do see examples of positive social transformation in Europe too. For example, in the city of Nottingham, Christians prayed earnestly that God would work in their city and bring a new peace. As a result, crime decreased significantly, and even the police noticed that God answers prayer. They even began to send specific prayer requests to the Christians.

What would industrial relations be like if both trade union leaders and employers enjoyed a living fellowship in the love of Christ? Would government forces abuse their fellow citizens or people of another ethnic background, if they were all revived believers in Christ? Violence withers in the presence of Jesus and his Spirit.[1]

Should gender make a difference?

Back in 1992, one of my books[2] needed another reprint. It seemed a good opportunity to revise and update it. Even in those days I was shocked to see how much things had changed in Christian perception since its first publication ten years earlier. The earlier edition was riddled with gender-exclusive language, all of which had to be painstakingly changed to make the book acceptable in the early twenty-first century. As a preacher, too, I have observed how important it now is to use terms like 'humanity' rather than 'man' when both men and women are included.

In America there is a marked divide on this subject, between more conservative evangelicals and other people. As an Englishman I am surprised by the careless use of gender-exclusive language by some of my friends in America, and in their books. On the other hand, with my less conservative friends and relatives there, such language would curl their hair. It is not only in politics that Americans can be divided. And we have to remember that gender-exclusive language was accepted everywhere without question just a few decades ago.

Male chauvinism is, however, increasingly rejected in the world of today. This has forced Christians to re-examine the biblical teaching on the role of men and women. As is often the case with relatively new debates, even committed biblical Christians hold radically different views. Many advocate the equality of women and men in the ministry of the church, but even in this there are some who strongly disagree. This debate has come to prominence particularly through the question of the ordination of women and then later the appointment of women bishops. The episcopacy issue has further raised the question whether ecclesiastical and household headship is reserved for men. Or can women also be in a position of leadership over men? Debate rages as to whether the biblical term 'head' in this context means 'headship over', or the 'source' of something, as in the head of a river.

Much printers' ink has been dedicated to books concerning the role of women in the church.[3] Key controversial passages (e.g. 1 Corinthians 11 and 1 Timothy 2) demand careful exegesis. Sometimes conservative Christians can assume that the traditional understanding of such passages is the only allowable one. But we need to re-examine the biblical teaching carefully without prior prejudice.

Many today point out that the foundation for a true understanding of this whole question must issue out from God's original creation, in which his ideal is to be seen. The harmonious equality and co-operative helping of one another in the Garden of Eden is, however, shattered by the fall in Genesis 3. In the original creation, status and power play no part in Adam and Eve's relationship. After the fall, however, God's curse determines that now, in the fallen world, the woman's 'desire will be for her husband' and 'he will rule over her' (Genesis 3:16). But in the new redeemed creation, the ideal image of God is being renewed within us (Colossians 3:10), so we are to develop mutual, non-dominating relationships which mirror the image of God's relationships. In the Trinity, all that any one Person does is equally the work of the other two Persons. It is false to talk of the Father as the unique source of creation, the Son as the only Redeemer and the Holy Spirit as the one sanctifying power in us. Although there is a clear distinction between the three Persons of the Trinity, there is also a total oneness in work and purpose as they serve and honour each other in humility.[4] This is surely the model for Christians in mission, as indeed in all our Christian life.

In the past, it was generally assumed that mission leaders should always be men, and some missions still follow this old pattern. But increasingly in this century, biblical understanding is changing, and patterns of mission leadership change, too. All over the world, women with spiritual gifts of leadership are being frustrated in not being allowed to exercise their God-given gifts. This is especially true in places with smaller mission teams. It is often hard to find a man with leadership gifting within a small team, so gifted women may suffer under inadequate male leadership. Some Christians are tempted to wish that God would stop giving women natural ability and spiritual gifting for leadership! But if God gives gifts, surely he expects them to be exercised. The church worldwide will miss out if it does not make use of all the gifts God has given to his people, both men and women.

More traditional mission leaders sometimes point out that we have to relate to Asian and African cultures, in which male leadership is assumed. This relates particularly to mission among Muslims. But sometimes they may fail to notice how things are changing also in those societies. Indonesia, the largest predominantly Muslim country in the world, has had a woman as president. The Philippines, Sri Lanka, Bangladesh, Pakistan and India have also all had women presidents. It is not just in western countries like Britain, Norway and Israel that women are chosen as leaders. The whole world is changing.

In mission we always have to ask how to relate to culture in the countries where we work. Should we be *avant-garde* leaders, encouraging those who follow our leadership to become more up to date? Or, if we feel that we should adjust to what is traditionally and, still today, acceptable in society around us, are we to relate to globalized youth, to traditional older people, or to whom? It is not easy in practice to know exactly where to pitch our cultural tents.

For example, uncertainty has raged in relation to some Christian fellowships which are issuing from a Muslim background. Some divide the sexes in their worship, as is done in Muslim mosques. The men worship in the main part of the building, while the women meet behind a curtain out of sight of the men. In Orthodox Jewish synagogues also, the main section of the sanctuary is reserved for men, while the women congregate in the gallery above. Some, more modern, young mission workers react strongly against such gender inequality, feeling that the good news of Jesus Christ must break down such cultural barriers of gender prejudice. As a matter of biblical principle, therefore, they reject forms of worship in which the men are in front and the women remain out of sight at the back.

Even some British churches which insist on men as pastors face strong debates. Can a woman help pass round the bread and wine at the breaking of bread? Can a woman be appointed as a deacon, or even as an elder? Can women be elected as members of the church board? Many of us react negatively when presented with a solid phalanx of men at the front when the Lord's supper is being administered.

If the church of God moves too fast in what are considered radical decisions, then we are likely to lose traditional members and we cannot attract ordinary people to our church. But if we remain too conservative and out of touch with the changing cultural mood, we shall lose our youth and young married couples. We shall again find it hard to attract non-Christians. This is equally true whether our mission is to the West or in other continents.

But biblical obedience must always stand above mere cultural adaptation for the sake of relating effectively to contemporary society. We are therefore challenged to engage in disciplined and serious study of the Scriptures with open hearts and minds. Some years ago, in a lecture, John Stott succinctly commented that 'all theology is contextual'. This may also apply to our understanding of the biblical texts concerning the role of women in the church and in mission. How far has our biblical interpretation been influenced by our particular tradition or culture?

The writing is clearly on the wall for all to read. There is a growing trend culturally, socially and also in biblical understanding towards gender equality. This applies to leadership, as also to other roles and ministries within the church.

Racism

Apartheid has been defeated. National Socialist concepts of race superiority have been largely discredited. Racial prejudice is decried by almost all people today. Yet, with the influx of large numbers of asylum seekers and refugees, neo-Nazi racism has again reared its ugly head. Jewish synagogues and cemeteries are being attacked in various European countries. Racially motivated murder and violence are increasingly common. And inter-ethnic and inter-community strife constantly threatens to erupt.

Terrorism in the name of Islam forces governments and police to target Muslim communities in their investigations, but this could inflame anti-western tendencies among moderate Muslims. In our multi-ethnic societies, harmonious intercultural relations have become essential for the well-being of our nations. In their teaching and preaching, churches need to underline that Christ 'has made the two one and has destroyed the barrier, the dividing wall of hostility' (Ephesians 2:14). Jews, Gentiles and indeed people of every ethnic background are called to live in peace together. Christians can give a lead in encouraging good relationships as we befriend and serve people from other communities.

With the growth of the church in all continents, mission, too, has become international and any form of racial prejudice must be discarded. No longer can white superiority be tolerated. Missionary domination denies the reality that we all have equal 'access to the Father by one Spirit' (Ephesians 2:18). Mission and church leadership must be in the hands of those Christians who demonstrate God's calling and gifting, whatever their ethnic background. It no longer matters whether God calls westerners or those from other continents and cultures.

We have to confess, however, how easily racial prejudices slip into our attitudes. Westerners can fall prey to old attitudes of colonialist pride, in which it is assumed that others lack the maturity or capabilities necessary for effective ministry. And post-colonial Africans or Asians can occasionally be so keen to assert their independence that they reject their white sisters and brothers. Happily, these colonial prejudices are now fading into the mists of history and the Holy Spirit binds his people together more easily in loving mutual esteem and humility.

Every culture has both strengths and weaknesses; this relates also, of course, to Christian churches. In inter-ethnic relations, it is easy to observe others' weaknesses in areas where our culture is stronger. But sometimes we fail to note their strength in areas where our people are weak. The teaching of Jesus about 'specks of sawdust' in other people's eyes and great 'planks' in our own (Matthew 7:3–5; Luke 6:41–42) applies not only to individuals' hypocrisy, but also to critical and judgmental prejudice in inter-ethnic relationships.

Speciesism and environmentalism

In the struggle against colonialist racism, the former Liberian leader Leopold Senghor proclaimed the battle-cry, 'Black is beautiful.' Although this slogan still carries weight, today's world faces further challenges on top of the old ones. Today's clarion call declares, 'Green is beautiful.'

The mind-numbing devastation of the Boxing Day 2004 tsunami reminded us forcefully of our human impotence before the forces of nature. Earthquakes, volcanic eruptions, droughts and floods sweep through whole areas of our world with fearful suffering and disaster. With all our modern technology and wealth, we can only attempt to put a little sticking plaster on the gaping wounds of suffering humanity. We can do relatively little to prevent some of these disasters, but we desperately need to heed the warnings concerning global warming and its consequences. Meanwhile, we seek to alleviate the post-trauma suffering.

In Christian mission we are surely called to play our part in such humanitarian aid. Christian organizations like Tearfund, World Vision, Cafod and Christian Aid stand among the pre-eminent agents in this work. As is evident from Jesus' manifesto for his ministry (Luke 4:18–19), God has a particular concern for a hurting world. In his teaching he describes the righteous, those who 'are blessed by my Father' (Matthew 25:34–36), as the ones who cared for the hungry and thirsty, the poor who need clothing, the sick and those in prison. He surely rejoices when his people are involved in loving care for those, too, who are suffering from environmental disasters.

In a fallen world, some natural disasters will happen whatever we humans do. But we have become increasingly aware that we ourselves are causing many of the difficulties. Our misuse of the world's resources is producing climate change to a tragic degree. This in turn affects the world's weather patterns, resulting in still further natural disasters. Our scientists and other leaders have still not faced the pressing question of how less developed societies can move forward without further damaging the environment. With the huge and accelerating economic development of China and India, with their combined populations of almost 2.5 billion people, global warming looks likely to increase. The United States' greedy squandering of energy resources stands shoulder to shoulder with the increasing fossil-fuel consumption in China and India as major threats to the very survival of our planet.

While Christians rejoice in the eschatological vision of a new heaven and a new earth, we are also called to work now towards this goal. We dare not twiddle our thumbs, merely criticizing the Americans and waiting passively for Jesus' second coming and the fulfilment of God's final purposes. Just as the vision of a new redeemed humanity from all nations and peoples already compels us to active evangelistic mission, so also our sure hope of a new creation motivates us towards active environmental concern.

The phenomenal growth of A Rocha, a Christian environmental mission movement, is surely symptomatic of people's burning concern for green issues. As a member of A Rocha's initial Council of Reference, I remember when it started, with a small centre in Portugal for the care of birds. After just a few years, new centres have mushroomed in many different countries as far apart as Finland, North America, Lebanon, Kenya and India. A clear message of God's concern for his created world is joined to professional ornithological and other environmental activity. Such patterns of holistic mission appeal strongly to this generation of Christians and also give an attractive testimony to the world outside. It is important today for the witness of the church and for God's name in the world that Christians are seen to be green.[5]

A Rocha has particular expertise in ornithology and the care of other living species. In our Christian mission we are to remember that God created everything, both the animate and the inanimate. In asking Adam to name the animals, God gave him responsibility for them – in contrast to the Muslim creation account, in which God himself names the animals without delegating this responsibility to Adam. We know that our heavenly Father so cares for birds that he feeds them (Matthew 6:26), and in his final purposes he desires peace for the animal world: the wolf with the lamb, the leopard and the goat, the calf and the lion, the cow with the bear, the lion and the ox (Isaiah 11:6–7). Indeed, this includes human children finding safety while playing with the cobra and the viper (Isaiah 11:8–9). What an ideal picture of harmony in the created order! Christian mission is called to work towards such peace among human beings, between humanity and the created order, and in natural harmony in the creation. And the climax is that 'the earth will be filled with the knowledge of the glory of the LORD, as the waters cover the sea'. In Habakkuk (2:14), these prophetic words relate to all the nations of the earth coming to know the Lord, and therefore to international evangelistic mission; but in the similar wording in Isaiah (11:9), their context is clearly the reign of God's peace in the animal world.

In Christian mission we are called to oppose racism, the abuse of one race by another. Likewise, sexism is now taboo, with its oppression of one gender by the other. Now we are also challenged to stand against the cruel misuse of other living species by human beings. We may well shudder at the newly invented word 'speciesism', but it accurately describes a sin in our world today. Holistic mission requires us to demonstrate God's love and concern for all his creation – men and women of every nation and people, and the created order, both animate and inanimate.

What about evangelism?

'Most so-called holistic mission is actually far from being genuinely holistic,' declared someone who had worked as a missionary in the Indian subcontinent and had wide mission experience.

In his view, contemporary Christian workers are reacting against a perceived lack of social concern among earlier missionaries. As a result, the pendulum has swung too far in the opposite direction. Now, so-called 'holistic mission' involves social, political and environmental issues, but often lacks heartfelt spiritual passion for evangelism or church ministries.

The first Lausanne Conference, in 1974, affirmed the priority of evangelization in the task of mission. It underlined the wide spectrum of ministries in the overall calling of God's people to mission, but evangelization still maintained its priority. Socio-political and environmental work should never be separated off from the preaching of the gospel and church-planting, as if they were totally separate entities. But in every activity under the wide umbrella of mission, the biblical calling to preach the gospel of Jesus Christ must always remain primary.

I am deeply aware that the number one need of Jewish people is for Jesus the Messiah. People may talk much of friendship for Jews and for Israel, or even of migration from the former Soviet Union to the land of Israel. But still the Jewish people's greatest need is for Jesus; he alone can impart the fullness of life and salvation through his cross and resurrection. This truth applies equally to all other peoples all over the world. In obedience to the word of God to us in the New Testament, we must never allow our concern for holistic mission to exclude or sidetrack the proclamation of Jesus and his good news.

Discussion starters

1. How can your congregation widen its ministry to become more holistic in its mission?
2. What can we do to demonstrate God's concern for his creation? What practical steps can we take to live in a more environmentally friendly way?
3. What gifts do you have which could contribute to holistic mission overseas?

Notes

1. For further reading on this topic see F. Beckett, *Called to Action* (Collins, 1989), and *Rebuild: Small Groups Can Make a Difference* (Crossway, 2001).

2. M. Goldsmith, *Islam and Christian Witness* (OM Publishing and Paternoster, 1982, 1992, 2004).

3. For example, M. Evans, *Woman in the Bible* (Paternoster, 1983); J. Hurley, *Man and Woman in Biblical Perspective* (IVP, 1981); E. Storkey, *What's Right with Feminism* (SPCK, 1985), and *Created or Constructed? The Great Gender Debate* (Paternoster, 2000); R. C. Kroeger and C. C. Kroeger, *I Suffer Not a Woman: Rethinking 1 Timothy 2:11–15 in the Light of Ancient Evidence* (Baker, 1992); A. Perriman, *Speaking of Women: Interpreting Paul* (Apollos, 1998).

4. For further discussion of this, see M. Goldsmith, *Jesus and His Relationships* (Paternoster, 2000).

5. The *Church of England Newspaper* (22 July 2005) reports that 'churches have responded to the challenge of climate change ... in trying to become more environmentally friendly'. In Britain, the diocese of Hereford has urged congregations to improve and promote energy efficiency, while a church in Essex is quoted as having introduced ecologically friendly areas for wild flowers, birds and other flora and fauna.

12 Tailor-made mission – make it fit

Back in the early 1980s, debate raged concerning more contextualized patterns of evangelism and church-planting. This had started with the mushrooming of new Jewish churches in America. Jews were in the forefront of the hippy flower-power movement in California in the late 1960s and 1970s. Some of these rebellious young Jews found new life in Jesus as their Messiah and Saviour. But they were still culturally Jewish and could not easily fit into the very Gentile traditional American churches. So new churches sprang into being to worship Jesus in obedience to the Bible, but seeking to accommodate more traditional Jewish cultural and worship forms into their new Christian faith. Traditional Hebrew chants were sung with tears in the eyes. These might be followed swiftly by lively Israeli worship songs with joyful dancing. The ancient synagogue benedictions and prayers were Christianized and added to Sabbath worship. As in the synagogue services, so now in messianic congregations, the Scriptures might be paraded in honour round the congregation. The prayer shawl and *kippah* were also carried over into the new religious practice.

But Jews form only a tiny minority in the great populations of the world, so this new movement made relatively little impact on the wider mission scene. Then Phil Parshall published his *New Paths in*

Muslim Evangelism.[1] In this book, Parshall used his own experience of planting more contextualized churches in a strongly Muslim context in the Indian subcontinent. Muslims form some 20% of the world's population, so the question of contextualization now impinged on mission debates more widely.

At that time Christian mission among Muslims seemed to be hitting its head against a brick wall, but it appeared that perhaps more contextualized approaches to mission were proving more fruitful. Was this the answer? Despite much prayer, dedicated preaching of the gospel and the building of loving personal relationships, most traditional evangelism among Muslims remained largely fruitless. My own experience of such evangelistic work in South Thailand in the early 1960s fitted exactly into this overall picture. Christian workers inevitably asked themselves serious questions. Why did God apparently not answer their prayers for fruitfulness in their ministry? Was there something fundamentally wrong with their spiritual life or with their mission strategy and methodology? How could we experience the dynamic growth of the church as described in the book of Acts?

Some confidently asserted that we just needed the sweeping revival work of the Holy Spirit. I remember a mission director leading our South Thailand mission conference and powerfully preaching the need for repentance and the filling of the Spirit. The team of tired missionaries wept their way to the Lord in repentance. With relief they claimed the power of the Holy Spirit to fill them and flow through them. It was reported that revival had hit our missionary team. But actually there was no more fruitfulness after the conference than there had been before. We were still hitting our heads against a Muslim brick wall. One by one, many of the 'revived' missionaries became disillusioned and lost hope. One by one they left South Thailand and returned to their home countries.

Into this questioning situation came the new debate on contextualized mission. Some grasped it eagerly with both hands and began to put it into practice. Contextualized churches with Islamic cultural forms have grown in the Indian subcontinent, but some more conservative churches have felt they are compromising deceitfully with Islamic practices and failing to stress biblical values. In the Middle East, some Christian workers have called themselves 'Muslim', using the literal meaning of the term (one who submits). Others object, saying that 'Muslim' is always understood to signify someone who follows the religion of Islam, believing in Muhammad as the ultimate prophet and the Qur'an as God's final book of revelation. And so the debate has continued to rage even into the twenty-first century. But, as in all debates, we need prayerfully and carefully to discern the biblical basis for our acceptance or rejection of contextualization.

Jesus was contextual

Whereas John's emphasis rests on the universality of Jesus becoming 'flesh' and thus relating to all humanity, Matthew and Luke, from their outset, immediately reveal Jesus in his Jewish context. He is born into a particular family at a specific time in history. He grows up and lives in the Jewish culture, religious milieu and philosophical framework of first-century Israel. The life, teaching, relationships and work of Jesus can be properly understood only when observed through the lens of his earthly context.

So the traditional credal statement that he 'became human' represents only half the truth. He became not only 'human' in general, but also a particular first-century Jewish man.

In our desire as followers of Jesus to become increasingly like him, we also want to be fully identified with one people and culture and yet at the same time to relate to all humanity. Following the model of Jesus, in our mission we dare not have an exclusive blinkered vision for one people only. This can be a danger for followers of the 'hidden peoples' movement, with their emphasis on the call to one specific ethnic group which has not yet heard the gospel. We may indeed concentrate on one people, but our mission concern must still embrace all peoples everywhere.

The incarnation of Jesus can only amaze us with its miraculous reality. We are excited at the fact that God not only condescended to become human like us and thus to relate intimately with us, but he also identified miraculously and totally with a sinful human society and culture, while remaining absolutely sinless and perfect in holiness. Although in his incarnation he remained fully divine, he was nevertheless entirely human in every way. He became an integral part of a corrupt human society and environment, identifying fully with us despite all our sin and inadequacy. Yet he remained incorrupt and sinless.

Jesus remains the model for Christian mission. We, too, are called to identify fully with the society and people among whom we live. Our life and message are to be definitely contextualized, yet we are still to follow Jesus in godly holiness without compromise. Sinless holiness and contextualized identification do not easily go together, but that is Jesus' high calling to us in mission. Jesus' contextualized incarnation remains the pattern for our mission.

The Bible is contextual

We have observed that, in his incarnate life, Jesus relates contextually to his family, culture and religion in first-century Israel, but at the same time he has universal significance for all peoples everywhere and throughout history. The Bible as God's written Word parallels the contextualization and universality of Jesus, the incarnate Word.

Could you imagine the prophet Jeremiah writing the Gospel of Luke? Or Luke writing the book of Jeremiah? The very questions are ridiculous. It is obvious from the content of his book that Jeremiah was writing several hundred years before the coming of Jesus Christ. And Luke was clearly writing after Jesus' death and resurrection. God's Word in those two books relates to particular historical contexts. Likewise, the character of the writers determines the content of the revelation. Jeremiah was lacking in self-confidence, so God reassures him: 'Do not be afraid of them, for I am with you and will rescue you' (Jeremiah 1:8). Such words of comfort run through the book like a golden thread. (How different from the gifted, golden-mouthed Isaiah, to whom God is revealed as the holy one, 'high and exalted' [Isaiah 6:1].)

Luke's medical interest as a doctor influences the way he views Jesus' healing miracles. And his ministry with Paul, the apostle to the Gentiles, gives him a deep interest in Jesus' wider relationships beyond the borders of Israel. Some critics even think, therefore, that Luke may have been a Gentile, but the many Hebraisms and the Jewish thought patterns in his gospel would seem to deny this. Clearly, however, the personalities and backgrounds of Jeremiah and of Luke influence the very content of the word of God through them.

The Bible, then, is a contextual book, and God's revelation is contextualized. But it also has universal application. Like the incarnate Jesus, the Bible too is God's Word to all humanity throughout history. Like Jesus' divinity-humanity, not only is the Bible written by fallible and sinful human beings, but we believe that it is also God's perfect Word. 'All Scripture is God-breathed' (2 Timothy 3:16), Paul affirms. Although it is obviously written by men in all their sinfulness, it also emanates from God by his Spirit.

So both God's Word incarnate and God's Word written demonstrate the amazing miracle of being thoroughly human in identification with sinful contexts and at the same time perfectly sinless and without error.

It is self-evident that mere human beings like ourselves can never match this miracle. Our words of preaching or prophecy will never be perfectly immersed in and relevant to our local context. Likewise, we shall never attain the sinless perfection of absolute truth and holiness. Some of us stress our acculturation in order to relate relevantly, but find it hard to maintain Christlike holiness. Others of us hold firmly to an uncompromised biblical theology and the demands of holiness, but may fail to identify contextually. Yet others of us seek a balanced middle way, in which we are to some extent contextually related while maintaining some standards of truth and holiness. But none of us attains to the perfection of Jesus Christ or the Bible.

In our mission calling we should seek to acculturate and identify cross-culturally, but we must not lose our biblical teaching and holiness of life. It is biblical and Christlike to contextualize, but to do so always striving to hold on unswervingly to truth and godliness. Our slogan should be 'Contextualization without compromise'.

In biblical mission we cling faithfully to our belief in God's unchanging revelation in his Word and we long to share that Word with the world. But we are also very much aware that our understanding of God's Word is at best fallible, for we 'see but a poor reflection' (1 Corinthians 13:12). Our vision of God's revelation is clouded by our sinfulness and inadequacy. We therefore constantly bring our lives and our understandings back to the plumb-line of Christ and the Bible. As we do so, we seek also to apply the Word of God to our needy world. The church of God can never escape God's call to witness. This compels us to look at our faith through the eyes of those to whom we are ministering. We begin to see the Christian faith from the standpoint of their culture and religion. We start looking for answers to *their* questions and needs, not just to ours. Otherwise, in our mission, we shall only answer questions which nobody else is asking. We believe that Jesus Christ brings 'good news', 'the gospel', to people of every age and every culture.

This theory of biblical contextualization has to be applied very practically in our different cultural and religious situations.

Christianity in the western world

Christianity has been firmly established for many centuries in the western world. It has initiated the development of education and popular thought, so that the western worldview is still shot through with Christian foundations. For any appreciation of the history of western literature and art, one needs an understanding of Christianity. Law, ethics and social relations have all developed with a Christian background.

While this Christian background has been considerably eroded in the last century or so, its influence remains. That influence is unfortunately seldom recognized for what it is, but nevertheless we cling to it as a precious heritage which we lose at our peril.

In witness within the western world, we have to recognize that our Christian faith has also been determined, not only by God's perfect revelation, but also by our western cultural and philosophical backgrounds. Until recently – and still, in some Christian circles – rationalism influenced our approach to the Bible and to the Christian life. We have found it hard to include the miraculous, dreams and visions or the casting out of demons in the practice of our faith, although in some circles in recent decades the pendulum has swung in the opposite direction. Likewise, we have allowed western individualism to determine our understanding and practice. We have interpreted every biblical 'you' as addressing several separate individuals, every 'we' as basically meaning 'I'. So we have downplayed the essential role of human relationships in God's purposes, concentrating on each individual's personal relationship with God in Christ by the Holy Spirit. Again, some have sought to rectify this with a renewed study of relationships,[2] and we have incorporated into the English language the new American word 'relational'.

Feudalism and the class system were also incorporated into the very structures of the church. There is some validity in Karl Marx's bitter stricture that the landlord and the parson go hand in hand. Church hierarchies reflect the feudal order, with the bishop or abbot paralleling the role of the lord of the manor. In English villages the Anglican church was frequented by the upper classes in the morning and their servants in the evening, while lesser folk attended the nonconformist chapel.

Materialistic capitalism has brought us under its sway, with an emphasis on power, wealth, pleasure and greed. The search for pleasure and 'fun' weighs against self-sacrificing Christian discipleship, in which we are called to be slaves of the Lord and of each other.

In New Testament times, slavery was still very common and terribly oppressive. To be a slave meant a degrading lack of any human rights. Nevertheless, the apostle Paul, following Jesus Christ's example (Philippians 2:7), even boasted of being a 'slave of Christ Jesus' (Romans 1:1, NRSV mg.) and of making himself a 'slave to everyone' (1 Corinthians 9:19). Slaves have no rights, status or dignity. But in the western world today, we find that suffering and pain have become an offence, which we find hard to embrace. Economics and money have become the tail that wags even the Christian dog.

Over the centuries, the western churches have contextualized to such a degree that the Christian faith merged happily with everyday life and society in our countries. But this contextualization did involve some compromise of biblical teaching, so that the dynamic life and witness of the first-century church seems far distant from the church of today. Can you imagine the apostle Paul, or even Jesus himself, fitting comfortably into the pomp of a cathedral church? They might be rejected as 'fundamentalist fanatics'! How would they have reacted to a bishop's 'throne' in a cathedral? A mitre would hardly fit on such biblical heads!

Western cultures have changed and continue to change at an ever-increasing rate. Our churches face a renewed challenge to contextualize in every department of their life and witness. Some of the new charismatic churches are making determined efforts to relate to modern expressions of culture, but still face the challenge of keeping such cultural contextualization together with quality biblical teaching and holiness of life. While some other churches' music and worship relate to several centuries ago, theirs often stems from the 1970s and 1980s. The challenge to keep changing and remain culturally up to date never leaves us.

In the past, in Britain, the Methodists represented the cutting edge of contemporary Christianity, with a burningly relevant message. Now the Methodists, too, have become a very traditional church. Later the Brethren and some other evangelicals became the expression of up-to-date, contextualized Christianity, but again we see the danger of 'cutting edges' becoming fossilized. More recently, the various Pentecostal denominations and now the new charismatic churches have stood at the forefront of contemporary relevance. Will they also succumb to the dangers of traditionalism, mistaking their particular forms for the necessary expression of Holy Spirit life?

What contextualized outworkings of Christian faith will arise in the coming years? There are encouraging signs that some of the mainline denominations are developing new expressions of witness and the life of the church within their traditional structures.[3] Hasten the day when western Christians break free from the trammels of comfortable materialism and unsacrificial rationalism with a lively and relevant witness! Perhaps we need to remember Paul's constant emphasis on 'boldness' (*parrēsia*), with its courageous testimony based on assured confidence in the truth of what we believe.

In the western world we need that combination of renewed traditional structures, contextualized life and witness, strong biblical exegesis and a definite emphasis on loving relationships and holiness. That combination must surely be the goal of our churches if they are to cut ice in mission. The western church, like all churches everywhere, faces particular challenges in contextualizing for the twenty-first century.

Contextualized buildings

Church buildings reflect the theology of their people. Old European churches banished God to the far end of the church, mirroring a faith in which God is remote and unapproachable in his holiness and glory. This led to awe-filled worship which resonated with beauty but lacked the warmth of an assured personal relationship with God through Jesus Christ. The threefold focus of attention at the front underlined the importance of communion table, pulpit and lectern. Thus attention was drawn to Word and sacrament. And the Word was to be both read and preached to the people, while the central reality remained the death of Jesus Christ which we proclaim in the Lord's supper. Unlike a mosque with its non-trinitarian monotheism, where there is only one focus of attention in the front, traditional Christian churches demonstrated by their furnishings a faith in the Trinity.

More recently, modern churches have often been built with the communion table down in the body of the church. There it stands surrounded on three sides by semi-circular rows of chairs, demonstrating the contemporary emphasis on God's loving presence among his people. The fellowship of God's people in loving relationships is shown by the intimacy of a seating arrangement where people can look at each other face to face.

Some theologically less careful churches have replaced the centrality of the communion table, pulpit and lectern with a stage for the band and a large screen for PowerPoint presentations. This pattern underlines the central role of worship with contemporary music and communication, but may reflect inadequate emphasis on the atoning death of Christ and biblical teaching or preaching with good theology.

In many parts of Africa, Asia and Latin America, quaint little English-style churches adorn the scenery. Their style of architecture speaks clearly of the colonial background of the church. In such countries the primary objection to the Christian faith lies not in the death or resurrection of Christ, but in the perception that Christianity is a western religion. In such situations it is vital that we teach church history properly, with a due emphasis on the fact that Jesus and the early church originated in the Middle East, not in Europe or America. Indeed, it took many centuries before the various European tribes were won for Christ through dedicated and sacrificial mission work.

It is important today that our church architecture demonstrates the biblical truth that Jesus relates incarnationally to all cultures. Churches should be built with local architectural styles. Both the external structure of the church and the internal furnishings should be indigenous, although the latter should also mirror theological truth – the Trinity, and Word and sacrament together. We may wonder how our churches can symbolize both the absolute burning holiness and distance of almighty God, and at the same time the intimacy of Immanuel.

Together with the larger theological significance of our church furnishings, we also need to relate culturally. For example, should a church have pews, chairs, or just carpets on which people squat? Local custom will need to be respected, for we want people to feel at home in the church. Saddled with edifices from a previous era, many western congregations struggle to adapt their buildings to more contemporary theological emphases and to form a milieu in which people feel comfortable.

Indigenous music

'Remember that they lack worship songs, so you will find it helpful to teach them some new ones.'

This advice rang in my ears as I set off to train Ukrainian Pentecostal missionary candidates in my first visit to that country. But at the same time I recalled their long church history and their tradition of beautiful national music. So I felt slightly mystified.

The discomfort of having no water to wash with in my fearfully cold bedroom was exacerbated by the sounds that wafted through the thin walls. The Ukrainian students were desperately attempting, with their guitars, to master some new English worship songs they had been taught previously. But, finding our metre and forms of melody hard to master, they generally mangled the songs.

So it was that in our times of worship I found it a relief when they sang some of their traditional Ukrainian songs. Their throat muscles now expanded with their lusty and enthusiastic singing, while the words of these local songs resonated with theological truth and devotional passion. Finally, I urged them to ignore English songs and concentrate on their own music. I also encouraged them to write new songs, but with Ukrainian metre. Feeling a new sense of liberation, on our final morning together they asked for a prolonged time for worship and sang one Ukrainian song after another with gusto and joy.

Attempting to squeeze these Ukrainian Christians into our western forms of music and worship ran the danger of stifling their own heartfelt expression of love for the Lord. It could so easily subvert a truly national church and make it a mere reflection of something foreign.

In many Asian countries, and in parts of West Africa, tonal languages further complicate the scene. The translated words of western songs often do not fit the music. Where a word's tone goes up, the music goes down, or vice versa.

The dangers of musical imperialism stare us in the face. Wycliffe Bible Translators have set a noble example in seeking to develop ethnic music in the various cultures in which they work. In their work internationally, ethnomusicology has been given considerable prominence. In Mali, it has been found that, on the second day of a funeral, women gather together from even distant villages to mourn within the context of the wider family. On such occasions they sing one traditional tribal song after another, whereas in ordinary life there is little singing. These much-loved traditional songs with their heartfelt emotion can be used to inspire new Christian worship songs. They will tug at the heartstrings in a way which no foreign music can rival.

Fifty years ago in Thailand, a leading musician became a Christian through the work of the Overseas Missionary Fellowship, and wrote many songs and hymns in traditional Thai musical style. Their style of music differs radically from western music, and fits the tonal language. These songs have been much loved in the Thai churches and have significantly helped Christians to worship the Lord with all their heart. They have also helped the Thai churches gain an indigenous image rather than sounding too foreign.

While the need for culturally relevant music remains clear, we also have to take globalization into account. However much we may dislike it, all the world is listening to modern western music and being fashioned by pop culture. No longer are younger Asians and Africans alienated by modern American and European worship music and the sometimes rather sensual body movements associated with it.

We remind ourselves of the fundamental principles of contextualization as modelled in the incarnation of Jesus himself and in the revelation of Scripture. Identification goes hand in hand with uncompromised holiness and truth. In musical contextualization, too, we are called to identify both with traditional national musical forms and with modern western imports. But we also have to struggle with maintaining holiness and truth. We need to be aware that traditional music may have its roots in another religion and can lead to religious syncretism. So we face the challenge to teach adequately by the Holy Spirit, who leads his people into all truth.

Modern western music is often associated with the club scene and can lead to rebellious immorality under drug-culture influence, so again it must be accompanied by a strong emphasis on holy living and submission to the lordship of Christ. It can also bring with it current western spiritual emphases. Thus a strong individualism and even self-centredness reveal themselves in the common and repeated use of the first person singular, 'I'. Modern Christian songs reflect today's longing for a God who is warm and welcoming, embracing us in love. It places little emphasis on the God who is unapproachable light or who is so burningly pure that nobody can see God and live (Exodus 33:20). So the emphasis is on 'Jesus', not on 'Christ' or 'Lord'. Is this spiritual approach contextually relevant in a Muslim context, in which God is incomparably great (*akbar*)?

Contextualized worship

We have already touched on the need for contextualized worship forms, but all over the world Christians are struggling with this question. So it may do no harm to refer to it again.

Jewish Christians have had to face the question of how to worship the Lord in a culturally relevant way. We transfer rapidly from joyful songs, with lively dance, to tear-jerking Hebrew dirges and back again. But traditional western worship finds it impossible to move so quickly from one mood to another. And modern charismatic worship would not enjoy the dirges. Symbolic foods also play a major role in Jewish worship, but Gentile worship does not use food with such significance in its services. The one exception is the Lord's supper, with its morsel of bread and its *Schluck* of wine. In midweek meetings and in coffee times after a service, as also in the Alpha course, eating together encourages fellowship. The liturgical meal for the Jewish celebration of Passover may form a model for the development of Christian worship in Jewish circles. For some other cultures, too, eating together holds enormous significance and should be part of our church worship. Jewish worship will also include considerable visual symbolism.

As we have seen, missionaries among Muslims have also debated the contextualization of worship forms in their contexts. But relatively little work has been done on worship in Hindu, Buddhist or other eastern religious contexts. Corporate worship services are not their common practice. But they have particular forms of prayer, both individually and together with others.

A Thai student asked me whether it is allowable for him as a Christian to use a Buddhist form of prayer. Could he still hold his hands with his palms together in an attitude of prayer? Following the threefold Buddhist *Tripitaka*, could he as a Christian divide his worship and prayer into three sections? It was easy to remind him of the threefold Christian Trinity and encourage him to have a section of worship and prayer which concentrates on the Father. Then he could base the second and third sections of his prayers on Jesus Christ and the Holy Spirit. The Buddhist posture for prayer can be easily Christianized, as can the Buddhist tendency to bow humbly before the Buddha. In humility before God, we too may benefit from such attitudes in prayer, and it may be good to bow physically before the Lord. As with Muslim prostration, body movements can impact our heart attitudes.

It is not easy, however, to determine what Buddhist or Hindu forms can be safely introduced into the Christian faith. Many today question whether we may use yogic body movements and breathing exercises in prayer. Are they too inseparably connected to a philosophy of losing all self-awareness and denying oneself in either empty nothingness or some internal Buddha spirit?

Many Christians have found that eastern meditation practices have been significantly helpful in their relationship with the Lord. In our frenetic lifestyles, meditational worship can bring much-needed peace and contentment. But we need to be careful to ensure that the underlying theology is biblically true. We abjure all meditation in which the self is denied. A Buddhist concept of peace through non-being (*anatta*, and thus *sunyata*, the void) contradicts the biblical revelation of God as the 'I am', the One who *is*. And since God has created us in his image, we too *are*. Our desire as Christians is not to escape from being, but rather to attain perfect, fulfilled eternal life. In the fullness of eternal life, we realize to the full what we truly are, the essence and reality of our inmost being. In our Christian meditation, therefore, we concentrate our conscious thought and prayer on the realities of God and his revelation, which is true existence.

Whether in the West or in other continents, we need constantly to examine our worship and prayer forms to make them contextually relevant for our surrounding culture in the modern world. But again, as with contextualized music, our worship forms must not compromise the biblical revelation in Jesus Christ. Our slogan remains 'Identification plus truth and holiness'.

Contextualized leadership patterns

The first Christian churches were, of course, Jewish. It seems that their leadership patterns were based on the model of the synagogue. This involved a teaching rabbi, who also played a key role in pastoral guidance and in leading the synagogue worship. But decision-making lay in the hands of the synagogue elders, who ran all administrative matters and determined the day-to-day life of the community. So, when the church was almost exclusively Jewish, its leadership followed a Jewish background pattern.

In Philippians 1:1, Paul writes of a plurality of *episkopoi*, seemingly a merging of the Jewish and Gentile leadership approaches. The term *episkopos* is used in both Jewish and Gentile leadership structures in New Testament times. In the Jewish background, *episkopoi* were a group of elders together. It was considered unacceptable and danger-ous for too much responsibility and power to lie in one person's hands.

In Greek usage, the term *episkopos* is commonly used for the power exercised by the gods, as well as for human overseers in various social functions. So Jesus points the finger at the Gentiles, criticizing the fact that 'their high officials exercise authority over them' (Mark 10:42). In saying this, Jesus is attacking authority, not just authoritarianism, in leadership. Jesus strongly rejects this pattern of leadership, and declares, 'Not so with you.' He then teaches his disciples that primacy means being 'slave of all'. Jesus himself gives the model of serving rather than being served. He comes, not to save his own life, but to 'give his life as a ransom for many' (Mark 10:43–45). While it is true that these last words teach that Jesus offers himself as a sacrificial offering in our place, this is not the main point of his teaching here. He is underlining that Christian leadership should not include the exercise of authority, but rather should be characterized by self-sacrifice.

Jesus was following a traditional Jewish approach to leadership here. But as the Gentiles increasingly dominated the church, their patterns of leadership obscured the Jewish background, and one-man leadership with authority became the standard pattern. And now in our time it is almost unthinkable that the western church could possibly live with leadership which did not have any authority except the authority of God's Word.

So we see that the early church assumed that their leadership patterns should be based on the accepted forms of leadership in their non-Christian background. As we saw earlier in relation to South Thailand, in our mission today we may need to study the leadership structures of the mosque, temple or gurdwara as the model for a contextualized church. In Britain, too, in more up-to-date churches, leadership patterns have evolved over these past decades in line with our changing culture.

But in the New Testament there were also some basic principles of leadership which stood above all cultural influences.

Such principles fit into two categories: the leaders' life, and their teaching. Christian leaders should be above reproach (1 Timothy 3:2), so that they earn the respect of others (1 Timothy 3:8). Both the *episkopoi* and the deacons are to be married, each with one wife, who like themselves, is 'worthy of respect'. The wife should know how to guard her tongue, for a wife's malicious tittle-tattle can seriously damage a church.

1 Timothy assumes that leaders will be married men, for in New Testament times the Rabbis forbade women to study[4] or to gain education. It was also highly unusual for men or women to remain unmarried. So church leadership naturally lay in the hands of married men. In today's world it is common for people to remain single, and leadership does not necessarily require marriage. But the principle

remains true that Christian leaders are expected to give a model of good attitudes and behaviour in relationship to their family (1 Timothy 3:4). In Jesus, we have the perfect model of a single man who showed loving care for his family.

Although it was unusual in the first century for women to have studied and thus to be ready for church leadership, already in the New Testament we see examples of women in positions of church leadership. Thus in Romans 16, Paul places Priscilla before Aquila, and calls Junia,[5] evidently a woman, an apostle. But the New Testament principle still holds true that people should not be appointed to church leadership without adequate knowledge of biblical teaching.

1 Timothy is very practical in stating that the leader must not be over-fond of the bottle, or 'a lover of money'. It is surely good that Christian leaders should not be paid too much, lest people seek to become leaders for the sake of financial security and well-being. Too much money also easily leads to pride and a sense of status. Is this a danger in some European countries where state-church ministers are well paid by the government and have security of tenure? It may also be a problem when local workers in international agencies receive overseas salary rates despite a much lower local standard of living.

Christian leaders are indeed to be humbly 'gentle' (1 Timothy 3:3), serving and giving sacrificially of themselves. They are not to be self-seeking in any way. Such high standards demand that Christian leaders should not be new Christians, but should have proved themselves within the life of the church. Normally, therefore, a leader will have considerable maturity and not just be young. Timothy is evidently an exception, so he has to be encouraged not to let anyone look down on him because of his youth (1 Timothy 4:12).

We are bound to question the traditional European and American patterns of leadership, in which young people are chosen and trained theologically and are then let loose on our congregations, teaching and pastoring Christians who are often older, more mature and more experienced spiritually than they are. One young Anglican curate remarked to me that he was 'only number two' in the congregation where he was serving. It was a large well-taught church, with many mature, godly and biblically well-read members. He was somewhat shocked when I suggested that actually he was merely number seventy-seven!

Are we right to export our patterns of Christian leadership overseas? In mission we are beginning to seek more suitable patterns, particularly for cultures where age is respected above youth. Thus many Pentecostal churches in South America expect their members to climb through various church ministries before they can become ministers. Open-air witness, Sunday-school teaching and actually planting a church themselves are three of the preliminary stages of discipleship before they can become ministers. While gaining ministry experience in this way, future pastors also have to demonstrate in their lives and in their family relationships that they will give good models to their congregations. The weakness is that they often lack biblical and theological training, so their teaching remains somewhat thin in content.

As we have seen, Christian leaders carry no authority in themselves. But their biblical teaching and preaching convey the authority of God's Word. In the context of not being despised for his youth, Timothy is instructed to 'command and teach' (1 Timothy 4:11). The Greek word used for 'command' was a military one for soldiers passing an officer's message down the line. It was not used for the officer commanding the men, but merely for passing on his words of command. In those days, the army lacked electronic means for conveying an officer's commands, and so depended on the ordinary soldiers relaying his word to their fellow soldiers. God, through his Word, is our officer. We merely pass on his Word through our preaching and teaching. His Word has authority, not us!

So in mission we shall want to relate our patterns of leadership to the religious and cultural backgrounds in which we are placed. But still we must maintain fundamental biblical principles of leadership. Incarnational mission must always follow Jesus Christ in cultural identification, but without religious or moral compromise.

Throughout this chapter – and indeed throughout the book – we have assumed the overarching authority of the Bible as God's written Word and therefore, too, of true biblical theology. But we have to confess that our understanding of the biblical revelation is always fallible and to some degree in error. This is equally true of the church's attempts to formulate theological beliefs as taught by Scripture. We are deeply grateful to God for the host of spiritual and intellectual Christian heroes through the centuries who have grappled with Scripture and attempted to produce biblical theological formulations. We have much to learn from them.

Like ourselves, however, all these past biblical scholars have belonged to their own age and context. They, too, have been imperfect in their understanding as well as in their practice of the Christian faith. They have sought to answer the questions and problems of their age, but in changing cultural contexts we have to put some question marks around their credal formulas. Their biblical understanding and theology were contextualized for their particular time and situation. Now we are challenged in our twenty-first-century mission to re-examine Scripture and formulate theology anew. We learn from the past, but are not blinkered by it. In the next chapter, therefore, we shall attempt to look at biblical and theological contextualization for the twenty-first century and in various contemporary contexts.

Discussion starters

1. What tensions do you see in your context between the need for relevant identification and uncompromised holiness and biblical truth?
2. What spiritual and theological emphases underlie the Christian hymns or songs used in your church or Christian Union?
3. What patterns of Christian leadership do you feel are needed for your cultural or religious context?

Notes

1. P. Parshall, *New Paths in Muslim Evangelism: Evangelical Approaches to Contextualization* (Baker Book House, 1980).
2. For example, M. Schluter, *The R Factor* (Hodder & Stoughton, 1993).
3. The Archbishop of Canterbury, Dr Rowan Williams, has called for new forms of church outside the traditional parochial approach. Some churches are experimenting with new styles of youth church; others are meeting in pubs for spiritual discussions, or in supermarkets. Some churches in Malaysia have adapted their witness to the traditional

emphasis on filial respect by holding special dinners for Christians' parents. Others have offered free tuition to satisfy the hunger for education.

4. It is noteworthy that Paul goes against this rabbinic teaching in asserting that a woman *should* learn, and it is in this context that he does not 'permit a woman to teach or to have authority over a man' (1 Timothy 2:11–12).

5. As Leon Morris notes in his commentary on Romans (*The Epistle to the Romans* [Eerdmans and IVP, 1988]), the NIV 'makes the second name that of a man, but this seems unlikely. The patristic commentators seem to have taken the word as feminine ("Junia").'

13 No more biblical blinkers

It was back in the early 1970s, in the dark days of rampant apartheid in South Africa. I was invited to give some lectures at a white evangelical Bible school. The students were enthusiastically open to all I taught them, and the staff were warmly friendly, too. After my lectures, the Principal kindly spared me some time to show me round the college and tell me more of their work.

After a while, I asked in what ways the multinational context of South Africa influenced the content of the syllabus. The atmosphere changed and electricity ran round the room. Defensive hostility replaced the warm friendliness.

'It makes no difference to our teaching,' he growled. 'After all, Calvin *is* the truth.'

I realized that my naively innocent question had appeared to be barbed. But I was shocked not only by the racist attitude, but also by the idolatry of his statement. I had always believed in someone else as 'the truth'! Even the great Calvin was merely human, and did not share any 'papal infallibility'.

But I was also challenged to ask myself how far our international mission context influenced the teaching of the Bible and theology in the college where I worked. As a result, I introduced a course on theological developments in Africa, Asia and Latin America. Back in 1973 this was still radically innovative.

But what should we call this new course? 'African, Asian and Latin American theological developments' was too long to fit on the timetable. I decided on the politically incorrect title 'Non-western theologies', although no-one likes to be defined by what they are not. Many students brightly suggested 'Contextualized theologies', but I refused. Such traditional courses as those on the theology of God, the church or eschatology never called themselves 'western theologies'. We could not escape from the fact that all theology is contextual. For example, in the traditional church creeds we affirm that Jesus 'was born of the Virgin Mary' and 'suffered under Pontius Pilate'.

Did nothing of significance happen between Jesus' birth and his crucifixion? Half the New Testament describes the intermediate time. Was there nothing theologically important in his life, relationships and teaching? But the creeds were relating to specific theological issues which raged in the first few centuries of the early church. They are not an objective statement of the fullness of biblical theology, valid for all time.

The South African incident rang bells with me in my own personal experience. Although I am Jewish, my Christian background was entirely Gentile. It was through the witness of Gentiles that I came to life as a Christian; my church was Gentile, and I did some theological studies in an entirely Gentile college. All the Christian books I read were also by Gentile authors.

As a result, I loved the Lord Jesus and the gospel, but always had the feeling that the Christian faith did not quite fit me. It was like buying a jacket off the peg, beautifully cut from fine material, but not quite fitting on the shoulders. The Christian faith was entirely beautiful, but I felt my shoulders were wrong. Then, in Indonesia, I met churches which had been without western mission workers for many years and had unconsciously developed a more Asian character. I felt wonderfully at home at last.

This started me on a lifelong process of searching for a more Jewish expression of my faith, a Jewish understanding of the Bible and of theology.

The Reformation context

A Jewish Christian leader recently expostulated to me, 'Why should we Jews be forced to interact with the Reformers? They are irrelevant to us and our Christian history.'

Yes, the Reformers, too, were brilliantly contextualizing the gospel for their particular time. They were facing a corrupt Roman Catholic Church, in which relationship to God was said to depend on our religious and moral good works. The Reformers therefore majored on a theology of justification by faith, not by works. In doing so, they ignored the fact that Paul was actually opposing justification by works of *torah*, law – not merely justification by good works. In Jewish belief, Israel relates to God because of his election of the Jews to be his people, and on the basis of his law revealed to Israel through Moses. Paul is declaring that if justification were indeed through the works of the Jewish law, salvation would be only for Jews, and for proselytes who join themselves to the people of Israel. But, as apostle to the Gentiles, Paul strongly declares that justification is by faith in Jesus and so is for 'Gentiles too' (Romans 3:29–30). So Paul underlines the fact that we are justified not by works of the Jewish law / *torah*, but by faith in Jesus Christ. This means that the good news of Jesus Christ is available for people of all nations who put their trust in him.

Of course, the Reformation deduction from Scripture is also true, even if it is not what Paul was primarily arguing. We cannot be saved on the basis of any supposed good works, for we are all sinners. Judaism would concur with this statement, for redemption through the Passover precedes the giving of the law on Sinai. Israel's people were welcomed into God's loving grace when they were redeemed from slavery in Egypt. This clearly came before the giving of the law. As Christians, we know that it is indeed only through the redeeming grace of God in the cross and resurrection of Jesus that we can come into relationship with him. The Reformers' contextualization of the gospel contained truth which we can rejoice in. And Judaism, too, would share this belief in God's gracious mercy as the basis for our relationship with him.

But the Reformers' contextualization failed to see the international implications of Paul's teaching on justification by faith and not by works of the Jewish law. Therefore, international mission has always been a small extra in Christian biblical teaching, not the central theme which it should be, according to the New Testament.[1] For example, international cross-cultural mission hardly features in systematic theology or the teaching of Christian doctrine.

Europe and America, with their Reformation background, have dominated biblical study and theology for many centuries. Other, non-western, Christians struggle in these days to disentangle the gospel from its western context and reapply it to their cultural and religious backgrounds.

Viewpoints on time and history

We have already seen how western individualism has shaped biblical interpretation and therefore theology. Western views of time and history also underlie all biblical understanding. This will inevitably affect our mission practice, too. Thus the emphasis on individualism leads to forms of mission in which we expect only *individuals* to repent and to be converted, baptized and discipled. In Indonesia, however, we experienced *group* conversions, and had to learn a different approach to mission. Just before our time in Indonesia, our church had led a whole battalion of the army to Christ. We ourselves witnessed a ward in a hospital, several extended families and various village housing areas turning as groups to Christ. Together they came into repentance and faith. Together they were prepared for baptism and were duly baptized. Together they were discipled and grew in their faith, sharing a communal witness to the life-changing work of God's Spirit.

In the West, it is assumed that a straight-line view of time must be the biblical one. But actually, Hebrew views of time are more event-orientated. And an event may be partly in the past, partly in the present and fully in the future. But it remains one event. Thus the salvation event lies partly in the exodus from Egypt, partly in Israel's release from Babylonian exile, wonderfully in the coming of Jesus the Messiah and, finally, completely in the glory of our future salvation. These different happenings are all one salvation event. So Paul declares that 'God raised us up with Christ and seated us with him in the heavenly realms in Christ Jesus' (Ephesians 2:6), and Isaiah calls Cyrus 'his anointed', literally messiah (Isaiah 45:1). With a Hebrew view of time, it is true that Cyrus, God's instrument of salvation and liberation for Israel, was already a messianic agent. And Paul is quite correct in saying that we are already seated with Christ in heavenly realms, for we are already caught up in the salvation event. Hebrew verb forms fit this, for they are not easily related to past, present or future tenses.

Asian worldviews are sometimes accused of being cyclical, but actually they see time evolving in a spiral. There is not just a continuous repetition, but also a development in history.

As the Kenyan theologian John Mbiti has pointed out in his books,[2] Bantu African peoples consider that everything is moving increasingly into the past. Western assumptions that the world progresses inexorably towards the future enter the Bantu consciousness through western education, but they are not natural to the Bantu background. For them, people start life in pristine purity as small children, then steadily grow older. Increasing age naturally brings degeneration, until it climaxes in death. After death, we become remembered ancestors, living therefore in the recent past. Finally, we slip into oblivion as long-forgotten ancestors. So we all progress further and further into the past.

Bantu languages reflect this worldview. They have many verb forms describing various aspects of the past, a form that describes the present, and another tense for the immediate future. But they have no verb tense to describe an indefinite future or any more distant future. How then are we to describe the second coming of Jesus in those languages?

Some years ago, a Bantu African student came to bid me farewell at the end of his studies. Cheerfully, he said that one day we should surely meet again. So I asked him how he would say that in his language.

He was embarrassed, admitting that he would not want to say such a thing in his language. After much thought, he announced that in his language he would tell me that we would meet again next year.

I pointed out that my diary was full for that coming year and I would not be going to his country. And he had no money, so he would not come again to England. So it was not true that we would meet again during the next year.

He said that in a year's time he would again say that we would meet 'next year'.

My mind went to the traditional Jewish hope: 'Next year in Jerusalem.' And I thought of the Christian hope that Jesus is coming soon. For 2,000 years Christians have been saying 'soon', and one day it will come to pass.

Is it allowable to interpret the Bible and formulate our theology in terms of an Asian spiral or a backward-moving Bantu view of time? In our evangelism in those contexts, must we teach another view of time before we can preach the saving message of Christ? The very question is clearly ridiculous. If it is possible to view the Bible and theology from a European, straight-line view of time, surely it must also be allowable to contextualize the gospel in the light of other understandings.

Black and liberation theology

Theologically, in Africa, one always has to distinguish between black theology and African theology.[3] The latter is represented by theologians like John Mbiti, Kwame Bediako[4] or Bolaji Idowu,[5] who are seeking to develop theology in the context of African traditional religion and African philosophical worldviews. Black theology was originally formed in the context of South African apartheid and the struggle for black identity in a world dominated by whites. Such theology is built on the foundation of Léopold Senghor's old affirmation of 'Negritude', 'Black is beautiful.'

One aspect of black theology is based on the Trinity, in which the three Persons are distinct and yet entirely one. The Father is not the Son, nor is the Son the Holy Spirit. Yet they are equal and entirely united as one God. So black and white should be different, but entirely equal in status and united. In this emphasis they consciously reject what James Cone[6] called 'whitenization', the attempt to make blacks become like whites. In the colonial era, blacks could gain position and respect only if they dressed and behaved like whites. But in the Trinity, no Person seeks to lose his own identity in order to become like another Person. The unique identity of the three Persons 'grows out of and is expressed in their unity'. As humans, we are made in God's image and thus also reflect that same unity in diversity, all of us being who we are.

In the struggle for equality, 'freedom' inevitably takes centre stage in their theology. 'It is for freedom that Christ has set us free' (Galatians 5:1). Paul's next words ring all sorts of bells in black consciousness: 'Do not let yourselves be burdened again by a yoke of slavery.' While Paul is thinking in terms of freedom from trying 'to be justified by law' (Galatians 5:4), being circumcised and obeying 'the whole law', black theology applies this more to political and social freedom. We are to stand firm in steadfast faith in the liberating Christ, resisting anything that again reduces people to a position of inferiority. With the background of African society, we are not surprised by their theological affirmation that freedom must be in the context of relationships. It can only be in relationship to God and to others that we can find true identity and freedom. Martin Buber, with his relational theory of 'I–Thou', would surely have agreed: there can be no true 'I' without a 'Thou'.

Clearly, black theology is related to and influenced by the South American liberation theology. As such, it is unashamedly a situational theology, issuing out from a background of oppression and inequality. Although one might feel that black theology should have lost its relevance with the demise of apartheid, actually it still has considerable validity in every situation of injustice.

Liberation theology's foundations coincide with the revolutionary era of the late 1960s and early 1970s. Robert McAfee Brown of Stamford University declared that with the publication of *A Theology of Liberation*,[7] Gustavo Gutiérrez, the prophet of liberation theology, became 'one of the most important voices on the world theological scene'. Gutiérrez himself calls it a 'theology of the Signs of the Times'.

While Gutiérrez lays the foundations, Jose Luís Miranda applies his principles to biblical interpretation, and Sobrino looks at a liberation Christology.[8] Gutiérrez unashamedly asserts that the situation of poverty and oppression is his primary theological reference point. In this he followed the WCC Uppsala Conference's 1968 slogan 'Let the world determine the agenda.' He resists what he considers to be the traditional western theological selectivity, which, he says, is biased because of a capitalist and oppressive mentality. Rather, he insists on theology emerging from the existential realities of historical situations.

He cites Israel's exodus from slavery and oppression in Egypt, which became the foundation for all future biblical expression.

It is, of course, true that New Testament theology is never divorced from its contemporary issues. Thus the great credal statement of the incarnation of Christ in Philippians 2 issues out of a particular local problem: Syntyche and Euodia were quarrelling. Therefore Paul instructs his readers to be like Christ, looking not to their own interests only, but being like-minded, one in spirit and purpose. So Paul's theology is situational, yet at the same time it relates objective revealed truth to that situation. Western Christians need to be reminded that unrelated systematic theology has no biblical basis, but perhaps our liberation-theology friends need the reminder that situational theology must be based on revealed truth.

Asian theologies

Whereas African, black and liberation theologies all arose in relatively recent times, definitely contextualized approaches to biblical and theological studies have been current in Asia for at least 200 years. Particularly in India, great Christian theologians struggled with the issue of how to relate the gospel to the various streams of Hindu philosophy.[9] Some (e.g. Nehemiah Goreh, 1825–95) continued with a more traditional western understanding, but sought to express it in Hindu philosophical language and thought-forms. Others related to the everyday forms of *bhakti* (devotional) Hinduism (e.g. A. J. Appasamy in the first half of the twentieth century, and the famous Tamil poets, Krishna Pillai and N. V. Tilak). A few (e.g. Brahmaband-hab Upadhyay (1861–1907)[10] realized that they needed to relate to the highest form of Hinduism. They therefore engaged in the extremely taxing task of expressing the Christian faith in Advaitin (non-dualist) terms, in which everything is the great Brahman. As humans, we have no separate identity, but are merely part of Brahman. And there is no distinction between one person and another, for all are Brahman.

One of the major questions refers to John 10:30. What does Jesus mean when he declares that 'I and the Father are one'? How do we understand the unity of the three Persons of the Trinity in the context of non-dualist Hinduism? Are the Father and Jesus two persons within the one God, or does this verse follow a Hindu non-dualist approach whereby both are identical, without any separate identity?

But Hinduism flows in a multitude of very different streams, so within Indian Christian theology one finds a great variety of expressions. Unless they are conversant with Hinduism, it may not be easy for western Christians to walk in these various theological shoes. And it is noteworthy that even the singularly brilliant theology of Upadhyay is virtually unknown in the West, where even most theological professors would never have heard of him. There is a real danger that our theology, as also our church history and other studies, can be sadly insular and blinkered. And if their theological expressions seem irrelevant to us, might it be that our theology could be irrelevant to them?

In relationship to Buddhism, the Christian church has again to distinguish between the different streams of Buddhism. Just as some have found it helpful to divide Hinduism into the two major streams of *bhakti* (devotional) Hinduism and the more philosophical Advaitin (non-dualism), so also it may prove convenient to think of three major movements in Buddhism. The Christian faith needs to be related to the context of each of these.

Theravada or Hinayana Buddhism is often thought to be the stricter form of Buddhism, but actually it is generally interlaced with remnants of local traditional animistic religion. Theravada Buddhism is predominantly practised in Sri Lanka, Thailand, Laos and Myanmar (Burma). Mahayana Buddhism is by definition syncretistic, mixed with other religious systems. Thus, in South Korea, Confucianism and traditional Korean shamanism are part of everyday Buddhism, while among the Chinese, Buddhism is mixed with Confucianism, Taoism and traditional Chinese religion. In Japan, it is again Confucianism which plays a major part in life, but here it is added to traditional Shinto, Mahayana Buddhism and Japanese local religion. Christians have made significant progress in relating the gospel to these two major streams of Buddhism, but little effective theological work has yet been done in relationship to Lamaistic Buddhism (e.g. in Tibet).

In relationship to Theravada Buddhism, the Thai theologian Wan Petchsongkram[11] has struggled with the biblical fact of God as Creator. Buddhist teaching seems to imply that everything is just illusory (*maya*), and we all need to gain awareness that nothing truly exists. There is a story of the Buddha dismantling a chariot. As he removed one bit after another, he asked his disciple what it was – a wheel, an axle, and so on. Finally, he threw away the last section of the chariot and asked: 'Where is the chariot?'

The answer came back: 'There is no chariot, Master.'

Similarly, the Buddhist should seek to become aware that ultimately nothing is. All apparent existence is just an illusion which binds us to the constant chain of reincarnation.

To the Buddhist, all creation is just illusion and is of negative worth. The Creator must therefore be more satanic than divine, because he is just making that which binds us all to the suffering of reincarnate life. Petchsongkram does battle with this Buddhist view in advocating the biblical Creator God who is also utterly good.

Many Christian converts from Buddhism were first drawn towards Christ by the story of God's creation of the world. It gives a wonderful assurance that there is a beginning to everything, and consequently there may also be a final conclusion. Life is not just a 'constant wheel of becoming'. So Petchsongkram's Buddhism-related theology of a good Creator is enormously important. It is noteworthy that in the only two sermons to Gentiles in the book of Acts (chapters 14 and 17), Paul stresses the fact of creation. With Jews this emphasis was not necessary. And in the West today we have been forced away from an emphasis on creation in our evangelistic witness because we might then be sidetracked into a debate on evolution.

In Sri Lanka, Aloysius Peiris[12] has done battle with the Buddhist philosophy of *anatta* (non-being). He has sought to develop a Christian approach to *anatta*, in which we find true existence only when we lose ourselves and are in Christ. In this context we have to ask what Paul meant when he declared: 'I have been crucified with Christ and I no longer live, but Christ lives in me' (Galatians 2:20). What is the 'me' which Christ now indwells? What does Paul mean when he affirms that he no longer lives, when he also goes on to talk of 'the life I live in the body'? Does the crucified self relate only to our selfishness, rather than to our fundamental being?

Theravada Buddhism faces Christians with deep questions which may not be relevant to the West. However, with the growing influence of Buddhism in Europe and America, such questions become increasingly pertinent. But it is not easy to do our theology in a Buddhist context. Yet somehow, in mission among Theravada Buddhists, we are compelled to struggle with such problems. Otherwise we shall leave ex-Buddhist Christians with a schizophrenic faith. I have observed this with some Thai students. When they started their studies in England, they seemed still to have an underlying Buddhist worldview and philosophy, but with a committed Christian covering. A vital part of their training was to help them to make their Christian faith interact with their underlying Buddhist assumptions. The light of Christ needs to shine into every area of our thinking.

In relationship to Mahayana Buddhism, the Japanese theologian Kazoh Kitamori[13] has been enormously influential (although the most popular Christian writer and thinker in Japan has been Kanzo Uchimura).[14] Kitamori was deeply aware, not only of the traditional emphasis on suffering in Japanese tragedy plays and popular art, but also of the fearful aftermath of pain from the Second World War. Suffering is central to Buddhist thought as the fundamental problem in human life.[15] As a tutor, I always asked my Japanese students to read Kitamori's *Theology of the Pain of God*, and over the years each of them told me that this book spoke directly to the Japanese mind.

For Kitamori, Jeremiah 31:20 represents the heart of the Christian message, the Japanese equivalent to the western Christian's John 3:16. It is the gospel in a nutshell.

'Is not Ephraim my dear son,
    the child in whom I delight?
Though I often speak against him,
    I still remember him.
Therefore my heart yearns for him;
    I have great compassion for him,'
                declares the LORD.

Suffering pain is the outworking of love combined with wrath – which we can express as a simple formula:

L (love) $+ W$ (wrath) $= P$ (pain)

Soft, grandfatherly love without the admixture of holy wrath knows no pain. Even if the child is naughty, there is no need to punish – just give it back to the parents! Without holiness, love takes no deep responsibility and is not hurt by the other's evil. Likewise, holy anger without love allows us to tut-tut critically, but again it causes us no pain. But if the criminal is our own beloved child, then his or her sin causes us much pain. God loves deeply, and his love goes hand in hand with total holiness. His love and wrath combine to produce deep pain in the very heart of God. He suffers because of us.

In Jeremiah 31:20, Ephraim is God's 'dear son' and the Lord 'delights' in him with 'great compassion'. But Ephraim has rebelled against God and fallen into fearful sin. So God says, 'My heart yearns for him.' The Hebrew word translated 'yearns' is *chamah*, which connotes suffering and pain. It is used for a decapitated chicken whose torso flutters desperately and writhes in agony until it finally dies, and for a wave breaking with the water splashing all over the place in chaotic disorder. God's heart *chamah*, yearns, because of the sin of those he loves. The Luther Bible translates this verse as saying that God's heart breaks, while the old Authorized Version declares that God's 'bowels are troubled'!

In a direct line from Luther's theology of the cross, Kitamori sees the sacrificial death of Jesus as the expression of God's suffering pain on our behalf. He strongly rejects a liberal theological approach which underplays the wrath of God and the sin of humanity in its desire to stress God's unconditional love. Likewise, he denies the opposite extreme and resists any theology of a God who is so glorious in his majestic splendour that he can stand independently above all human or historical involvement. Kitamori stresses that God's love is firmly connected with the incarnation of Christ and his suffering on the cross. Kitamori declares that, in the Bible, the love of the trinitarian God is always expressed in relationship to humanity and through the cross.

Kitamori's disciple Kosuke Koyama[16] has developed his theology to relate to Thailand's Theravada Buddhist context, but in some ways it may be said that he stands somewhere between the two contexts of Thailand and Japan. One major mission in East Asia has felt that Koyama gives such a helpful insight into a more Asian approach to theology that it has asked all its new mission workers to read his *Waterbuffalo Theology*. Koyama underlines Kitamori's emphasis on

God relating directly with the world, but emphasizes the holy wrath of God rather than Kitamori's divine pain. He strongly attacks any idea of a remote, passionless God who sits on high in unperturbed *apatheia* (non-feeling). The very fact of God revealing himself assumes that God relates in history and is involved with us. If God remained unrelated to us in isolated glory, human activity would become independent of God and of no real significance.

Holy anger can never be tamed or controlled by us. So in his wrath God resists all human attempts to 'domesticate' God and control him. He is not just a helpful, tame divine spirit. No, he is an utterly independent personal power who acts of his own volition in history. Whereas Buddhism sees the ultimate solution outside history, and the Stoics looked for imperturbability within the order of history, our God is no timeless 'apathetic God beyond history'. He gets his hands dirty, involving himself with our affairs. And his wrath ensures his sovereign independence. We humans cannot just rub him in prayer like an Aladdin's lamp, whereupon his Spirit will emerge to do our bidding.

Thus Koyama also opposes Buddhist *anatta*, non-being, for he points out that non-being is the ultimate state of imperturbable *apatheia*. He asks the pointed question, 'How indeed can "no-self" be perturbed?' Unlike the coolly unemotional Buddha, our God, and we as his followers, are to be fully involved in history.

Koyama also gives us a delightful model of a more Asian style of communication. He does not adopt the dry theoretical pattern of doing theology, but uses rich pictorial language. The very titles of some of his books reflect this. *No Handle on the Cross* shows us the danger of neat formulations concerning the cross of Jesus, which is actually much bigger than our pigeonholed formulas. As soon as we think we have got a hold on the cross, we find that it eludes our simple understanding. And Koyama's autobiography, *Mount Fuji and Mount Sinai*, tells how he has sought to transfer the biblical faith from its Jewish origins to his own Japanese context. As Christians, we need to develop a much richer and more graphic language in our mission teaching and preaching of the gospel. In Jewish tradition, teaching may come in two forms, *halakhah* and *haggadah*. *Halakhah* is legal teaching in direct non-pictorial language. But the more common and popular form is *haggadah*, which includes stories, history, parables and dramatic action. In many cultures, haggadic teaching will prove more appropriate and effective.

Conclusion

We have touched lightly on a few examples of contextualization of theology. Many other examples could have been quoted. In themselves these various writers and thinkers are not important, but I hope they give us a model of contextualizing the gospel for the various contemporary religious and cultural contexts in which we may find ourselves.

In cross-cultural ministries, Christians are called to adapt their message and forms of communication to fit other backgrounds. The primary task of contextualization must always remain firmly in the hands of local people. But if foreign workers have learned the language well and gone deeply and empathetically into the local culture, they can at least ask relevant questions and suggest possible lines of contextualization. And as they study African, Asian and Latin American contextualized theologians, they will also have their minds widened and may gain insights which can be of help to local Christians in the culture they are associating with. They can therefore encourage and stimulate people to venture biblically and theologically into the often uncharted waters of contextualization in their own context.

Such contextualization has relevance not just for Christians in Africa, Asia or Latin America. In our contemporary world, cities everywhere contain rainbow societies with people from all over the world. In our evangelistic witness to people of different religious and cultural backgrounds, we shall need to contextualize the gospel of Christ. This applies also to our biblical and theological teaching within ethnic-minority churches. Such Christians are deeply aware of their ethnic identity and will respond warmly to teaching which is stripped of its western clothing and takes on more contextual forms.

In closing this chapter, we remind ourselves that our ideal is to remain entirely faithful to the biblical revelation of Christ himself, but at the same time to relate contextually. In thinking through our faith, we shall ask ourselves what questions people today are asking and what needs they feel they are facing. As we move forward in this twenty-first century, the church must not be an exotic ghetto. We dare not live in splendid isolation, irrelevant to the currents of our day. The Christian church is not only to be indigenous, with local people as its leaders rather than foreign missionaries. It is also to contextualize with uncompromised truth and holiness in its buildings, worship and music, leadership patterns and structures, biblical understanding, communication and theology. That is the mission challenge for God's people in every country and continent, among Jews and Gentiles of every nation and people.

Discussion starters

1. In what ways is traditional western theology contextualized to past religious and philosophical situations?
2. Try to think through a more contextualized expression of the Christian faith for your particular context: postmodern or secular, Muslim, Buddhist, Judaistic, Sikh or whatever it may be.

Notes

1. For further study of this theme, see M. Goldsmith, *Good News for All Nations: Mission at the Heart of the New Testament* (Hodder, 2002), and *Matthew and Mission: The Gospel Through Jewish Eyes* (Paternoster, 2000).
2. For a good description of African theological developments see G. Molyneux, *African Christian Theology: The Quest for Selfhood* (Mellen Research University Press, 1993).
3. ibid.
4. For something of Bediako's theology see his *Theology and Identity* (Regnum, 1992), *Christianity in Africa: The Renewal of a Non-western Religion* (Orbis, 1995), and *Jesus in Africa: The Gospel in African History and Experience* (Regnum Africa, 2000).
5. For something of Idowu's theology see his *African Traditional Religion* (SCM, 1973).
6. See J. Cone, *Liberation: A Black Theology of Liberation* (Lippincott, 1970), and *Risks of Faith: The Emergence of a Black Theology of Liberation* (Beacon Press, 1999).

7. G. Gutiérrez, *A Theology of Liberation* (Orbis, 1973).

8. J. L. Miranda, *Marx and the Bible* (Orbis, 1974); Jon Sobrino, *Christology at the Crossroads* (SCM 1978), *Jesus the Liberator* (Orbis 1993).

9. For a brilliant overview of Indian theology see R. Boyd, *An Introduction to Indian Christian Theology* (CLS, 1969).

10. See J. Lipner and G. Gispert-Sauch, *The Writings of Brahmabandhab Upadhyay* (United Theological College, Bangalore, 1991).

11. W. Petchsongkram, *Talks in the Shade of the Bo Tree* (privately published, n.d.).

12. A. Pieris, *Love Meets Wisdom: A Christian Experience of Buddhism* (Orbis, 1988), and *Fire and Water: Basic Issues in Asian Buddhism and Christianity* (Orbis, 1996).

13. K. Kitamori, *A Theology of the Pain of God* (SCM, 1966).

14. For an introduction to K. Uchimura see H. Miura, *The Life and Thought of Kanzo Uchimura, 1861–1930* (Eerdmans, 1996).

15. For an overall introduction to Japanese Christian theology see C. Michalson, *Japanese Contributions to Christian Theology* (Westminster Press, n.d.).

16. K. Koyama, *Waterbuffalo Theology* (SCM, 1974), *No Handle on the Cross* (SCM, 1976), *Three Mile an Hour God* (SCM, 1979), and *Mount Fuji and Mount Sinai* (SCM, 1984). For a good introduction to the thought of K. Koyama see D. T. Irvine and E. Akintunde, *The Agitated Mind of God: The Theology of Kosuke Koyama* (Orbis, 1996).

Conclusion

Kendall Soulen,[1] of Wesley Theological Seminary in Washington DC, helpfully argues that God's ultimate aim for his created world is to bring his *shalom* to all. Soulen describes God as 'the Consummator' as he works to lead the world into the fullness of his *shalom* 'in unsurpassable fashion to the mutual blessing of all in a reign of wholeness, righteousness and peace'.

Soulen affirms that this consummation comes through relationships of difference with mutual blessing: God and humanity, Israel and the nations, male and female, different generations. Each contributes to, and itself finds fulfilment in, the other. Even God gains pleasure in graciously giving the fullness of life to his people.

In his granting of complete salvation, the whole history of Israel and the incarnate life, relationships and teaching of Jesus play a vital part. Soulen warns against jumping too quickly from the first three chapters of Genesis to the incarnation and redemption of Jesus the Messiah. God's gift of *shalom* is already being worked out within the history of Israel, as well as in the life of Jesus. And throughout biblical history God has set his sights on all peoples everywhere. In calling Abraham and his seed in the people of Israel, God always has his eyes fixed more widely on all nations. God's blessing is to flow through Israel as his gateway to the Gentiles.

Jesus, too, is called to 'the lost sheep of Israel' (Matthew 15:24), but in that very passage he finally brings healing also to a Gentile

Canaanite woman's daughter. And the healing of that Gentile leads on to the feeding of a Gentile crowd in 15:29–39.[2] He had already fed a Jewish crowd in 14:13–21, so he is now giving his disciples a model of God's concern for all peoples – in fact, a model for international mission. We are called to feed the crowds of both Jews and Gentiles of all nations and peoples everywhere.

It should be noted that the feeding of the first crowd follows immediately after the death of John the Baptist. Jesus therefore has his own sacrificial death definitely in mind. So Matthew carefully uses verbs which remind us of the last supper and therefore of Jesus' atoning work for us: he took bread and looked up to heaven, he gave thanks, he broke and gave; and they all ate (Matthew 14:19–20). Jesus feeds the crowds, not only with bread and fish, but also with his saving work on the cross. Our mission is also to feed crowds of all nations both materially and spiritually.

In passing, we may also note that, for the Jews, Jesus' feeding of crowds of Jews and Gentiles constitutes a messianic sign. For this reason the Jewish leaders challenge him to give them not only an ordinary earthly sign, but also a 'sign from heaven' (Matthew 16:1). But Jesus had shown by the twofold feeding of crowds that his witness was reliable. In Old Testament law a testimony is reliable if supported by two witnesses. And of course the feeding of the crowds was clearly miraculous.

It is in this context of feeding Gentiles as well as Jews that Jesus talks of the 'sign of Jonah' (Matthew 16:4). In the Old Testament, Israel was not called to go out to the Gentiles to preach the message of their God. Rather, they were commanded to live as the people of God in obedience to his law, so that the Gentiles would be attracted in to Zion to worship the Lord. Thus Israel was called to be an attractive magnet, a light to draw the Gentiles to God, honey to entice the Gentile bees to suck the sweetness of Israel's God.

But Jonah is the one Old Testament exception. He is commanded to go out to preach to the Gentile city of Nineveh. So Jesus here gives the 'sign of Jonah' in the context of his feeding the Gentile crowd[3] to show that his ministry (and therefore ours) is not limited to just the Jewish people.

So the New Testament emphasizes the international purposes of God to bring his *shalom* in the salvation of Gentiles as well as Jews. In

Romans 9 – 11, Paul struggles with the situation, even in his day, whereby the church was becoming increasingly Gentile, while the majority of his own Jewish people were rejecting Jesus and his salvation.

Having shown in the earlier chapters of his letter that both Jews and Gentiles are equally justified by faith in the redeeming work of Jesus Christ on the cross, he inevitably has to ask whether God still has special purposes for the Jewish people. Paul feels deep sorrow as he thinks of his own people, who are largely rejecting their Saviour (9:1–5). He prays for them and longs for them to be saved (10:1). His heart burns with the question, 'Did God reject his people?' (11:1). They have rejected him, but has he washed his hands of them? Has God thrown his covenant promises to Israel out of the window? Of course, to Christians such a thought is anathema. If God could discard his Mosaic covenant with Israel because of their sin, might he not also cancel his new covenant with the church in the blood of Christ? After all, the church has also not been totally without sin in its history!

In Romans 11, Paul finds an answer to his questions. He is given renewed faith in God's continuing purposes for Israel, while at the same time seeing the movement of the Holy Spirit among the Gentiles. So he asks of the Jews, 'Did they stumble so as to fall beyond recovery?' (11:11), and answers the question with the strong negative, 'Not at all.'

Paul develops the theme that the transgression of the Jews has opened the door of salvation for the Gentiles. This may be seen in Acts 13:44ff., when Paul and Barnabas experience Jewish opposition and therefore boldly declare: 'We now turn to the Gentiles' (verse 46). If the Jews' sin leads to such rich blessing among Gentiles, what blessing would their full salvation bring!

Paul then argues that the salvation of the Gentiles is in order that they may provoke the Jews to jealousy and thus bring the life of Christ to some. Thus we observe the opposite of a vicious circle, namely a blessed spiral. The sin of Israel allows Gentiles to come into life in Christ – the salvation of Gentiles provokes Jews to jealousy and some of them are saved – salvation of Jews leads to yet greater blessing among Gentiles – more Gentile blessing means that more Jews come to faith in the Messiah. More Jews means more Gentiles; more Gentiles means more Jews. And so God's kingdom grows.

Paul concludes with this picture of growing salvation as an olive tree, a common representation of Israel. Some of the Jewish branches are pruned away because of their unbelief. New, Gentile, branches are grafted in and joined to the trunk. Finally, the tree contains, not only all those unnatural Gentile branches which have been added, but also the original Jewish branches that are re-grafted into their own tree.

So Paul comes to his climactic statement. He looks forward to that great day when 'the full number of the Gentiles has come in' and thus 'all Israel will be saved' (Romans 11:25–26). There is evidently a parallel between the *plerōma* (fullness) of the Gentiles and the *pas* (all) of Israel. Neither suggests that every individual Gentile and every individual Jew will be saved. But *plerōma* and *pas* do imply considerable numbers of both Gentiles and Jews of every sort and background. Paul would seem to be prophesying a mass movement both among Gentiles of every nation and people, and among Jews of every background. How we look forward to that vision being fulfilled! And we are called to work to bring God's wonderful purposes into reality, for we are designated 'God's fellow-workers' (1 Corinthians 3:9; 2 Corinthians 6:1).

In passing, it may be noticed that Paul does not talk of the olive tree of Israel being cut down and replaced by a new tree; only of some of the branches being cut off for a time and finally brought back into the life of the great tree. The Gentile branches are added to the Jewish tree trunk and it becomes a tree with both Jewish and Gentile branches. It still remains the old tree of Israel, but now it is multinational. There is no basic divide between the people of Israel and the New Testament church. Indeed, the very word *ekklēsia* (church) is used in the Greek Septuagint translation of the Old Testament for the 'congregation' (*qahal*) of Israel. There is a clear continuity from the congregation of Israel to the church. Sometimes, in Gentile Christian circles, one hears that Pentecost was the birthday of the church. But the church was born at the call of Abraham, or perhaps even at the creation of Adam and Eve.

So God's call comes to his church to reach out to both Jews and Gentiles with the redeeming message of Jesus Christ.

As the final book of the Bible, Revelation promises God's special blessing to those who read and take to heart 'the words of this prophecy' (Revelation 1:3). The book of Revelation is a prophetic work, looking ahead to what God is planning to accomplish in the coming times. It concludes by warning people to stick closely to 'the words of the prophecy of this book' (Revelation 22:18–19). Only then does the Lord reiterate his glorious promise that he is coming soon.

This book gives many prophecies of what God is planning for the future. But perhaps the central vision is of heaven itself. Both in chapter 5 and chapter 7 we have revealed to us God's ultimate purpose, in which there will be 'a great multitude' of people from every nation, tribe, people and language (5:9; 7:9). In chapter 7 these multitudes are in addition to the '144,000 from all the tribes of Israel' (verse 4). As we saw earlier, the 144,000 = the 12 of the Old Testament tribes of Israel × the 12 of the New Testament disciples of Christ. And in Jewish thought, 1,000 signifies a huge but limited number. It therefore means a large number of Jewish believers in Christ from both Old Testament and New Testament times. So heaven is peopled by a great multitude of the redeemed both of Jews and of Gentiles.

The Revelation description of these great multitudes of Jews and Gentiles shows them to be active in worshipping the Lord. Great songs of praise swell into a paean of praise to the Lamb, who sits on the throne of heaven. In this worship they stand together as one united choir before the presence of God. What a picture! All disunity is annihilated and all human barriers are removed in the glory of being with the Lord himself. Although Jesus informs us that in his Father's house there 'are many rooms' (John 14:2), we smile at the old joke that each denomination will have a separate room to itself. Charismatic Christians will not be divided off from Reformed Christians, but somehow will rejoice in combined worship together at the foot of the heavenly throne. There will be no heavenly police to ensure that the various Christian groupings never have to encounter each other. In the huge and vital task of worldwide mission, we must stand together as we seek to pull down all fortresses which stand against our Lord and Saviour. And as we unite in mission, we shall actually become more prepared for joining that beautiful heavenly choir to praise our God for ever and ever.

It is the purpose of this book that we should all dedicate our lives anew to hasten the day when God's purposes for the world actually come to pass. Only then will the Lord Jesus come again. So our appeal to him – 'Come, Lord Jesus' – at the very end of the Bible (Revelation

22:20) demands that we preach his gospel to all people everywhere, both to Jews and to Gentiles of every nation and people (cf. Matthew 24:14). For this great undertaking we need the power of the Holy Spirit, so that we can effectively 'witness in Jerusalem, and in all Judea and Samaria, and to the ends of the earth' (Acts 1:8).

Luke develops this theme in the Acts of the Apostles, telling the story of the powerful working of the Holy Spirit through the first apostles. By the Spirit they went first to their fellow Jews, then to the mixed race of the Samaritans, and then more widely to the Gentile world. The book of Acts introduces us to the start of the history of the Christian church in its increasingly wide outreach into the world. Now we in our day are called to play our part in this great work, until the multitudes from all peoples have been brought to faith in our Lord Jesus. No wonder the Bible ends with the vital prayer, 'The grace of the Lord Jesus be with God's people. Amen' (Revelation 22:21).

Notes

1. R. Kendall Soulen, *The God of Israel and Christian Theology* (Fortress, 1996).

2. For further exposition of this passage see M. Goldsmith, *Matthew and Mission: The Gospel Through Jewish Eyes* (Paternoster, 2000). For further exposition of the Jew–Gentile emphasis of Scripture, see M. Goldsmith, *Good News for All Nations: Mission at the Heart of the New Testament* (Hodder, 2002).

3. In Matthew 12:39–40 Jesus uses the sign of Jonah to prophesy his own death, burial and resurrection. Jesus uses the sign of Jonah more than once and with different meanings.

Further reading

K. Bediako, *Theology and Identity* (Regnum, 1992).

D. Bosch, *Transforming Mission: Paradigm Shifts in Mission Theology* (Orbis, 1991).

R. Briggs (ed.), *Global Action: A Personal Discipleship Manual for the World Christian* (OM Publishing, 1997).

R. Dowsett, *The Great Commission* (Monarch, 2001).

M. Goldsmith, *Good News for All Nations: Mission at the Heart of the New Testament* (Hodder, 2002).

——, *Matthew and Mission: The Gospel Through Jewish Eyes* (Paternoster, 2001).

——, *What About Other Faiths?* (Hodder, 1989, 2002).

P. Heslam (ed.), *Globalization and the Good* (SPCK, 2004).

D. Hesselgrave, *Planting Churches Cross-culturally* (Baker, 1980).

P. G. Hiebert, *Anthropological Reflections on Missiological Issues* (Baker, 1994).

T. Jeffery and S. Chalke, *Connect!* (Lifestyle and Spring Harvest, 2003).

A. J. Kostenberg, *Salvation to the Ends of the Earth: A Biblical Theology of Mission* (Apollos, 2001).

K. Koyama, *Waterbuffalo Theology* (SCM, 1974).

J. D. Lundy, *We are the World: Globalization and the Changing Face of Mission* (OM Publishing, 1999).

G. McDermott, *Can Evangelicals Learn from World Religions?* (IVP, 2001).

C. Partridge (ed.), *Lion Handbook of World Religions* (Lion, 2005).

D. W. Smith, *Against the Storm: Christianity and Mission in an Age of Globalization* (IVP, 2003).

———, *Mission After Christendom* (Darton, Longman & Todd, 2003).

R. Tiplady, *Postmission World Mission by a Postmodern Generation* (Paternoster, 2002).

R. Valerio, *L is for Lifestyle* (IVP, 2004).

G. Verwer, *Out of the Comfort Zone: Grace! Vision! Action!* (OM Publishing, 2000).

A. Walls, *The Cross-cultural Process in Christian History* (Orbis, 2002).

C. Wright, *Thinking Clearly About the Uniqueness of Jesus* (Monarch, 1997).